FEB 2 8 1968

LET DONS DELIGHT

LET DONS DELIGHT

BEING

VARIATIONS ON A THEME IN
AN OXFORD COMMON-ROOM

BY

RONALD A. KNOX

Plus c'est la même chose, plus ça change. —Remark still waiting to be made by someone.

LONDON
SHEED & WARD
1939

LF509 .K6

PRINTED IN GREAT BRITAIN
BY PURNELL AND SONS, LTD.
PAULTON, SOMERSET
AND LONDON
FIRST PUBLISHED FEBRUARY, 1939
BY SHEED AND WARD, LTD.
FROM 31 PATERNOSTER ROW, LONDON, E.C.4

To
DAPHNE
All this Waste of Time

CONTENTS

CHAPTER		PAGE
I.	In Which I Drop Off	1
II.	Hannibal Ad Portas: 1588	13
	Notes on Chapter II, from Anthony à Wood and Bishop Challoner.	
III.	Cakes and Ale: 1638	44
	Notes on Chapter III, from Anthony à Wood.	
IV.	The Pigeons Flutter: 1688	79
	Notes on Chapter IV, from Thomas Hearne's Diaries.	
V.	Lost Causes: 1738	111
	Note on Chapter V, from Boswell's *Life of Johnson*.	
VI.	The Unchanging World: 1788	145
	Note on Chapter VI, from the *Edinburgh Review*.	
VII.	False Dawn: 1838	173
	Note on Chapter VII, from Mark Pattison's *Memoirs*.	
VIII.	A Rear-guard Action: 1888	207
	Note on Chapter VIII, can it be Mr. Nicolson?	
IX.	In Which I Wake Up	245
X.	Chaos: 1938	254

LET DONS DELIGHT

CHAPTER I

IN WHICH I DROP OFF

It was said in my hearing, over dinner at All Souls': "How curious it would be if the Day of Judgement came at a quarter to eight on a Sunday evening, to find all the dons carousing in Hall, and all their wives eating cold shape at home." It is doubtful whether, in the general disturbance of values, this act of culinary infidelity would over-burden the most scrupulous conscience. But the observation on Oxford manners is certainly an accurate one; nor is it only the fear of that questionable shape which drives the learned men back to the haunts of their bachelordom. Sunday night, when there are no cinemas open; Sunday night, when so many former undergraduates have come up for the week-end, with mature views on banking, or hair-raising rumours from the Foreign Office; Sunday night, when it is still fashionable to edify the junior members of the College by looking as if you had been to Chapel—a hundred considerations combine to make it guest-night everywhere. This is all very well, except for hangers-on of the academic world like myself, who have other fish to fry on most evenings, and can only afford to breathe the pure serene of Common-room on this one day of the week. How are we to sample, when the rare invitation comes our way, the flesh-pots of other foundations, without guiltily absenting ourselves from the familiar company of Trinity (or wherever it may be) ? I am not, for this reason, much of a diner-out; but when, the other day, a friend asked me to dine with him at Simon Magus, I could not resist the allurement. Who could resist the port of Simon Magus, whether it be considered as an end in itself, or as a means to an end—that is, to the brilliant flow of soul for which the College is equally famous ?

Simon Magus occupies, for many reasons, a unique position in the University. It is the only foundation, unless you count the finishing-off of Christ Church, which dates between the dissolution of the monasteries and the death of the eighth Henry. It is the only one, unless you count the later and less fortunate experiment of Keble, which is built, as to its main portion, in red brick; the only come-back we have to the Cambridge man who boasts to us of the mellow glories of Queens'. And the accident of birth which is perpetuated in its architecture was reflected in its early history. It had no remote memories which could chain it, however tenuously, to the ages of faith when the Pope's word ran in England just as it did elsewhere; nor was it, like Jesus, bound up with the nascent fortunes of Protestantism; nor yet, like Trinity and St. John's, did it represent a deliberate effort to hark back to the older order of things, made in the brief years of Queen Mary. A man of the new nobility, Sir Piers Collett, founded it with the ill-gotten gains he had derived from the looting of various Yorkshire monasteries; induced thereto by the proverbial bad luck which followed (in his case) with a swift blow of retribution. In memory of his two sons, who died from wounds inflicted on one another in a fatal brawl, he instituted at Oxford what was meant, evidently, to be an old-fashioned chantry foundation, but was governed by statutes prudently designed to advertize the New Learning. So exactly did it represent the spirit of its age, that the changes of religion which followed left little mark upon it. By the time Queen Elizabeth came to the throne it was, like England in general, halting between two opinions; accessible to Puritan influences, yet ready on the least provocation to go back to old ways which memory recalled, and loyalty had abandoned with reluctance.

In these days, Simon Magus does not rank high among the Colleges; for the outer world judges them by undergraduate standards—that is, by the difficulty of obtaining admission to them; and it must be confessed that Simon Magus undergraduates are neither expensive nor particularly athletic. But the dons have the reputation of being good company; and certainly they ought to cultivate the amenities of life, for their lot is cast in pleasant places. Even those who have never penetrated beyond the front Quad carry away endearing memories of the College. The fortunate vandalism of the later seventeenth century ordained that the brick-work should be plastered over to look like stone; and when the repulsive veil was stripped away, some thirty years back, the bricks came out of their imprisonment with all the mellowness of age untempered by any suspicion of decay. Once the sun catches them, those little, rough bricks of the Tudor period, almost more pink than red, have a domestic charm which only the most perfect stone can rival; nor do they need, as stone does, a grass plot to set them off in contrast with the ground. The odd, high, twisted chimney-pots are not all original, but at the worst they are good copies. The building is only of two floors (though I believe a disastrous proposal in the nineties to add an extra story was only defeated by one vote), and the area of the Quad itself is proportioned to the height of the surrounding enclosure, in what I take to be the right ratio; viz. that the western block does not shut off the sunlight from the windows opposite until a time of day when sunlight is too weak to be worth encouraging.

What makes this Quad yet more attractive to the summer visitor is the round-headed gate set in the archway opposite the front lodge. It is of iron, very beautifully figured, and has that indefinable tint, midway between light-blue and light-green, which sits upon old iron-work as if it were a natural hue. Through its wide loops and fantastic spirals you catch a glimpse of the Fellows' garden immediately beyond, of lawns smooth with three hundred years of cultivation, flaming poppies or delphiniums, sober yews that defy the sunlight. It is my custom to stop for a minute or two in the gateway taking in the effect of all this—but not just before Hall, when the undergraduates are standing about in the lodge reading the notices, or exchanging mysterious confidences with the porter. Undergraduates, at such a time, always give me the impression that they feel sure, from the look of me, I have been directed to the wrong College, but are too polite to say so. I went straight through into the Quad and up to my host's rooms; it was Charles Mordaunt, the ancient history tutor. I was offered the inevitable sherry, and refused it, knowing that at Simon Magus, as in every other College, sherry is the only thing you will get to drink before the end of the fish course. Mordaunt had no other guest, and we sauntered across into Hall without hurry; they make no fuss and bother there about being in time for grace.

I am inclined to date all my odd experiences that evening from the moment when I looked up at the wall opposite me (I was sitting with my back to the undergraduate tables), and became aware of a portrait hanging there which seemed unfamiliar. Rearrangement of some kind had been going on; and, partly from a prejudice in favour of old landmarks, partly because I found it difficult to break the ice with the scientist on my left (I felt sure he was a scientist, but didn't know what his line was; I wish dons wore labels), I asked whose the portrait was, and where it had come from. It represented a very old man in the costume, as I judged, of the later eighteenth century; like most portraits of that time, it seemed mostly wig and fancy dress; the face framed in these accessories suggested the appearance of a man who is surprised that the artist should be taking such a liberty as to paint him, but supposes it is all right. I learned that the picture had hung in a dark corner of the Provost's Lodgings; that recently, when it was sent to be cleaned, an expert with no axe to grind had suggested the possibility that it might, at least in part, be the authentic work of Sir Joshua; and that it had been transferred to this place of honour in Hall to be at best a College treasure, at worst a convenient topic of conversation.

"Not but what," added the scientist, "there is something to be said for having Jonathan Shillett hanging over the High Table. I don't think you can say he was a distinguished man, but he was something of a patriarch, and a don who has a long innings generally acquires a sort of bogus value in the College annals. As a matter of fact, I take off my hat to any man who reached eighty in those days, considering the way they used to put away the claret. No, old Shillett never became Provost; but he was more identified with the name of Simon Magus than most of our Provosts have been. You see, he was a fellow here long before the '45, and lived to see the French Revolution."

"It must have been a curious span to have bridged," I suggested. "I mean, one always gets the impression that Oxford changed less in those years than in almost any other period of its history. A man who had that sort of record now might almost have been dandled on the knees of Dr. Routh, and all that sort of thing. And he would be full of rather dreary reminiscences about the way Oxford had changed within his own memory. But your Shillett, after all those years of un-progress, or whatever the word is, must have thought of Oxford as something wholly immutable; a museum of the past, and a Minimax (please God) of the future."

The scientist looked at me narrowly, as if to ascertain whether I was expressing my own sentiments, or those which might reasonably be attributed to the old gentleman in the portrait; but I kept my own counsel, and I do not remember that we canvassed the subject much further. But afterwards, when we moved into the Common-room, I had a look at a much younger Jonathan Shillett, in a print that hung there; and in the smoking-room, falling into the hands of an antiquarian enthusiast, was introduced to many other figures of the past; for the College loves to do honour to its former members. I heard, and resolved to forget, innumerable facts about the bewigged or chokered old gentlemen who look down reprovingly from those walls upon what they evidently regard as a degenerate array of successors.

The smoking-room at Simon Magus was formerly the Common-room; and I have never quite been able to understand why the change was made (just before the War, I believe), unless it were that this old room is somewhat dark in the day time, and perhaps cast an added shade of gloom over the proceedings at College meetings. As it is, it is seldom used above once a week; which seems a waste of that curious panelling, rich in semi-classical grotesques, which runs all round it except for the deep embrasures of the windows. The dons boast that hardly any change has ever been made in the room since the middle of the sixteenth century, when it was built. Electric light has been put in, of course; but otherwise there is nothing, you imagine, that would make one of the original fellows feel a stranger if he could walk into it to-day; he might warm his hands at the same hearth, open the window with the same catches, spill his wine on the same oak floor.

Nobody *had* opened the window, that evening; and fires in the late spring do make a room feel drowsy; nor do I deny that a glass or two of Simon Magus port, recently introduced into the system, intensifies and mingles with that feeling of drowsiness, almost making a man forget that he is in the presence of the best set of talkers in Oxford. The grotesques on the panelling danced a little before my eyes, as things will before eyes that are in danger of closing; my pipe went out once or twice, a bad sign. Still, I do not think I was in any danger of forgetting my position, if Mordaunt had not been summoned to answer an urgent trunk call on the telephone. There was no instrument nearer than the one at the lodge, but it only meant ten minutes' absence, and he did not think it necessary to depute any of his colleagues to attend, during that short interval, on my needs. Thus I found myself, for the moment, dropping out of my human surroundings; there was conversation on my left, conversation on my right, but the lie of the furniture did not make it imperative that I should register interest in either. I listened on my left, and heard the fellows of Simon Magus discussing some intricate piece of University business, in which the name of the Ashmolean kept on figuring; I never could understand University business. I listened on my right, and heard the fellows of Simon Magus discussing the relative merits of two different types of cars; I never could distinguish between different types of car. The grotesques on the panelling seemed to be executing a positive war-dance. A friend, who was sitting on the other side of the room, assures me that at this point I closed my eyes. It seems to be a legitimate conjecture that I may have gone to sleep.

If I dreamt, I managed my dreaming very ill. Your good dreamer will transpose all the details of his surroundings; if he has fallen asleep in a train, the motion will be represented in his dream-world by that of an aeroplane or a boat, the noise of the wheels will turn into the drone of monotonous music, or the roar of a waterfall. But I, if I dreamt, was unimaginative enough to dream myself back into my real surroundings, not otherwise than that famous inhabitant of Crewe who dreamt he was eating his shoe.[1] The chairs I was looking at may have been different chairs, but they were in exactly the same positions in which my waking consciousness had left them; the attitudes of those who were seated in them did not seem to have altered; the buzz of their conversation was, at first, the same kind of buzz. Only, were they the same people? You know how it is in dreams (mine, anyhow); you do not see people's faces, you just *know* that the man you are talking to (or throwing downstairs) is Such-a-one, belonging to your acquaintance. It may be that in the course of the pro-

---

[1] He woke up in the night in a terrible fright and found it was perfectly true.

ceedings you look at his face, and find that it is the face of somebody quite different; this does not puzzle you in your dream, only afterwards; at the moment, you are content to let A act as a symbol (I think they call it) of B, and it is with an A-faced B that you round off the cycle of your adventures. So it was with me, that evening. The figures in the chairs wore the faces of twentieth-century people I knew, all of the academic world; nor would those faces maintain themselves as the dream went on, but the man sitting on my right would now be Dash of Magdalen, now Blank of Christ Church. Only I knew he was not really either Dash or Blank; his identity was something distinct from either, and something, I could not tell how, intellectually known to me.

Intellectually known—I do not see how else I can express my meaning; they were concepts of the mind, not mental images. Yet they were all docketed and labelled by some process of which the intellect could give no account; I knew every speaker's name as he spoke, and what office he held in the College, and how long it was since he had taken his degree, and what his sympathies were in University or in national politics. And I knew that they were not men of our day; was conscious, as if by some internal time-instinct, when the scene shifted from one century or one half-century to another. My dream came to me in a series of episodes, and that series followed the order of time. As each episode came to an end, I woke up again and immediately dozed off again—at least, I thought I did, though

IN WHICH I DROP OFF

my friend opposite assures me that my eyes were closed the whole time. Let it not be supposed that this gross discourtesy of mine lasted very long; Mordaunt assures me that he got his call immediately, and that the business, whatever it was, needed little discussion; he is positive that he was not away from the room for as much as a quarter of an hour, and that he found me there with my eyes open exactly as he had left me.

People have asked me, when I tried to recount this experience to them, whether I was not conscious all through it of changes in costume. For (they say) if you thought you were listening to a set of Elizabethan fellows talking, and then later on to a set of early Victorian fellows talking, they cannot have been dressed in the same way; was it not, perhaps, a change from ruffs to lace, from full-bottomed to short wigs, from chokers to stiff collars, that enabled me to guess what century I was in as the thing went on? It may have been so, unconsciously; but the fact is I have a wretched memory for costume, and that dream-world, in which anything may happen and anybody may meet anybody, produces in most of us a complete incuriousness about detail. All I know is that I carry away no visual impression of what passed, only an oddly accurate memory of what was said, and who said it, and the tones of the competing voices and the gestures with which they were accompanied. Another question I have been asked is, whether I myself took any part in the conversations to which I listened? As well as I remember, I tried to, but found myself in the predicament of the ghosts (was it not?) in the Aeneid, *inceptus clamor frustratur hiantes;* I would open my mouth, frame sentences, but could not be certain whether any sound resulted, and did not greatly care, since it was evident that the dream-characters heard nothing, or at least took no notice of me. I suppose I must be a secret admirer of my own conversation, for I am by no means strange to such an experience.

In reporting what I heard, I have taken the liberty of reducing it all to the form of dramatic dialogue. This expedient, while obscuring for the reader, I am afraid, the sense of reality or of quasi-reality, saves an infinity of bother over inverted commas and conversation-rubrics generally. "The reader," I say, making the assumption that some will be at pains to follow my dream (if it was a dream) through all its stages. Those who prefer to confine themselves to every-day fact will do well to neglect all the chapters which follow except the last two, in which this narrative returns to waking life; to the existing glories of Simon Magus in this age of fulfilled hopes, and of achieved finality.

CHAPTER II

HANNIBAL AD PORTAS: 1588

MR. TAVERNER. I hear Puccius hath recanted, and is become the Pope's man again.

MR. RICHARDS. That is very like; I was told lately he was in Poland, where the Jesuits have made much head; he and Dr. Dee were for raising the devil, and other the like superstitious practices; which their low creeping sort would not stick at, for the better overthrow of religion.

MR. TAVERNER. Nay, Mr. Richards, you have been told the tale bottom foremost. This Puccius came of a very bigoted Papist stock, but was himself brought to another way of thinking, and embraced the gospel sincerely enough in the city of Lyons. Whereupon he came over to Oxford and went out Master of Arts here, having the name of a very painful student of divinity. He was after that bosom friend to Socinus, and wrote somewhat dangerously of universal redemption. That he hath been in Cracow, the Jesuits were nothing answerible for it; with whom, indeed, he tried a fall or two in theology, but busied himself rather in the affairs of Dr. Dee and Mr. Edward Kelley, who were for raising the spirits of the dead (and not devils, as your story goes) in those parts. But, as I hear, the Pope's nuncio taking these their doings amiss—or whether it were, as some say, that the spirits themselves gave Puccius a warning, that the whole world should shortly become Catholic, in which case he was like to have had short shrift from his own countrymen—he is returned into Italy and reconciled with his own Church, and hath set about studying for the priesthood.

THE PROVOST (*it is a feast-day of the College; otherwise he would not be in Common-room*). I think this Dr. Dee is a Cambridge man? I do not remember any of his name that hath been admitted here. This Puccius was a slight fellow; I remember well the noise that was made about him.

DR. HEYWOOD. Certainly Dr. Dee was a Cambridge man; I do not know where else he would have been brought up so detestably. This is what will come when you let men souse themselves in mathematics; it breeds so great a lack of judgement, as that before long they will be busying themselves over *Abracadabra* and *Rebus Rubus Epitepscum*. I warrant that his spirits will have told him this and much other foolery.

THE PROVOST. Kelley was an Oxford man; I cannot remember of what house. But I do not think he came to much here; he went to Glastonbury, and it was there he found his elixir.

DR. HEYWOOD (*snorting contemptuously*). He was a man of very unsettled wits, and addicted to chymistry. He is besides an Irishman, and Dr. Dee a Welshman; I hope when I am gone hence, if my spirit must return, it will find itself in more honest company. I am sorry, Mr. Richards; I had forgot you were from Wales.

MR. RICHARDS. English or Welsh, Oxford or

Cambridge, I think they do very ill to meddle with such matters. It little availed King Saul, when he had Samuel out of his grave; and I think Dr. Dee will come to no good, nor his seer either.

DR. WOLVERIDGE. Dr. Dee is getting to be an old man now; like enough he is doating. But God forbid you should speak as if it were all one whether he is raising spirits, or casting horoscopes and whatever else is proper to a mathematician. He hath made some very notable predictions, and I hold him for a man of science, these later infantilities notwithstanding. Besides, it is not long since that he was much in men's mouths as a geographer. It was he that set on Sir Hugh Willoughby and Richard Chancellor to find the North-East Passage; wherein if they had persevered, my belief is many good men's lives had been spared, that have perished trying to sail round the Americas. It was he, as I think, who shewed that there is much profit to be had if some man will search out the kingdom of Lochac; which should be a great continent in the southern hemisphere, very rich in gold and other precious commodities.

DR. HEYWOOD. Why, you are for making the man out a worse moon-calf than ever. He hath but crazed himself with reading of old authors that were yet more doltish than he. He is a man that would not be content with finding out new markets for our merchants overseas, but was for sending out colonies of Englishmen to settle down in the waste places of the earth which the Spaniard had wisely left alone; as hath been most disastrously done in these last years in the place they call

Virginia. He came to such a pitch of ranting, if I mistake not, as he would talk of a British Empire beyond the seas.

MR. FENTON (*he is a junior fellow of the College, but speaks in a reprimanding tone as if expecting the others to defer to him; which indeed they do*). This is very strange, Dr. Heywood, that you think a man to be maggoty-headed because he would see this little and great country enlarge her borders somewhat. As for the plantations overseas——

THE PROVOST (*breaking in nervously*). Nay, Mr. Fenton, Dr. Heywood's meaning was, that English people will never be hearty colonists, because our climate fits us ill for southern adventures, and we are catched easily by the fevers and distempers of those parts. Let the Spaniards and the Portingales garrison these outlandish coasts, to keep the beastly inhabitants under, and we will ply for trade between their ports, when the world is more settled again. I think Dr. Heywood spoke only in that sense.

MR. FENTON. You say well, Mr. Provost, " when the world is more settled again ". But it shall not be long, as I hear from one that is very close to the person of my good patron, the Chancellor. He tells me there are dispatches come in that have quite removed all ground for these late alarms over a pretended invasion. (*Raising his voice a little.*) It will, I doubt not, much comfort the heart of the Fellows to hear that the Duke of Medina Sidonia is clean contrary to the King of Spain's projects; and hath told him, his ships underwent last year such a drubbing from our captains, as that it were midsummer madness to make any attempt to come at us.

THE PROVOST (*a little wearily, as if he had heard this kind of thing before*). Why, God be thanked for it.

MR. FENTON (*rather too obviously quoting from official instructions*). And whereas divers persons, whether of their natural fearsomeness, or with intent to comfort the Queen's enemies, will still be putting about rumours of great peril impending, whereby simple folk are much dismayed and confounded in their wits, the Queen (I hear) is greatly displeased thereat, and will have all such authors of sad reports given up to correction. (*He looks at Dr. Heywood, who shifts a little in his chair but does not speak.*) Well, Mr. Provost, I have to wait upon a gentleman who makes but a short stay in the City; I hope the Fellows will have me excused.

(*He goes out, and there is an immediate sense of tension relaxed as he shuts the door behind him. He is not a spy, for everybody knows what his position is in the College, but a kind of Government commissar in whose presence they studiously avoid topics of national importance The Provost shakes his head, and there is silence for a little.*)

MR. TAVERNER. It is not to be doubted but the Spaniard is on the high seas.

DR. HEYWOOD. It is rumoured, he hath touched already at the Scillies.

MR. TAVERNER. This is a pretty harvest the Queen hath reaped, for taking upon herself to be the defender of the reformed religion. I do not know that the name of England hath ever been so blown upon, in the lifetime of the eldest man living. I was in London lately, and saw the poor fellows that had come back from the wars in the Low Countries, some fifty ragged wretches complaining that there is neither food nor help sent to our armies there, and driven away without ceremony by the Lords of the Council, that they should not come at the Queen's person. Small wonder if they of Holland cry out on us for treachery; to let Sluys be taken was worse done than to lose Calais in Queen Mary's time.

DR. HEYWOOD. It is God's truth; we are to be notoriously punished for our so long blowing hot and cold in matters of religion. These years past, we might have been comforting the Netherlanders against King Philip, and all we did was to mumble and let occasion slip. We have threatened the King of Spain, and made promises to his enemies, taking no thought how we could bring to pass one or the other. We have talked loud of peace, and let the manifest peril of war blow up against us, counting it all gain if we could harry a few merchant ships plying on their lawful occasions from the Indies. If the Duke of Parma should land to-morrow in Essex, it is no more than what we have deserved.

MR. RICHARDS. Well, we are all in God's hands.

DR. HEYWOOD. No, Sir, we are not in God's hands. That is, we are subject to his near vengeance; but we can look for nothing from his mercies, who have so often abused his patience and man's with our continual piratical injuries.

DR. WOLVERIDGE. I take that to be piracy, which makes prizes of foreign ships when there is time of peace. This is not so now, when, though there be no open declaration of it, all the world knows the King of Spain is our enemy. What Sir Francis Drake did last year in the harbour of Cadiz was no more than to prevent the designs of the Spaniard against us, by being beforehand with him; this was not piracy.

DR. HEYWOOD. You would do as well to say, that a man may rightly hamstring his neighbour's horse if he feared this same neighbour had designs upon his wife. No, Sir, we must not anticipate the wrong done; we shall all go back to savagery else. It is besides observable, that this meddling with Spanish matters is not at all a thing of yesterday. We were already taking prizes out of Spanish bottoms these many years back, when they were carrying goods to France, at which time it was generally agreed that France, not Spain, was our chief enemy.

DR. WOLVERIDGE. And may we not carry off cargoes as well from those who are comforting our enemies, though they be at peace with us, as from our enemies themselves?

MR. RICHARDS. For my part I would make no distinction; French or Spanish, they were all papists together, and we are not bound to be respecters of such.

DR. HEYWOOD. That is right Lollardy, Sir, when you will have us believe that a Frenchman or a Spaniard hath no right of possession over his own cargoes, because he is not one of God's elect. Have a care, Mr. Richards, or you will yet stand at the stake for an Anabaptist. I am no more ready than you, God knows, to have papists and foreigners for my bedfellows; nevertheless I say we should have let them alone, and not provoked them by these bitter injuries to levy war upon us.

MR. TAVERNER. Well, it is all one; be the fault where it will, the King of Spain has us at his mercy.

DR. WOLVERIDGE. So they of Athens said, when the invasion of Persia was presently expected. Nevertheless Themistocles told them, according to the oracle, that they should be saved by their wooden walls, that is, by their ships. The Duke of Medina Sidonia must still try conclusions with Lord Howard and with Sir Francis Drake before he will put his troops on land.

DR. HEYWOOD. Sir Francis Drake? Why, he is for nothing but prize money. See if he do not leave his place in the line, the first time he sees one of the enemy's ships at a disadvantage, to tow it into Plymouth and make plunder of the captain's dinner service.

THE PROVOST. Sir Francis hath a fine spirit, but little judgement. He is not an Oxford man; I would that they had more Oxford men now in the fleet. Sir John Hawkins, they say, hath been very negligent since he was Treasurer, so that all our ships are rotted away most villainously. If we had Sir Humphrey Gilbert, now,—he would have made all well. But he is dead these five years, a great ornament of the University.

DR. WOLVERIDGE. Very like, Mr. Provost, if you had the care of the realm, you would advance Sir Walter Raleigh, that was his half-brother?

THE PROVOST. What, Raleigh? No, he came to no good here, nor will elsewhere. I hear he is trying to plant potatoes in Ireland. You will not teach the potato to grow in Ireland; it is very marshy and boggy soil there.

MR. TAVERNER. It is all one, who is in command; it is

not possible but that the Spaniard should have the best of it. See how little a work they made of Strozzi's force, that was in the Azores. Our captains will slip in and out of a harbour, doing great mischief to the shipping before they are catched; but on the high seas he who can board his enemy with greater force must needs come off bettermost. Call me a vain prophet if we do not see King Philip proclaimed here before summer is out.

MR. TAVERNER'S GUEST, *one* MR. LEE. How is that, Sir? Are you so confident in your opinion that King Philip has an itch to rule in England again? It is thought that he hath had his bellyfull of it. There are those besides among the exiles—I had it myself from one that is a friend to Mr. Allen—who are making great influence for the King of Scots; it being generally thought that he would embrace the religion of his late sainted mother gladly enough, if he could put the Tweed between him and the presbytery. For my part, I think King Philip is a true son of his own Church, and more eager to see the wrongs of religion righted than to take any vengeance for the loss of a few cargoes. If we had in these islands a Catholic King, such as would not help the rebels to make head in the Low Countries, I doubt not he would be well content.

MR. RICHARDS (*a man of clear-cut ideologies*). I cannot see that it makes any great matter whether the King of England be Philip or James, or Simon or Jude, if he brings back the Mass with him. It will be an end of true religion; and I thank God I have good friends at Basel who will shelter me.

THE PROVOST. You are a young man, Mr. Richards; and you young men will always be for making nice definitions over this and that. For myself, I was fellow here in King Henry's time, when we sang the Mass lustily enough, yet the Pope's word never ran in Oxford, no, nor in the whole of England. And then King Harry died, and we were hard put to it to tell whether there was Mass in the chapel or no; it was Kyrie eleison to-day and Lord have mercy on us to-morrow, with much expense to the College in continual procuring of new service-books. But it did not last long, Sir; when Queen Mary came in, we went back nothing loth to our old mumpsimus, and the realm was at peace.

MR. RICHARDS. Peace, Mr. Provost? I will answer you out of the mouth of Jehu the son of Namsi; what peace, so long as——

DR. HEYWOOD. Sir, contain yourself; Mr. Provost is speaking.

THE PROVOST. What was I saying? Ay, I was talking of Queen Mary's time; but that did not last long neither. As for her present Majesty, she hath blown hot and cold, but now we have all one mass again, and we must use that until she or some other send us a better. But you will find it is all one; the times go backwards and forwards, and no man can tell what will be the end of it. Honest men should put their coats about their ears for a little, and follow with the fashion of the time, not running off to Basel this day, and to Rheims the next, as if salvation should depend on an Ave Maria.

DR. HEYWOOD. It is well said, Mr. Provost; but you

are of the old vintage, and can turn parson or priest as the times serve. I was ordered priest with Queen Elizabeth's book, and if we are to have the Mass back by the autumn, it is time I went to school again and learned my primer after the old fashion. Should I not look a brave fool, think you, to begin putting on massing-vestments at my time of life and cry Dominus vobiscum, who have been bred to nothing other than the new book, and have had it pat on my tongue these twenty years?

THE PROVOST. You will find it comes wonderful easy with use, Dr. Heywood. I doubt not but I am something rusty in the manner of it myself; " Orate fratres " . . . let me see, what was that that was said after " Orate fratres "? It is no matter; I warrant you a little use would bring it back to me. You shall do well enough, Dr. Heywood, you shall do well enough.

MR. TAVERNER. It is fearful to think what havoc will be wrought of men's consciences, when so many ministers must needs put away their wives, or else starve. I thank God the statutes have made us into as good celibates as ever the Church of Rome boasts; we had been in great trouble of spirit else. Do you think it shall suffice his Holiness to absolve the realm from schism, Mr. Provost, and thereupon all go merrily, or must Dr. Heywood and the residue of us be admitted to orders anew? They tell me there is much pother made now among the Catholics over the ordering of priests.

MR. LEE. It is very certain, Mr. Taverner, we shall be nothing the better for it, who have been ordered after the Queen's fashion; we are no massing-priests, you and I.

MR. TAVERNER. One thing is certain; there are so many chances of damnation in this unquiet world, it will be a comfortable thing to have St. Peter on our side, when the account is taken. What, Mr. Richards, are you leaving us thus early?

MR. RICHARDS (*evidently disliking the turn which the conversation is taking*). Your pardon, but I am to preach before the University this Lord's Day coming. I am much exercised over that of St. Paul to the Thessalonians, where he speaks of the Man of Sin, who is none other than the Pope of Rome, to my thinking. Who, then, is he that letteth? There is here, I think, much room for controversy. (*He goes out.*)

DR. HEYWOOD. It shall go hard but this shall prove to be the Spanish King, so long as St. Paul hath Mr. Richards for his interpreter. This will do us no good, Mr. Provost, if things go as it is probable, to have the name of Simon Magus bound up with such uneasy firebrands as Mr. Richards is.

THE PROVOST. He will grow milder with years, Sir, and frame himself after the fashion of the times; you will see all shall be well. It exercises me more, what is to become of the fellows who left us for Douay, in these ate years, and will now be fetched back again to the College, as I suppose, full of quidlibets and quodlibets after the old fashion of the Schools. I doubt we in Oxford shall seem very rusty and moss-grown to such as were our pupils formerly. There was Mr. Lewis, as I think, and Mr. Loseby; I cannot remember if there were any more. (*Turning to Mr. Lee.*) Were there many from your house, Sir, that went overseas for religion?

MR. LEE (*with an embarrassed smile*). Why, no, Mr. Provost; I believe I am the first. (*In answer to a general dropping of jaws.*) Since these two gentlemen have left us, who are of the new way of thinking, nothing forbids but I should be open with you; I believe myself to be among friends. Mr. Lewis, when he was of this College, was my very good friend; and I will not deny but I have had some exchanges with him by way of letters since he crossed the seas. He hath persuaded me, or at least taught my conscience to persuade me, that there was never any true religion among us since the Queen put out the old bishops that were in her sister's time; and that neither I nor any other man here, Mr. Provost excepted, can offer to God any agreeable sacrifice. Since I have thus resolved my mind, there are no two ways of it; I take ship to-morrow, before the ports be so hindered and watched as that passage may be altogether denied me.

THE PROVOST (*as if humouring a child*). Yes, you young men will always be for going overseas.

MR. TAVERNER. Good God! Mr. Lee, Mr. Lee, it was this you would say when you told me you looked to be absent for a good while! Why, the bustle and confusion of these times must have crazed your wits, that you should be for leaving Oxford behind, and these pleasant walks of Simon Magus, and the company of men your equals, to coop yourself up behind seminary walls, in a forgotten town of Flanders, and wear out your manhood over knotty questions of the schoolmen. This is not well thought of, Mr. Lee; indeed it is not. Ask these gentlemen now, that have longer experience of the world than you and I, whether you be not set on a wild-goose chase, you that are so regarded in the University, and like to be one of the proctors for next year.

MR. LEE. I am sorry, Mr. Taverner; I have broke this news to you something more suddenly than our long and dear acquaintance hath deserved. But what would you? Oxford is a town full of whispers, and a man can scarce speak his mind to himself but he goes in danger of being betrayed. Look you now, how is it that you and these other gentlemen are so ready to welcome back the Mass and the Pope if the King of Spain bring them to your doors to-morrow, yet will raise so much cry about it if I go abroad to seek them, and that to-day? Is it a matter that can be decided by a puff of wind on the seas, whether the Mass is Christ's Body and Blood, or rather a blasphemous fable?

DR. HEYWOOD (*energetically*). Ay, Sir, but I will retort your dilemma on you; I will rebut it with due forms of logic. If the Mass be what you think it is, can you not in God's name wait till the autumn of the year to enjoy it, when the realm hath wanted it these thirty years past? Come, Sir, either the Duke will speed well, or he will go to the bottom and all his force with him. If he prosper in his design, either the Queen herself will turn Catholic or some other of that faith shall sit on the throne instead of her; in such case, you shall have your Mass in St. Mary's. Or else he shall be repulsed; which if God grant, the new religion shall yet stand as heretofore, and you, if you find your stomach too queasy for it, shall go abroad at your good leisure, no man letting you.

MR. LEE. Sir, I think Prometheus saith, in the play Aeschylus wrote of him, it is no great matter to give good advice to men in trouble, so you be outside of it yourself. My case is other than yours. I find no fault with the conscience you in Simon Magus have, albeit this reformed religion of yours seemeth to me a strange thing, which to-day is and to-morrow is cast into the oven. But for myself, I hold that if the Pope of Rome will be Christ's Vicar come Michaelmas, Christ's Vicar he is even now; and I am on my way to him.

THE PROVOST. I cannot see what you young men will be after, to be evermore talking of the Bishop of Rome. For the Mass, now, that is a different matter; there was little complaint made about that, so long as we had it, and there is less reverence had to the clergy since Tom, Dick and Harry could understand all that was said in the prayers. These English prayers are besides very wordy stuff; it was Dr. Cranmer, I think, who had the making of them, that was a good scholar indeed, but wrote after a very tedious fashion. I would say the Mass again right merrily, if I could find what is become of the old books; but it sticks in my head they were burned when my Lord of Barchester made his visitation, and quite took away all that was left from Queen Mary's time. But I was speaking of the Bishop of Rome; he was no more thought of in the University than Prester John, at what time Simon Magus was founded. Yet Mr. Taverner here is continually telling us we shall have the Pope back; I cannot understand it that he should speak so.

MR. TAVERNER. I spoke of the University, Mr. Provost; you will not deny, as I suppose, that the Pope's word ran in the University before King Henry gave himself out to be head of the Church. And as for Trinity and St. John Baptist's, they were founded both of them in Queen Mary's time, to the very end they should further the Pope's cause; and it was great prejudice, as I think, to the University that the intentions of their founders were so lightly set aside. Who will build Colleges now, when he cannot say what purpose his benefactions shall be put to, while he yet lives?

DR. HEYWOOD. For that, Mr. Taverner, you are in the right; and there is no doubt but that the continual disquiet of these times, through the shutting of men's purse-strings, is much to blame for the decay of learning and neglect of the arts in this University. But I am not yet finished with Mr. Lee. What the plague ails you, man, that you would go off and join yourself to the Pope and Mr. Allen, at the very time when the Pope, as is most certain, and Mr. Allen, as it is commonly credited, are putting on King Philip to invade your country? Did not Aristides, when he was exiled by his fellow-citizens, nevertheless discover to them the practices of the Persian king, choosing rather to seek the good of his country, than to take a private vengeance upon Themistocles his enemy? And would you, for no better a cause than these your uneasy scruples over a matter of Church government make common cause with the Queen's enemies, at the time of her most need? This is no sort of honesty, nor conscience neither.

DR. WOLVERIDGE (*who has been sitting with his head judicially cocked on one side, drumming on his knee, and now turns round to take part in the conversation*). Why, Dr. Heywood, I like your taste in honesty. Here are the Pope and Mr. Allen, as you pretend, levying war upon us, and Mr. Lee is resolved to throw in his lot with them, whether their cause shall prosper or no, betaking himself for that end to some foreign port, at the great hazard of his life and good name. Whereas you will sit comfortable here in Common-room, waiting till you see which way the wind blows, and anon crying huzza for King Philip, or damning him for a lousy papist, as need shall serve. You will not easily persuade me that your part is the more heroical.

DR. HEYWOOD. No, Sir, this will not serve. I am by God's grace a minister of religion; and I hold it the duty of all such to live peaceably under whatever king Providence may send us, and to draw others thereunto. I will exercise my ministry, God willing, in this chapel, under the form which may from time to time by lawful authority be prescribed. You will not find me slinking about from one country to the next, stirring up foreign enemies without and civil dissension within. I will not be bold to meddle, Sir, in the affairs of princes.

DR. WOLVERIDGE. God forbid I should ever be a prince; but if I ever were such, I would not wish for a better subject. But come now, Dr. Heywood, let me set forth a parable. I hear there was a stage-play lately enacted in London, I have forgot who it was that put it out, upon the career of Dr. Faustus. Some think it glanced a little at Dr. Dee, of whom we were but now speaking. However that be, it seems this Dr. Faustus did sell his soul to the devil, who undertook to do all his bidding until the time was due for calling in the said bond; with such comical effects as might be expected. Now, Sir, if you were even now in Dr. Faustus' case, tell us what fortune you would send to the Duke of Medina Sidonia and this armado that sails under his colours? Would you grant them fair landing, or raise such a wind as should break them all to pieces upon some inhospitable headland in the Northern seas?

DR. HEYWOOD (*chuckling*). Why, that would be what old Wycliffe said, that God must obey the devil. I will open my mind to you, Dr. Wolveridge, since we are all friends here, as Mr. Lee says, and no word is to go beyond these walls, however luck shall serve us. If I had a familiar that would run such errands for me, the Duke should sink like a stone, and all his company, and all should go forward in England as heretofore. There has been too much chopping and changing, and whilst we are wrangling, the minds of the common people are quite drawn away from religion. You will remember that crazed fellow John Penry, that was formerly of St. Alban's Hall; he hath put out an address lately, wherein he says plainly that in Wales the common sort will not go to Church any longer, and live very loose. For my part, I would damn all papists and all Puritans, and order everything seemly, but so as shall be to the liking of the common man that has his place on the ale-house bench, and is neither saint nor sinner. Let us all in God's name be content with that, and there shall be neither burnings nor bowellings hereafter.

DR. WOLVERIDGE. Herein, I think, Mr. Taverner will much blame you.

MR. TAVERNER. Who, I, Sir? Oh, I am for peace, like Dr. Heywood; only that I would have the Mass back, and all made merry with holy days and processions as in the old time, and men shriven of their sins, not hardened in them or despairing of them as the more part of them are at present. As for the Pope, I think no harm of him if he would give over plotting against us, and making alliance with foreign princes to overthrow us. He should be Pope still, so he would suffer us in England to follow the old ways, and send no more Jesuits among us.

DR. WOLVERIDGE. You are too nice in what you ask, Mr. Taverner; I doubt you will find a devil in all hell that is powerful enough to order the world according to your liking. Take care but, if the Duke land, you will find the Pope an uneasy bed-fellow. It will be as it was after Queen Mary's crowning; if you will not burn with Dr. Cranmer, you must be the Pope's man with Dr. Gardiner.

THE PROVOST (*as if to himself*). I cannot understand what they are at, to be evermore talking of the Pope; this was not so in my time.

DR. WOLVERIDGE. There is no need to ask your mind, Mr. Lee. I think you would send Lord Howard and Sir Francis to the bottom, and no dirge said over them.

MR. LEE (*his head pillowed between his hands, as if to avoid looking at the others*). God knows I cannot say. You will think this conceit of mine very strange, but I do not think I would gladly see the Spaniard get the best of it. And that, perhaps because I am English born; yet I do not think so neither; I have little love for the rule of this present council at least. But my thought is rather this—If this realm were governed now by a Catholic prince, what manner of Catholic subjects would his be? Men like Dr. Heywood and Mr. Taverner, who would conform then, as they conform now, because they must. This were, to my thinking, a religion of show and of custom only, worth no more than a flower with a canker at the heart. The Church in these our days hath no need of lip-service; she cannot conquer, until men are brought to believe she is the Bride, and the Pope's Holiness the Vicar, of Christ himself.

DR. HEYWOOD. It is an ill matter, when men will stick over points of doctrine, and not rather read life as they see it. Here is the Bishop of Rome bidding the Queen's subjects lift up their hands against her; this had not Christ done, who told us we should love our enemies; and I say he hath a very unserviceable Vicar at this time. Why, you were but now saying yourself that you would not rejoice to see the Spaniard land; will you now tell us that the Bishop of Rome doth well to comfort him?

MR. LEE. You must forgive me, Sir, but I will not follow you into these matters; I have not the head for them. You are very confident now that the Pope doth ill; by that September come, if I understand you right, the case may be so altered that you will be confident the Pope did well. But as for me, I know not whether he doth ill or well; only I know that if he doth ill, Christ will judge him for a most unworthy Vicar; for he is but a man. But, Sir, it is not the man as he is a man that all good Catholics should reverence, for he may err in judgement. It is his office that all good Catholics should reverence; which office we in England have most wilfully left vacant, feigning instead that her Majesty is the supreme governor of the Church in these lands, which is blasphemy such as her ancestors never used. Since when, as I hold, the bishops that have taken the oath to her, with all such as acknowledge them, are no true part of the Church Catholic.

DR. HEYWOOD. Sir, I can see you have conned your brief well, but see where it leads you; to make a Catholic of yourself you will make an alien of yourself. You will become a stranger unto your mother's children, that is, to your fellow-countrymen, all but a few stubborn fellows, that will be as absolute as yourself over one point of doctrine.

MR. LEE. I will not deny what you say; I have weighed it already, and counted the cost. All these last weeks, I know not why, that of the shepherd in Virgil hath been coming back to my mind continually;

At nos hinc alii sitientes ibimus Afros:

we are exiled from you now across the seas, and we shall be exiled yet longer from your thoughts and memories in England, and most in Oxford. Anyone that will be absolute over a point of doctrine shall find himself a stranger here. And we above all, that will stick to the old religion, shall have no part with you. We shall be men marked down for hatred; why, I know not, unless it be that men hate more where they have done wrong than where they have suffered it, as the philosopher says that he who confers a benefit is afterward more loving than he who hath received it. It will not be aught we have done to you, whether the burnings in Queen Mary's time or the plottings, if there be any, at this present, that will be the food of your hatred; it will be as when a man loathes the sight of the mistress he hath cast off, you will wish us dead because we disturb you with a memory of what once you were. And though your fury against us abate with time, you will still reck little of us; and this that was said, because it was said by a papist, shall have the less credit, and he who will seek advancement in the realm must first be false to his own faith, or he will get no hearing among you. You in Oxford will be slow to strike in with new fashions, but evermore, though at a distance, you will follow them, and the old things will not return. You have reproached me, Mr. Provost, for that I go lightly overseas; do you think I have not understood what things it is that I leave behind? Or do you doubt my love for them?

THE PROVOST (*feebly*). You should have more patience, man, and trust to the event. All shall be well; believe me, all shall yet be very well.

MR. TAVERNER. Come, Mr. Lee, as touching all this that you have said, you are but dreaming. You have but forecast, according to the measure of your own dark fancy, how things shall go in Oxford if the Pope's cause be lost. Whereas it is plain from all we hear that the old religion is shortly to come back again, to the great contentment of many, and as I think of the more part, in this realm. Pray leave these your scruples for a little and continue your stay here for a few weeks at the least, until we see which way things will be falling out.

MR. RICHARDS (*re-entering suddenly, in great excitement*). I could not be content to withhold it from the fellows, how much I am eased in my mind with what hath befallen.

DR. HEYWOOD (*half-rising in his excitement*). Why, what is that?

MR. RICHARDS. It hath been made known to me, Sirs, who is he that letteth. It is none other than the King of France.

DR. HEYWOOD (*in disgust*). What, is there no news then come from London?

MR. RICHARDS. Oh, aye, I had forgot. There is a post come, that the Spaniard hath been sighted. I think they told me, he is a little way off the Scillies.

MR. LEE. Your pardon, Mr. Taverner; and you must make my excuses to these gentlemen. There is no other way will serve, but that I should take horse for London to-night.

NOTES ON CHAPTER II

It will naturally be asked, whether I have any independent authority for believing in the existence of these *revenants*, whom I saw in my dream, but only as one sees men in a dream; as personages, rather than as figures, so that when you looked at them intently their features began to dislimn and were exchanged for the features of later men, familiar to the dreamer in common life. Unfortunately, the early records of Simon Magus have been very badly kept; much has disappeared during the disturbances of the Commonwealth. There is one source, however, to which I naturally turned in the hope of gleaning some information about my dream-friends, Anthony à Wood's *Athenae Oxonienses*. Of course, this work only embalms the memory of those who left published works to the credit (or discredit) of their names. And it looks as if the fellows of Simon Magus in Queen Elizabeth's time had not been very ready with the pen; so that I have only been able to trace the careers of two by this means—Mr. Taverner, who afterwards became Provost, and Mr. Richards. The notices are somewhat meagre, as they are apt to be when Antony is dealing with men of the sixteenth century. But I cannot resist the temptation to reproduce even these shreds of corroboration. Here is the obituary of Mr. Richards:

"HENRY RICHARDS was born in Wales, and particularly in Denbighshire, the son of honest and sufficient parents. After what early nurture I know not, he was admitted fellow of Sim. Magus Coll. in the year 1585 or thereabouts, having the name of a sober student and one well grounded in divinity. Yet it appears he ever leaned so much towards enthusiasm, as that he could not reach any preferment in that society, which still hung after the old ways and busied itself little with controversy. Being forced, therefore, to seek room elsewhere for the proper employment of his talents, (for his mind was much set on preaching, and that in a high-flown fashion, with many fantastical subtilties of interpretation), he removed to the parish of Snailham, in Essex, and there passed the residue of his earthly life, as I guess, among clownish men that had a great conceit of him for the ranting style which he used in admonishing of them. His published works are,

The Ungodly cut off as Foam upon the Water, a Thanksgiving to Almighty God for our Deliverance from that frightful Armado which the Spaniard lately sent against us. Lond. 1589.

England's Powder-Magazine, a Discovery of those hellish Plots whereby the Bishop of Rome seeks daily our Destruction, shewing clearly what Peril this Nation is come into from harbouring of Jesuits, seminary Priests, and other sculking Nicolaitans, whom the Spirit of Christ bids us rather spew out of our Mouths. Lond. 1593.

God's frightful Judgements upon impenitent Sinners; shewing that the Number of those who will be lost is out of all proportion infinitely greater than of those few who shall be saved. Lond. 1598.

Our author, as he was at all times very hot against certain points in the Common Prayer, and was thought by his friends to be far gone in enthusiasm, so he made shift to comply with what orders were taken under Q. Elizabeth for the seemly performance of public worship, and wore a surplice, though 'twas thought very unwillingly, as often as he went into the chancel. He died by drowning in a channel or dyke, an. 1601, not without the suspicion that he had made away with himself; being at that time much addicted to melancholy, in so much that he was drawn into grave doubt concerning his own salvation. Yet 'tis certain that he received Christian burial, and lies towards the E. side of the church at Snailham, time having much defaced his epitaph."

Mr. Taverner's career was a more successful one:

"JOHN TAVERNER, the son of a father of both his names, entered upon his being in this world about the year 1565, in the parish of Wapping. To what favouring winds he owed his early advancement in the arts, it is not upon record; 'tis certain he was a battler of Sim. Magus Coll. in an. 1577, and afterwards scholar and fellow of the same society. At which time learning flourished little in the College, or in the University, so many of the more precious scholars of that age having withdrawn themselves overseas for the cause of religion; nevertheless, our author was thought to have laboured with some fruit in the study of natural philosophy, then much neglected in comparison of what we have seen in our day.

At what time Q. Elizabeth visited the University, an. 1592 (of which you shall see more elsewhere), he was one of those that busied themselves most in the matter of her entertainment; 'twas said he was the author, in part, of a play which was performed in her presence, and 'tis certain that he made a Latin speech, to the admiration of all, in which he rehearsed the singular great benefits received from Providence during her reign. It is reported by one, who wrote much in dispraise of our author, and manifestly bore him an extreme ill will, that the Q. herself made little matter of it, only asking one of those who stood near her, *Who that little rat was?* And indeed it does not appear that he came by any considerable preferment until more than a dozen years later; at which time he wrote very ingeniously in Latin heroick verse an epistle congratulatory to his Majesty, for having escaped the malice of his enemies intended against him by means of gunpowder treason. After this he was much employed by k. James upon secret business, and was made one of his chaplains. His defamer, of whom I wrote but now, hereupon gives him the character of a sneaking and obnoxious person, whose only study it was, through royal favour to insinuate himself into such preferment as was far above his merit.

But if it were so, it seems these arts prevailed less in k. Charles' time; when our author fell quite out of favour, although by that time he was become provost of Sim. Magus, and much regarded in the University. It is most likely to be conjectured, that he came to want the king's favour through the displeasure of Dr. William Laud, afterwards archbishop of Canterbury; for it appears he made some influence against the new statutes which were then brought in, chiefly through the contrivance of that prelate. So it was that he never came at the vice-chancellorship, although it was thought by some he would willingly have held it, being somewhat inclined towards shows and dignities of all sorts. His works are,

An Inquiry, how it is that the Moon draws the Tides, with some further account of the Influence which is exercised by her upon Phrenetick Persons. Lond. 1589.

O, quam te memorem, Virgo? sub quo titulo Elizabethae reginae, universitatem hanc Oxoniensem serenissimi sui vultus lumine jam tandem illustranti, catalogum beneficiorum illorum, quae per illam (Deo gubernante) in nos defluxerunt humillime recenset Joh. Taverner, A.M. Oxon. 1593.

PATESCUNT INSIDIAE, h.e. epistola congratulatoria regi nostro serenissimo Jacobo, a perfidis hostibus Graeci ignis detonatione jam jam excidium subituro, sed

praesenti Dei ope feliciter erepto, humillime dicata a Joh. Taverner, A.M. Oxon. 1606.

Besides this if he wrote anything, it is lost beyond the reach of discovery. Nor is there much more I can tell you about our author, who grew to be an old man and somewhat doating, yet did not live long enough to see the miseries of this nation brought about by the unnatural rebellion of the Parliament men against his sacred Majesty k. Charles; dying, as it appears, on the very day when that martyred king set up his standard at Nottingham; his distemper, the pleurisy. I cannot tell what scruple it was induced him to have those words inscribed above his resting-place, *Remember not the offences of my youth.*"

This is all I have been able to collect from the *Athenae Oxonienses*. But I may be allowed to add some further notice of Mr. Lee, which I came across in a catalogue of names less remembered, yet perhaps not less memorable—Bishop Challoner's *Memoirs of the Missionary Priests*. The entry is to be found under June 31, the feast of Saints Promiscuus and Miscellaneus; internal evidence appears to shew that our Mr. Lee is in question.

"Mr. Walter Lee, alias Forrester, alias Cartwright, was born in the first years of Queen Elizabeth; his father being a priest who had had the misfortune to lapse into schism under King Edward, and again after the death of Queen Mary, so far forgetting his sacred calling as to go through the form of matrimony with one of his parishioners. Their son, although from his infancy he was brought up to have no other sentiments towards the Catholic religion than those of horror and distrust, was endowed with a naturally pious disposition, which enabled him to follow the imperfect lights that were given him with remarkable fidelity. Having conceived the desire of embracing an ecclesiastical career, he went to Oxford, and there set about studying for the Protestant ministry; the name of his College has not been preserved to us.

Oxford had already at that time given many of her sons to the priesthood, and a few to martyrdom; but there were some still to be found among the fellows of Colleges who hesitated between the voice of conscience, which called them to go into exile overseas, and the fatal allurements of worldly prosperity. We have no record, how long or how difficult a struggle Mr. Lee may have undergone, before he received the grace to follow his true vocation; but it appears from the books of Douay College, then flourishing under the rule of Dr. Allen, that a Mr. Lee was admitted there late in the year 1588, and pursued his studies in due course for the secular priesthood. While he was at the College, he edified all by the cheerfulness of his demeanour and the unaffected simplicity of his conversation, the University of Oxford being then a school, not of foppery and elegance, but of plain living and serious study. He proceeded to England immediately after ordination, and laboured for some time in the county of Barset, where by his earnest exhortations he persuaded many temporizing persons to refrain from attending schismatical worship, as well as securing the conversion of some from their protestant errors.

He was for several years remarkably successful in eluding the watchfulness which the government of that time kept upon the comings and goings of Catholics, disguising himself now as a travelling tinker, now as a waggoner, now as a gentleman of quality, in his travels through the district. But at last, in the general alarm caused throughout the country by the news of the attempted gunpowder treason, a special search for priests was set on foot by the sheriff of the county, and Mr. Lee was apprehended as he came away from celebrating Mass in the house of a widow lady, near Silverbridge. When he was brought to trial, his accusers spared no endeavour to implicate him in political disturbances, saying that he had gone overseas at the very time of the Spanish Armada, and that he was personally known to Mr. Garnett, whose name had been brought into suspicion as being privy to the recent conspiracy. But, failing to convict him of any such treasonable activities, they were content to rest their proceedings against him on the ground that he had received ordination in a foreign seminary, had celebrated the holy sacrifice of the Mass, and had presumed to absolve the King's subjects from the guilt of heresy. On these charges alone he was condemned to suffer at Tyburn, observing, when the sentence was pronounced, *I looked for no other issue than this ; God be thanked for it.*

Shortly before his execution, a protestant minister was sent to reason with him and induce him, if possible, to abandon the tenets of our holy faith. A particular account of this is given in a manuscript letter which was preserved among the archives at Douay. It seems that the minister chosen for this purpose was, by mere chance, an old acquaintance of his during his time at Oxford. He had scarcely come into the cell, and his eyes had not yet become accustomed to the darkness of it, when Mr. Lee broke out, *Why, Mr. Taverner, are you yet at Simon Magus?* And, being assured that this was so, *Why, how do my good friends that I used to meet there, when I dined with you? And does the scent of the gilly-flowers come in yet by the windows of the Common Room, when you sit talking there after dinner?* Whereupon his visitor, conceiving that a man who talked so was but little concerned to prepare himself for death, replied, *Tush, man, you should not be thinking of these trifles ; but rather looking forward to eternity, and considering the horrible punishments you will there undergo, if you perish without repenting of your disobedience to the laws of this realm.* But Mr. Lee, with a very gay and cheerful countenance, put him aside from his purpose, assuring him, *That he thanked God he was well enough prepared for the difficult passage he was to make, having confessed his sins to a fellow-prisoner, and been shriven for them ; only he would know how Oxford did, for the pleasant memories of the place were with him continually.* And, to be brief, this Mr. Taverner went away in great disappointment, being unable to enter into any discussion of theology with him ; Mr. Lee guessing, I suppose, that no good could result from it.

He suffered very bravely, calling heaven to witness that he was a loyal subject of his Majesty, and died only for the ancient faith which had been the faith of England until fifty years back. Some portions of his clothing, sprinkled with blood, were carried off by a pious Catholic who witnessed his execution, and are yet preserved among the relics at the College of Douay."

CHAPTER III

CAKES AND ALE: 1638

MR. FULWELL (*a young fellow with a rather severe face*). Mr. Lilly, you have been smiling to yourself very secret this last hour gone; will you not tell us what cud it is your fancy chews upon?

MR. LILLY. Why, there is no mystery about it, save, if it please you, for the name of him that is most nearly concerned. I was this day rambling abroad with my friend Mr. Cotter of Magdalen Hall; and it was our humour to climb up over Cumnor Hill and so pass down the Long Leys to Bablock Hythe. The hawthorn was fully out, and there was a great smell of new summer about the hedges; the river flowed smoothly, as no longer swelled up with the late rains; it was a day for adventure and the renewing of old loves. The ferry-boat was moored at the further side, and the ferryman, as evermore he will be, absent from his duty. But there was in the boat itself a ragged-looking fellow of the common sort, with a cloak about him all in tatters, who sat there wetting his fingers in the stream, most childish to see. When Mr. Cotter and I holloa'd to him, he looked up without surprise, and set about pulling across to meet us. It was not until he was close to the Berkshire bank that we recognized him for the man he was; he, on his side, looked as if he would have withdrawn upon our nearer view; but, since that could not be done other than churlishly, he came on and greeted us as quietly as if we had been appointed to meet him. His name I must not bring back to memory, for he told us he would be best pleased when it was forgotten in Oxford. But you will remember, Dr. Berridge, what happened not long since about a bachelor of arts of this University; how he left his rooms and was seen no more among us, yet there was never any talk of foul play or of disgrace, only that he had wearied of Oxford and would rather live wandering about the countryside?

DR. BERRIDGE (*a man early bald, with something of a monkish look about him, though he would not like the suggestion*). Ay, I remember what you speak of, and I knew the fellow a little. He was a very sad, humorous man; not altogether without parts, but such as would never stick to his book, his mind hanging, as I was told, after easier and smoother studies than logic. He was soon forgot here, and I have not surmised above once or twice what was become of him.

MR. LILLY. Well, you shall hear at last; it seems this gentleman fell in with some roving fellows called *gypsies*, that had their encampment by Bagley Wood; and, for all they are at most times pretty close, and do not admit anyone of their brotherhood unless he be of their tribe at least by marriage, this friend of ours so worked upon them, being already much versed in such curious studies as are their delight, that they suffered him to go in and out with them, and even taught him some little of that hidden learning they have. I warrant you, Mr. Cotter and I sat there wide-eyed, with Thames at our feet, while he told us of the singular things he hath partly seen, partly heard with good ground for crediting of them. As, of a man taken up in the air and set down about the same time at a place many miles distant, and how they can read men's thoughts by the use of the beryl-stone. He told us also, what a glad exchange he had made of it, to be sleeping under a hedge, or beneath the eaves of a barn when winter comes, and how he hath learned from the gypsies to play their strange airs on the fiddle, which he will do at the village fairs till the folk dance their feet off for the great conceit they have of his melody.

DR. BERRIDGE'S GUEST, a MR. KINGSMILL (*he is evidently deaf, for he has sat with his hand cupped against his ear during the last speech, and only joins in the conversation at intervals*). That is very understandable. You in Oxford, as I have ever said, are on the high road to destruction; meaning thereby, to Woodstock, whither whenever his Majesty retires with the Court, you set on foot such merry-makings and junketings here as quite turn the hearts of the boys you should be training up in godly piety; so that those of them who will not go a-massing with the Jesuits will go a-fiddling with the tinkers. I hope Mr. Provost here hath more care of his charges in Simon Magus.

PROVOST TAVERNER (*roused to energy by any attack on the University*). No, Sir, for my part I think Oxford is not near in such bad case as formerly. In my young days, the boys would spend the more part of their time fencing and dancing, hunting the hare and stealing of deer and conies, with some wooing of wenches. All that is quite changed since my Lord of Canterbury was made Chancellor, who hath so plainly set out in black and white the ancient statutes of the University, as that no wrong-doer may plead ignorance of them. They are very painful, sober students here, Mr. Kingsmill, forward enough to read their book early and late.

MR. BERRIDGE. I think we are in more danger now of bemusing the young men's wits, with over-much studying against the time when they will be examined. To respond to a set of questions in the schools with a dozen or two of answers they have got parrot-wise is not to become learned men, nor yet to give proof of their natural parts and quickness of wit. There have been several notorious instances of late in this College of boys being plucked after we had expected great things of them.

THE PROVOST (*nursing an old grievance*). Ay, that is the fault of my Lord the Chancellor, though he hath notably enriched the University with his gifts. He is too stiff with us, and always for amending abuses out of hand. As witness the great influence he hath made, that none should determine before the statutory time; whence several Magus men have crossed over to Cambridge and determined there; a very beastly conclusion.

DR. BERRIDGE (*in a low voice*). Sir, Mr. Kingsmill is from Cambridge.

THE PROVOST. I meant no more, than that a man ought to determine at his own University.

MR. FULWELL. I hope Mr. Kingsmill will not find me contentious; but for my part I think the resolve taken by Mr. Lilly's friend, to go off and consort with vagabonds, is but a shift to which lively wits are driven, because they would escape from the overmuch sourness and heavy melancholy of the times. For, since the puritan sectaries came to their present pitch of boldness, every man is afraid of his neighbour's ill-looks, and dares not dance or sing or make merry as formerly they did. It is therefore that you find men overtaken with strange whimsies, such as that we were speaking of.

MR. LILLY. What, Mr. Fulwell, I did not know you were become so frolicsome. Shall we yet see you dancing a morris on the College lawn? Shall we ride out, a few weeks hence, to Fyfield, and will you give me news of the spicy nut-brown ale there, when young and old come out to play on a sunshine holiday?

MR. FULWELL (*evidently disapproving of this banter*). What you bring up at me was written by a puritan sectary; a Mr. Milton. He shall go a-maying with you, Mr. Lilly, and I wish you joy of your company. (*He lowers his voice, in deference to the views of Mr. Kingsmill.*) He is a poor, snivelling fellow, Sir, that will do much harm with his pen if he is cried up for a magazine of all the arts and graces, as he is like to be.

DR. BERRIDGE. The verses Mr. Lilly was making mention of were nevertheless ingenious. I do not look to find above one or two in a generation that are so ingenious as Mr. Milton. He hath put forth since a pastoral threnody which hath been much read; he called it Lycidas. I hope you will give some of your leisure to it, Mr. Fulwell; it may mend your opinion of its author somewhat.

MR. FULWELL. Sir, I have read the verses, and I find them very boisterous, lumbering verses indeed. " Where were ye, nymphs . . ." why, is not this a great to-do to be made about the death of one Mr. King, that had written some Latin verses at College? This is *exiguus mus*, a very slight argument for such general grief as the author supposes.

THE PROVOST. I am sorry to hear Mr. King is dead. I do not think he wrote any verses while he was at Christ Church.

MR. FULWELL. Sir, we were speaking of another Mr. King altogether, a Cambridge scholar that was drowned lately in the Irish Sea.

THE PROVOST. Why, then, we are well rid of him.

DR. BERRIDGE. Sir, Mr. Kingsmill is from Cambridge.

THE PROVOST. I am sorry. I meant only, that it was an ill-advised journey. I cannot understand what the young men are at, to be evermore going overseas.

MR. FULWELL (*pursuing his grievance*). And Mr. Milton asks, Sir, why the nymphs were not in the Irish Sea at what time Mr. King was drowned. Which easily moves the reader to ask, whether it had been a great negligence in them to be visiting the Lowland seas at that time, or the Caribbean seas, or any other. Moreover, when he hath stuffed his piece with gods and nymphs taken from the ancient authors, he did not well to conjoin them with the mention of Christian saints; this was never before done, I think, in pastoral.

THE PROVOST. It is a very hazardous thing, to write pastoral. You will not find anyone now to match Mr. Drayton.

DR. BERRIDGE (*fuming*). Sirs, what matter does it make, whether the young gentleman hath written good pastoral or no? His Lycidas is not such a piece as you can exactly measure *ad amussim*, with a foot-rule, bidding him go back and mend it, if here and here he have broken the canons of his art. I know something of this Mr. Milton, and I am very sure his geny is for something other than tickling men's ears with delightful conceits. He hath less care, I suppose, for such shepherds as do lie abroad in the fields and pipe ditties about their shepherdesses, than for those pastors whose much-wanting duty it is to feed the souls of men. That is why he brings into his verse the mention of Peter, mourning over Lycidas because there are few left like him, and there is great store of shepherds that will feed themselves only, suffering the sheep to go straying, or be catched by the wolf.

MR. KINGSMILL (*who finds it easier to follow when his friend is speaking*). That I know to be true of him; and moreover that he had a mind formerly to take upon himself the sacred function, but, seeing the great disorders that are in the Church at this present, and thinking he was not easily able to stomach them, he hath twitched his mantle blue, as he saith, and is gone off to other pastures. These are ill days, when a man of such learning and ingeniousness cannot proceed to orders, because his conscience will not suffer him. So he must needs occupy himself with writing of verses, for lesser men than himself to cavil the manner of the writing, because they cannot bear to look steadily upon the prophetic truth which is therein contained.

MR. FULWELL (*nettled*). For my part, I think there is charity shewn by honest men that will praise or blame Mr. Milton for his well or ill writing of pastoral, and not be searching about for prophetic meanings hidden beneath it. Else I think Mr. Milton might soon come to stand in the pillory, as Mr. Prynne did lately for a seditious libeller, because his *News from Ipswich* was written *sine fuco*, openly for all to read, and not wrapped up in a great deal of fantastic imagery about the tangles of Neaera's hair, and God knows what else.

THE PROVOST. Mr. Prynne was formerly much well spoken of at Oriel.

MR. LILLY. I do not think Mr. Milton hath let his meaning appear so openly as you pretend. What he said of those greedy shepherds put me in mind of the popish recusants; that is where, I think, his drift lies.

MR. KINGSMILL. That will not serve, Sir; for who then is the wolf? He brings in the massing-priests under the image of the wolf, that daily devours apace, and nothing said; meaning, thereby, that these same creeping enemies of religion have gained much boldness through the liberty granted them in these times by his Majesty's advisers, who are themselves, it is much to be feared, no better than papists at heart.

MR. FULWELL. It is false, Sir; there hath been no abatement of vigilance in that matter, no, not for an instant. My Lord of Canterbury, since he was Chancellor, hath ordered at all times diligent search to be made in the University for any that would snare the hearts of the young men; and if he comes to hear—as it needs must fall out now and again—that one is become the prey of the Jesuits who lurk hereabouts, he will have all the ports watched sooner than let such a one travel overseas.

THE PROVOST. It is difficult of comprehension, why the young men will always be going overseas. In my time, we heard little enough of it.

DR. BERRIDGE (*to Mr. Fulwell*). Either you are simple indeed, or you would wear a false cloak of simplicity, if you do not perceive that this sourness of the archbishop against the papists is but practise. He will make a great show of sacrificing these seminary priests to the just indignation of his countrymen, only that it may not light upon himself. This is what Medea did, when she chopped her brother Absyrtus small, to engage the attention of her pursuers. Even so these prelates who so willingly chop the Bishop of Rome in pieces are themselves but limbs of sorcery; ready to put the reformed religion into their cauldron, as befel Aeson, and bring it out again in all the lusty idolatry which clothed it aforetime.

MR. FULWELL (*scandalized*). Why, what wrong have our bishops done, that you should miscall them so villainously? Have they procured anything by their authority—that is, by the King's authority to that end committed to them—except only that the laudable customs of this Church of England, too long through factiousness and sottish negligence suffered to fall into decay, should be decently observed henceforward?

MR. KINGSMILL. Oh, ay, laudable enough, that a man is not to enter a Church without bobbing and bowing like a jack-in-the-green; though he were a proctor of the University, as happened to Mr. Corbet not long since, and could not endure to demean himself so childishly! Laudable enough, that he must bow again when the name of the Saviour is pronounced, as though the worship of the body availed anything, when there is none in the heart, or as if anything more were wanting, when that inner spiritual worship is truly present! Laudable enough, that the communion table should be fetched back to the end of the church, and there set lengthwise along the wall, after the very fashion of the idolatrous mass-altars which the Roman Catholics worship! I warrant you if old Parr, that went to Court three years back and died of it, had seen one of our new prelates at prayers, he would have vowed he was back again in his youth, *Consule Planco*, with King Henry the Seventh still reigning.

MR. FULWELL. Why, if we are to have a trial of rhetoric, we shall see the sun down before we come to any point between us. But I will not be led away into rantings; I will deal with you *ad strictos juris apices*, juridically, Mr. Kingsmill. That the table should be set lengthwise along the eastern wall, there is no innovation here, but it is plainly ordered by the Injunctions which Queen Elizabeth put forth; who, as she was the author of all our reformation in religion, so she must be thought to have known, what a table is and what an altar, and whether either the one or the other be idolatrous. And I will shew you in the same injunctions where order is taken that men should bow their heads whenever the holy Name of our Redeemer is found in the service. It is true, there is no like prescription for bowing the head when one comes into Church; but this is very conformable to all the discipline which is observed in this realm. If a man uncovers when he comes into the Church, why should he scruple to bow? The one is not more a sign of reverence than the other.

DR. BERRIDGE. Sir, you are young, and you see things after the fashion of the times; which is, to be very absolute over your determinations in argument, using the forms of law and logic with overmuch nicety. Mr. Kingsmill and I are older men; and we have learned with age this among other things, that it imports more to have regard to the scruples of men's consciences, than to any laws written with paper and ink. So Paul says, first Corinthians eight and thirteen, "I will eat no meat while the world standeth, lest I cause my brother to offend." There may very well be enactments, made these many years since for the ordering of public worship, which have been suffered to fall into disuse not from any contumacy, no, nor from any supine negligence either, but because it was judged better that men's consciences should not be troubled with the observing of them. For there was yet some hope, I conceive, *Elizabetha regnante*, that the papists would be prevailed upon to forsake their brutish superstitions the more easily, if a few remnants of corrupt custom were left still in vigour. But since it hath abundantly appeared that, do what you will, they remain stiff in their hellish opinions, there was no reason any more for retaining these foolish ceremonies, for all that authority had formerly prescribed them. It is these *umbrae et imagines*, these shadows and images of popery, that your bishops are seeking to restore once more among us, for no better reason than that they are courtiers bred, and think idly to please Almighty God by such flatteries and empty shows as he most evidently abominates.

MR. LILLY. Nevertheless, Mr. Fulwell hath some right in his cause. For these ceremonies you speak of are not like to draw men any longer into superstition, since they mean nothing but what any Christian man may soberly avouch. As for example, it makes no matter whether the table be set lengthways or sideways, while it is commonly agreed that in our Communion order there is no pretended sacrificing of Christ's Body and Blood. What queasy stomachs, then, must they have, who would lift up their hands and cry popery over things of little moment! If any such are scandalized, let them look to it that it is not their own over-niceness which doth breed dissensions in the Church.

DR. BERRIDGE. Sir, I will answer you in your own kind. If these outward ceremonies signify nothing, were it not better you should forego them, for peace sake? But if they signify anything, then I would ask Mr. Fulwell here (for I think you yourself, Mr. Lilly, are not much concerned in these questions of divinity) what it is they signify; and according to his answer we shall know whether our consciences will suffer us to travel the same road with him.

MR. KINGSMILL. Ay, and let me press upon this gentleman my own question, which I propounded to him but now. If a man entering a church doth worship God in his heart, to what purpose is it that he should worship also with his hips? And if he doth not worship God in his heart, what can it avail him, that he should make an empty show of reverence? Nay, will it not rather fetch him into the surer damnation, seeing he thereby proclaims himself a hypocrite, whose portion is to gnash his teeth in eternity?

MR. FULWELL. Gentlemen, I could weary you with my reasons. But one reason I will give, because it is of the chief weight, and is more apt to command your good will. These and the like customs were, as it can be proved by strict inquiry, observed in the early Church, before ever it was corrupted by ill example. So that it were little becoming in us to pretermit what holy men of former times did hold in honour, and such moreover as had drunk in their religion from the very fountain of apostolic witness.

MYSELF. . . .

MR. KINGSMILL. I bid you have a care, Sir; you are slipping your head into a noose; this will do you ill service, if you should fall into controversy with the papists. For it is the very marrow of their doctrine, that what they observe is what hath been handed down to them by the tradition of former times; and it is therefore that they are so curious to know what Clement said of this, or Polycarp of that, or how it was that Ignatius of Antioch demeaned himself when he went into Church. But for us who have received the pure light of the gospel it is enough to say, that we have the Spirit working within us as well as ever he did formerly, so that there is no need to be evermore casting back to those early times; in which, moreover, God suffered much confusion to prevail, as you may read in Paul's epistles.

DR. BERRIDGE. It is besides one of our chief tenets, that Scripture doth contain all that is necessary to salvation.

MR. LILLY. Doth not the Scripture say that every knee shall bow at the holy Name?

DR. BERRIDGE. Tut, Sir, that is but a figure. The scripture bids us work out our own salvation with fear and trembling, Philippians two and twelve. Yet would you think me crazed in my wits if you saw me shaking at the knees and shivering like one that hath the ague, as often as I came into the chapel here, and protesting I would be damned if I did not work myself into a St. Vitus's dance?

MR. FULWELL. Sir, Mr. Kingsmill, I mean—I did not think to find you so timorous and crouching, as that you would decline an open controversy with the papists. It is very certain that they must be put down; and this shall best be done, if we shew them that we have kept the old tradition of apostolic times more eagerly than themselves; which is what the archbishop did, when he put down Fisher the Jesuit, and other our divines have used the same way with them.

MR. KINGSMILL. I would have no man argue with the weasel that spoils his hen-roost, nor no more with a Jesuit; I would root them out. If the law were well enforced, they should have no space for argument.

MR. FULWELL (*mildly*). Yet there are other papists than those who lurk in his Majesty's dominions; upon the Continent of Europe especially. And many of them, I make bold to think, are less stiff in their opinions than these our fellow-countrymen; so that there is some hope we may yet disabuse them of their errors, and come to a better understanding with them over sundry points of divinity.

MR. KINGSMILL (*making a gesture as if to stop his ears*). See now if it be not as I said, and you and all those divines you boast of are but returning like a washed sow to your wallowing in the mire! What, have you comforted all these years the Flemings and Frenchmen who fled hither for conscience sake, and given them liberty to practice the reformed religion, and will you now make terms with the old Beelzebub and throw them to him to mangle? I tell you, Sir——

DR. BERRIDGE (*interposing quietly*). Come, Mr. Kingsmill, you must not make an arch-traitor of Mr. Fulwell; I warrant he is not altogether so blood-thirsty as you pretend. Though true it is there is grave reason to fear the Frenchmen in London are like to be disturbed in the practice of their religion, so hard doth the archbishop bear on all who will not be conformable to his manner of worship. But, Sir (*turning to Mr. Fulwell*), what is worse, you are for offending the consciences of your own countrymen, and of other the King's subjects, for what? Only to get credit with a rabble of foreigners, who will never be content until they see the reformed religion quite put out of his Majesty's dominions. Look now at the Scots, how the archbishop doth harry and vex them; and what uproar was made, when the new service was first read amongst them!

MR. LILLY (*flippantly*). O, the Scots! In God's name let them be vexed and harried; they will overrun all England else.

MR. KINGSMILL. Nay, but pardon me, Sir, the shoe pinches nearer than that. Do you not see how many there are in England that are driven to worship God in honest men's private houses, or even in the open fields, because they cannot receive the Common Prayer as it is at this time for the most part enforced? And these being hunted out, having no other refuge to turn to, must cross over to Holland, or else take ship and sail for the Americas, as that godly remnant did not long since, that sailed from Boston in Lincolnshire, and now languish as colonists in savage parts, among barbarians indeed, yet such as prove less unkind than their fellow countrymen.

THE PROVOST. I could never yet understand why men will be going overseas. I have heard the old Provost say, when I was but a young fellow here, no good should ever come of sending out English folk to be colonists in the new world, by reason that this climature of ours, which is dampish indeed but not unwholesome, maketh us unapt to bear the many distemperatures of southern regions. Which prediction of his hath been abundantly verified, as we see that they of Virginia came near to being quite extinguished, some years back, through famine and the beastly treacherous assaults of the Indians. We have little news, I think, from Maryland; but 'tis like that they are in no better case. We must not look to hear more of the English plantations overseas, nor of these Lincolnshire gadabouts neither.

DR. BERRIDGE. What is to become of the planters, is not much to our purpose. They are scarce like to thrive, in a country which yields little but the tobacco and other worthless grasses. What more concerns us, is to see England emptied of her best and godliest families, because no room can be found for them to worship God here conformably with their consciences. Meanwhile this Oxford, that should be the nurse of true religion, puts out nothing but a race of crabbed scholars itching for preferment; and the more part of the boys sent here to study run wild for want of correction, falling into very loose ways, as Mr. Kingsmill says. Sirs, it is commonly known that there are three hundred ale-houses in the town; and the proctors are grown so remiss that they walk little of nights to see how these are frequented. What is this but to nurture the young gentlemen to be soldiers instead of scholars? As if we had need, in these peaceful times, to recruit an army for his Majesty.

THE PROVOST (*who has already forgotten that there is a Cambridge man present*). What Dr. Berridge says is true;

there is a deal of loose living in the University. And we are like to see worse, now that they have suffered the Thames to be made navigable as far as this; which design I would willingly have overthrown, if I had had the Chancellor's ear, for it will make Oxford yet greater, that is too great already. When I proceeded here, a man could see little outside the walls but fields and marshes, and now they are building everywhere. Look you how fair a house Mr. Smythe hath made for himself, over by Grampool, near where the Friars Preachers had their lodging formerly!

DR. BERRIDGE. It was but this morning I was shewing the place to Mr. Kingsmill, as we went forth towards Hinksey. We were of one mind, that the wooden figures beneath the windows are little becoming a Christian man's habitation.

MR. LILLY. I cannot find much reason to think that the boys here will be drawn into loose living, if only a score or so of bargemen with their families should be added to the number of the townspeople.

MR. KINGSMILL. It is because you have not lived long enough, Sir, to see what ill example boys of fourteen or fifteen years may take from the neighbourhood of the common sort. Already God is much offended by the profaning of his sabbath, with the playing of football and at cudgels, with the holding of Whitsun ales and May-poles, and the ringing of Church bells. If your boys here fall into such evil uses, from the daily consorting with low fellows in the ale-houses, how will you have acquitted yourself of your stewardship, who have received this pleasant inheritance to be a nursery of all godly piety?

THE PROVOST (*stiffly*). Sir, I do not think you will catch any young gentleman of this house playing at football. Nevertheless, I would have a limit set to this continual enlarging of our borders.

MR. FULWELL. Mr. Kingsmill, I find in you what I have ever noted in my friend Dr. Berridge; that you will make a great to-do when any man would abridge your own liberty of conscience, as by bidding you set the communion table here and not there; yet, if a man will only shoot an arrow at the mark on the Lord's Day, you are instantly for having such a one clapped into gaol. Now, Sir, which way will you have it? Will you stand for the ordering of men's doings by public authority? And, if that be the case, whose authority will you do better to obey than the King's, who is set over you by God himself for the terror of evil-doers, and his bishops', men learned in divinity and in the history of former times, when they meet in their solemn assemblies to take order for the good of the commonwealth? Or will you, *per contra*, have every man follow his own conscience, to do whatever he think well and right, as answerable to God and none other? Which if it be the case, why will you put restraint on Mr. Lilly here, that he should not go morris-dancing on the Lord's Day, ay, or play at football, if he be in the humour for it?

MR. KINGSMILL. I will answer you very simply, Sir, according to the light God gives me. We will have none of your authority, save in so far as it may be needful for keeping of the peace and for defence of the realm, because it is authority exercised by carnal men, concerning whom we can have no assurance, whether they be regenerate or no. And as it is very certain that the unregenerate are displeasing to God, so neither ought we, no, nor will we, engage our consciences to serve them as of right. This and none other, I conceive, was the cause why our fathers would not rest until they had reformed the old religion. Was not Queen Mary true Queen? Were not her bishops learned men and exercised in affairs? Yet might they not prevail over men's consciences; so neither shall his present Majesty, nor those his bishops, who are set apart by the laying-on of men's hands, and not called by God, as was Aaron.

MR. FULWELL. You have but answered the half of my question. Since you will have liberty of conscience, to disobey what order the King takes for right government in matters ecclesiastical, how is it that you will put on Hob and Dick a yoke which neither they nor their fathers were able to bear? Shall there be no more cakes and ale, nor dancing on the green, nor catches sung round the fire when the evenings close in with the winter?

MR. KINGSMILL. There is here no parity of matter. It is written that the saints shall judge the world; and although the time be not yet, when things will be openly so ordered, yet must the consciences of God's saints, even in these heavy times of waiting for their redemption, be a rule for carnal men, to demean themselves conformably with it. And though the King be not a perfect man, and his council, that rules without Parliament, be a very synagogue of Satan, yet it must be our study so to overbear them with salutary counsels, as that they shall take away the high places and cut down the groves (for this maypole of yours is nothing other than a heathen image), and bring the Lord's Day into greater observance. Else we should be accountable for the heavy judgements which are fallen upon this nation, as the fire in London lately and the pestilence that hath of late been among us; and moreover for those heavier judgements yet hanging over our heads, of whose near approach many portents bear witness.

MYSELF. . . .

MR. LILLY. Why then, we are in very evil case; I mean carnal men like Mr. Fulwell and myself. For burn in hell we must, by your way of it; and if in the meanwhile we would take to ourselves some little comfort, with drinking and dicing and whatever else unregenerate men should, you and your friends will have none of it. *What*, say we, *cannot you be content to wait a little before you see us languishing in bitterness?* And you will not humour us in this, lest we by profaning of the sabbath should bring down God's hand upon us in some shape of pestilence; which you catching of us, should have too sudden a passage to everlasting felicity.

MR. KINGSMILL. Sir, I perceive that you are in the gall of bitterness. You do ill to make light of God's admonishment.

DR. BERRIDGE (*in the unwonted role of peace-maker*). Come, Mr. Fulwell, let me resolve your difficulty more to your liking; I can see that you and Mr. Kingsmill shall never agree well together. He hath given you no other ground for detesting loose manners, than that he and his friends have sat in judgement on the King's Declaration of Sports, and have found it wanting. This is to arraign you and Mr. Lilly before a tribunal you do not submit your case to; you would have the matter tried *de novo*, in a higher court. Will you not consent, both of you, to remit your pleadings to the highest arbiter man hath in this imperfect world; I mean, God's word revealed to us in the Scriptures? If the Scriptures forbid the sabbath to be profaned, then I hope there is no tyranny used, if the common sort be restrained from profaning the sabbath by law?

MYSELF. . . .

MR. KINGSMILL. Your pardon, Dr. Berridge; it is much to be feared that this similitude of yours will only serve to darken counsel. The Scriptures, to my thinking, should better be compared to such a written code of laws as they that sit on the bench are sworn to judge by; not the court itself but the ruling which the court must needs observe. It is by a living voice that such a frame of laws must be interpreted, if it shall be made of effect here and now.

MR. FULWELL. Sir, I am grateful to you. You have said what was at the tip of my tongue; but I doubt I should have been so absolute in the delivery of it. How then, what is this *vox viva*, this living voice whose office is to interpret whatever is found ambiguous in the Scriptures?

MR. KINGSMILL. It is in the heart, Mr. Fulwell. The

Spirit himself bears witness in my spirit, that this and none other is the sense which such a passage bears. It is a light that shines privily from within, so that no man sees it, not even he that has it, but only he sees where it falls upon the page that lies before him, and with that he is content.

MR. FULWELL. I conceive that if a man were cast away upon an uninhabited island, and by God's mercy a Bible were left to him out of the wreck of all his fortunes, he should do well to be guided by such light as comes to him from within. But where you have many men desiring to live together, as men must, by a common rule and a common order, what is this private light of yours but a very Friar's lantern, jumping hither and thither? Nor is there any art or shift by which an end can be put to the ceaseless unnatural jarring and jangling of men's minds over quarrels of religion, through which the world hath been set by the ears these hundred years past, but if the Church speaking in the person of her bishops, by lawful authority appointed, do judge and decide in all matters of faith and worship. And if any be so queasy of conscience that they cannot demean themselves conformably, then —why, it must be the old cry of *sitientes ibimus Afros*; they must find some new angle of the globe to lay their scruples in, and their bones as like as not.

THE PROVOST. Whose was that verse, Mr. Fulwell, you cited but now?

MR. FULWELL. Virgil hath it, Sir, in his first Eclogue.

THE PROVOST. Ay, the first Eclogue; I knew I had heard it elsewhere.

DR. BERRIDGE. I marvel at you, Mr. Fulwell, that you can lend yourself to a manner of argument which, if it be carried to any great length, will leave yourself and your friends naked and unarmed before the first saucy Jesuit that will enter upon controversy with you. What, Sir, do you not see that it is as easy to set one Church quarrelling with the next, as one man? Have we not in England, besides this Church established by law, a great riff-raff of sects, Brownists and Familists and Ranters and the like, that can never come to any point one with the other? Which is like to draw us into such confusion as that the slinking Roman fox, a *tertius gaudens*, will carry off the goose from under our noses. No, gentlemen; where the Scriptures have any need of interpretation, it must be for them that are learned in the Scriptures to make them plain by continual painful study; not for court prelates, nor yet for maggoty-headed enthusiasts. I know that I am now but a pelican in the wilderness; but in the latter end, when you are all wearied of controversy, this will be the way of it. In the meantime, the Church in this realm hath two nations in her womb, and I would to God she might find an easy delivery.

THE PROVOST (*rising*). Sirs, I have lived through fifty years in this College of Simon Magus, and seven times have passed over me. I was myself *calidus juventa* when my Lord of Leicester was Chancellor, and it did not then appear whether the old things might not come back again; there was great ado made, but it all came to nothing in the end. You will see more than I shall; but I warrant you the wheel of time will come round full circle, and all shall be as it hath been. I must needs wait on Mr. Vice-Chancellor, who hath received fresh complaints of the young gentlemen disturbing his Majesty's game; it is a troublesome business. I hope you will spend the remnant of the afternoon with better argument than these uneasy points of divinity to engage you.

NOTES ON CHAPTER III

In attempting to identify by research the dream-characters we have just met, I have been unfortunate so far as Dr. Berridge is concerned. Perhaps I dreamed his name wrong. Mr. Kingsmill is alluded to in one of the extracts printed below; I have not come across him elsewhere. Mr. (afterwards Bishop) Fulwell was an author, so was Mr. Lilly, and each has accordingly his niche in *Athenae Oxonienses*. I print the two extracts in full, despite their length, because they are so thoroughly in character.

"ELIAS FULWELL, the son (as I conceive) of a gent., although his arms do not anywhere appear, drew his first breath in this world about the year 1610, in the county of Rutland. He was put to school at Okeham, and entered commoner of Sim. Magus Coll. an. 1622. Who, as he was of a sickly complexion and much inclined to the ague, so he did not at his first coming to Oxon. raise any great hopes that he would adorn the university with fresh laurels. But, being of a sober and admirable disposition, he applied himself to his studies above what was common in that age (the statutes being not yet reformed, which was done when Dr. Wm. Laud was Chancellor, as you shall hear more fully elsewhere), and at last proceeded bachelor of arts to the admiration of all who knew him, for the quickness and judiciousness of his mind. And soon after taking upon himself the sacred function, he was much held in regard, having the character of a painful and edifying preacher.

Besides his exact performance of the duties of his fellowship, he had a charge of souls in the parish of St. Mary Magdalen's at Little Matchett, no great distance from Oxford. Where, finding the chancel fallen into great disrepair; the dampishness of the walls (by reason of the roof gaping here and there) breeding everywhere (as he writes) nothing but mildew and pestilence, the walls scribbled on, the grease from the candles standing in great pools, and all the furniture of benches &ctr. set kim-kam here and there; this stout and public-spirited person made a great purge of these and other sluttish negligences by which the worship of God had hitherto been profaned. Causing the Communion table to be set in its right place, together with proper and comely rails at the entering of the chancel; also a cushion for the table and a pulpit-cloth; and he repaired the old organ, that was silent many years past and had bats roosting in it. All which things were cast up against him before the Grand Committee for Religion (as 'twas called, but should rather have been called the Grand Committee for sneaking and factious sycophancy) set up by the Parliament after the King's cause was lost in these parts.

On which account, and also because he had bowed or curtsyed towards the said table, and preached in his sermons much salutary doctrine (as will appear from the titles of those he hath published, as I shall later rehearse them), he was put out of his incumbency and also of his fellowship, and 'twas for some time thought he had been made away with, so utterly was his presence unknown to those who were formerly his companions in the university. But the truth is, he remained yet in Oxford; lodging very privately at the house of a widow lady, and making shift to eke out his penury with driving a carrier's cart between Oxford and Little Matchett (where, as I have told you, he was minister aforetime). Afterwards he was an usher in a free school in the county of Middlesex, until what time k. Charles was restored to his father's sovereignty, and those who had suffered from the villainous and inhuman fury of the sectaries were enabled to come to their own again; whereupon he commenced to reside at Sim. Magus as formerly, but as for his parish of Little Matchett, I do not find that he laboured there any longer. And indeed, within a short while he was lost to Oxford through accepting of higher preferment, being made archdeacon and afterwards bishop of Barchester, which last office of emolument he adorned 'till his death. His published writings are,

The Power of Prelates in the Church not contrary to Christ's Word, but rather confirm'd by many Evidences to be certainly of his express Institution; in the form of a Dialogue between two Disciples, by E. Fulwell A.M. Lond. 1634. This book, which is now somewhat scarce to be come by, was at the time of its appearing much in men's mouths; he thought at one time to have enlarged it in a new edition, but after repented of his design, for what reason I know not.

The Fear of Death abated and abridg'd by the Testimony of a Good Conscience, a Sermon preach'd before the University in St. Marie's Ch., Oxon. 1636.

How shall this man save us? which Query, blasphemously propos'd in the time of k. Saul by those the Scripture calleth children of Belial, is by the Male-contents of these times yet more blasphemously insinuated. Lond. 1637. This was a sermon, as I conceive, preach'd at Paul's in London, but afterwards enlarged somewhat and armed with fresh stings against the sectaries, then making head in London against k. Charles' government. To which purpose he added in the following year another short treatise which he entitled,

Parliaments not prescrib'd by God's Word for the good Estate of Nations; and that Council, which was set up in Jewry at some time after the Return from Captivity, no true Council but rather a Latrocinium, as is by the New Testament abundantly made manifest, being a remonstrance lovingly dedicated to the people of this realm by their humble servant, Pleniputeus. Lond. 1638. I cannot find why it was that he did not put forth this work under his own name (which the Latin nevertheless insinuates clearly enough), unless it were his purpose men should think this was a new champion come into the field; what was not to be expected from so sincere and venturous a character. This charge was cast up against him by the sectaries when (as I have told you) he was examined at the time of the rebellion. It is more likely to be supposed that, as he was a man of much diffidency, so he bogled with himself whether this work should increase his fame among posterity or no. And indeed it is somewhat sourly written, being otherwise no unworthy fruit of so fertile a genius.

The Tower of Siloam, a Consideration whether the late devastation most lamentably wrought in the Church of Wydecombe near the Dartmoors, as also the harm done to certain churches in Kent by the great storm of this January past, are to be thought of as God's Judgements upon this or that, and not rather as the common effects of lightning, and part of those daily admonishments by which he reminds us in general of our miserable State in this present World. Lond. 1639. This was occasioned by the relation published (by R. Herford, and printed in Queen's Head Alley) of the death and destruction on account of a thunderbolt, or some other such cause, in the church above named, an. 1638, which event was much drawn to superstitious uses by the credulous.

Good Manners, how corrupted by evil Communications, four Sermons preach'd at St. Bartholomew's in Smithfield. Lond. 1641.

The Sin of Witchcraft, a Sermon preach'd before his Majesty in the Church of St. Marie at Oxford. Oxon. 1644.

The Men of Succoth taught with Thorns of the Wilderness and Briers, a Sermon preached before his gracious Majesty upon the occasion of his happy Restoration. Lond. 1660.

I do not know that he published anything after he was made bishop; preferring rather, as I think, to make the example of his life and conversation a manual of godly piety which all might read that were his familiars. It was ever observable in this admirable prelate, that he preached no other law than that he lived by, being much regarded both for his liberality to the poor, and for his devotion to the person of his late Majesty. At length, being cut off in a short time that he might not see the evils which were to come upon his people, he surrendered up his pious soul to the Almighty an. 1669, of an ague. He is buried at Barchester; the more part of his books was given to Sim. Magus, and is there disposed commodiously enough in the college library."

" ROBERT LILLY, son of Gervase Lilly of Snettisham in the county of Salop esq. by Anne his wife, daughter of Sir Francis Matcham of Over Picklebury in the county of Dorset, received his first being in this world on the xviiith of March in the year 1616, one of the greatest lights, as I conceive, this university had yet produced, if he had matched by painful study the early promise of his wits. He was educated as to the grammaticals in the free school at Wenlock, and afterwards by his uncle, one Mr. — Lilly, of Weoley in Gloucestershire. He matriculated, as I learn, at Sim. Magus College an. 1629, being then much accounted of for his forwardness and excellent parts. So that, finding in that soil a nurture proportioned to his disposition (the Coll. being at that time most prudently governed, and flourishing more than commonly), he was very soon declared to be a magazine of learning and a walking library. He being moreover of an uncommon lively disposition, his company was everywhere desired and loved. After he had taken the oaths as fellow, he laboured much over an English Theocritus, of which some that are yet living have seen the original in manuscript; for what reason unpublished, I was never able to learn. But not long after, being drawn away to philosophical studies (his geny being not less prone to this kind of enquiry than to the other), he wrote excellently of dioptricks, and exchanged letters for a time on that head with Des Cartes, a Frenchman.

He was stiff at all times against puritans, misliking them not so much for what they held concerning Church government, as for their melancholy and bigoted humours. Which led him (to the reluctancy of such as would have seen him benefit mankind by fresh examples of learning) to engage in controversy, not long before the unnatural rebellion of the parliament-men against k. Charles I, with one Kingsmill. This Kingsmill, as I find, was matriculated at one of the houses in Cambridge, although on account of some perverse scruples upon matters of divinity he never proceeded there. He was a pragmatical and mealy-mouthed person, not at all well matched with our author (as 'twas thought) in such a contest of wits; nevertheless, the sectaries making great head about that time in London, he made shift to support himself in his quarrel with the applause of poor-spirited men. But soon after, the voice of reason being silenced in the clash of arms, our author returned to his philosophical studies, although in a more rambling fashion than formerly, so as that he was thought by some that were his friends to have had his pate crazed by continual overmuch study. It was then that he put out his observations on the prophecy of Nostradamus, which have received the praise of some, as beyond doubt most ingeniously conceived, notwithstanding they were decried by others as the portents of a roving and inconsiderable mind.

At what time the court was in Oxford, he was ever forward to attest that loyalty towards the King's person which he had sucked in with the milk of the humanities. As for instance in the speech delivered before his Majesty (*Serenissime princeps* &ctr.) in which he shewed the Parliament-men to be no better than Homer's Thersites. Which boldness of his, as it was the occasion to him of engaging his Majesty's gratitude above the common, so it drew upon him the malignancy of those phanaticks, who not long after invaded the government of these dominions. So that he judged it prudent to retire himself from the university, and went to lodge in Eastcheap, where for some time he lent his services to a haberdasher of hats, and afterwards read sheets for one Holcroft, a printer. He hath written and published,

De metris Pindaricis, being a Disquisition on the excellent architectonick framing of the Pindarick Ode, by R.L. Lond. 1629.

A new Method of Dioptricks, wherein much is discover'd that the Ignorance of former times hath overlook'd, or their Partiality conceal'd. By Robert Lilly A.M., Fellow of Simon Magus College in Oxford. Lond. 1633.

David dancing before the Ark, being a brief Apology for Whitsun Ales, Stage-plays, Bear-baiting, Morris-dancing, and all other Sports and Delectations which the sour-fac'd

melancholy of these times holdeth abominable, in the form of a DIALOGUE between Hobbinol and Crop-pate. By T.Y. Lond. 1638. To which a reply being put out in the same year, entitled, *A Reproof for taking the Ark of God into Battle, wherein Misochorus remonstrates with T.Y., who after the manner of Hophni and Phineas makes men to abhor the offering of the Lord* &ctr. &ctr., our author returned most courageously to the attack, publishing at some time in the next year,

The Hand of Uzzah stretch'd out to defend the Ark of God, in which a Warning is offer'd to Misochorus, and all other the pestilent sectaries by whose means the Ark of God is kept out from its true Place, and detain'd for this time at the house of Obed-Edom the Gittite, by T.Y. Lond. 1640. Which work being now in the press, it seems the printer, or some other that contrived to come at them, did privately convey the sheets one by one to Mr. Kingsmill; by which dishonest practice he was able to put out his reply more expeditiously. This was entitl'd, *The Ark of God carry'd by unserviceable Oxen, that turn to the right and the left, and not upon the Narrow Way to Bethshemesh, lowing as they go; which lamentable Lowings were lately publish'd by one that calleth himself T.Y.,* under the title, The Hand of Uzzah &ctr. This so incens'd our author, who (it seems) guessed well enough by what means it was that his adversary had gained this advantage upon him, that he determined he would continue the cannonade with heavier pieces. So that it was a full year and more before he published his last rejoinder in this controversy, which he called,

The Linen Ephod, wherein, namely in our Justification as Christian people, we do well to dance, yea and will dance, all canting and ranting of all melancholy Fanaticks notwithstanding; and that there shall be cakes and ale yet, as dancing David gave them to his people, when the Ark

returned from its Captivity, to make both Misochorus and all humorous Conventicle-men roar with Envy. By T.Y Lond. 1642. Which as it was a work of more compass and import, and adorned with many weighty passages from the Fathers by way of proof, so it was not easy for Mr. Kingsmill, being but an empty and clownish person, to busy himself any further in this matter. Nevertheless that he did put out a reply, 'tis certain; whose merit is to be judged from the obscurity into which it has fallen; for I was never able to come by a copy of it, no, nor even to find out what title was given to it.

The Prophecy of that singular great Mathematician call'd Nostradamus shewing how wonderfully the times following upon his death have vindicated his Veracity; with further observations upon what he hath written concerning these times next coming, and the happy Event that is to be expected from his Majesty's present Troubles. By Robert Lilly, A.M., Fellow of Sim. Magus College in Oxford. Oxon. 1644.

Besides this, I do not know that our author published anything, unless it were under some feigned name. He died as he had lived, a stiff and severe enemy to all puritans. He was, upon the happy restoration of k. Charles II, received back with much rejoicing into the bosom of the society he had adorned. But, whether it were that neglect and indigence had damped his spirits, or perhaps from the breeding of some melancholic humour in his natural disposition, it was observable that he did not return to his former studies with any gust or aptitude, but was wont rather to sit long over his wine, and entertain his company with discoursing somewhat ramblingly over what was past. In which retired and lonish complacency he lived near thirty years, and at last paid his debt to nature an. 1688, of a chill he had catched when he attended the funeral of his long acquaintance, the former Provost of the Coll.; being buried about the W. end of the chapel, where those words, 'they toil not, neither do they spin', were (by his own direction) inscribed at the foot of his monument."

CHAPTER IV

THE PIGEONS FLUTTER: 1688

DR. GARSIDE (*a middle-aged fellow with an almost habitual frown of bewilderment*). If this is true that you have been telling us, then we are all at sea again. It was hard enough for honest men to resolve their consciences so as they might best obey his Majesty in all things lawful, whilst we thought it was for a time only, and we could look for redress to the Princess of Orange. Then the rumour sprang up and flourished, the Queen was expecting; as if the Crown should be settled on papists thenceforward. And now here is a fresh tale, in all seeming worthy of credit——

MR. TRUMPINGTON. There is no man of sense but will set it down for a palpable forgery. Men will lie readily, when their passions are engaged.

MR. LILLY (*now an elderly man, but well preserved, with a red face that suggests good living*). You may add, at such times they will believe their own lie. I think it is Shakespeare said, in one of his dramatic pieces, that the wish is father to the thought. There is no lack of men in England that wish the Queen childless, and I partly believe Dr. Garside to be of their number.

DR. GARSIDE'S GUEST, *a* MR. MITFORD (*he is a person of some age, and evidently of a scholarly bent, though he does not belong to the University*). I can but tell you, gentlemen, what was told me; adding this much, that the friend from whom I had it is a man of credit, and is much acquainted with Dr. Windibank.

MR. BLEDLOE (*making an effort to change the subject, which he dislikes*). Has Dr. Potts called upon Mr. Provost this morning?

DR. GARSIDE. He was with him above half an hour, but he says no art can stay the course of this malady. The lozenges appeared to afford some little relief, but we must not look for any present change in his condition. Dr. Potts says little, but I fear it goes ill with our friend.

MR. LILLY. The Provost? Oh, he will go out like the snuffing of a candle. When you have buried as many fellows of Simon Magus as I, you will read the death-warrant in a man's looks without much labour. Well, he was ever a man of sickly habit, and hath, these many years past, enjoyed but a prorogation of death. It would have better become him, as one that was ever a great lover of the College, to have hit upon some more seasonable time for his dissolution. We are like to be damnably circumstanced, if the provostship should fall vacant in these next days coming.

MR. BLEDLOE. You would not persuade us, Sir, that the King would send a mandamus to this house? Here is Magdalen altogether laid waste; here you have Dr. Massey at Christ Church and Mr. Walker at University outvying one the other in restoring the Mass; there can be no just cause adduced, why the Roman Catholics should have any new favour shewn to them.

DR. GARSIDE (*shaking his head*). There is no doubt but his Majesty is in these times shamefully ill advised. We hear everywhere fresh instances, how the Pope's cause is making head. You will scarce credit what whispering goes round even now among the busy-bodies, since Mr. Provost took to his bed. They have not stuck to name such men as Father Petre, and Mr. Penn the Quaker that was put out of Christ Church for non-compliance, to be the next Provost of Simon Magus.

MR. MITFORD. Mr. Penn is a man of very eminent parts. He has, besides, had some experience of the plantations overseas; I hope I shall not seem less than grateful for the honour of dining with the fellows, if I say that it is easy for you in Oxford to become ingrown in your habit of mind, so that you regard too little what passes in the world about you. Mr. Penn, now, is a man that has been bred in the same school with you; and yet his wits are become nimble through his many comings and goings between various countries. I do not say, gentlemen, that he is a fit man for so honourable a post as was mentioned but now; I say only that the Oxonian Muses might, without shame, welcome him back to their Helicon.

MR. LILLY. Of all Puritans, God defend us from a Court Puritan! Who is this Mr. Penn, but the son of old Penn that obliged his late Majesty in a matter of ten thousand pounds; old Penn that served under King James against the Dutch? For which good offices the son is evermore in high favour at Court, when he is not in gaol for his snivelling Quakerish disrelish to the established religion. Oh, let us have the most villainous friar that ever went barefoot, rather than Penn with his thee's and thou's, calling us *friend* and whining to us through his nose about the New Jerusalem.

MR. BLEDLOE (*to Mr. Mitford, as if apologizing for Mr. Lilly's outburst*). Our statutes, Sir, will not allow us to appoint as Provost one that has not yet proceeded to holy orders. And whereas this Petre has received the laying-on of hands, although it were shiftily, in a foreign seminary, Mr. Penn neither is nor could be (conformably I mean with the tenets of his own persuasion) an ordained minister.

DR. GARSIDE. He might yet be dispensed; there is nothing cannot be dispensed in these times.

MR. BLEDLOE. Would we then be free in conscience to act contrary to the statutes?

DR. GARSIDE. I am not persuaded of it. For, though it be in his Majesty's discretion to say that this or that man shall hold preferment in the University (as he did reasonably enough at Christ Church, since it is a royal foundation, and less colourably elsewhere), yet to say that such a dispensation gives me, Richard Garside, leave to prevaricate against the oaths I took when I was admitted fellow, is no better than papistical juggling. I believe there is no power on earth can dispense me from my sworn oath.

MR. LILLY (*who evidently delights in embarrassing his colleagues*). You would do well to tread carefully, Dr. Garside. Let us suppose now that his Majesty were put out from reigning among us, through some plot of his enemies that would make room for the prince of Orange or another, would you still be obliged, think you, by the oath you have taken to King James?

MR. TRUMPINGTON. I do not think King James will be easily put out. Things are not as they were in the martyred Charles' time, now that the throne has a standing army to defend it; and not an army only, but such a general officer, I mean Lord Churchill, as is like to win laurels on the Martial field. There are few kings have such a servant as Johnny Churchill.

MR. MITFORD. It is much to be feared that all causes, both great and small, must henceforth be decided upon the Martial field you speak of, and not triumph through their own justice, or the will of peoples. All our modern panoply of war, since powder was commonly used, gives much vantage to the power that is in possession, and little hope to the rebel. It is the more extraordinary that the late Mr. Milton in his divine epic made powder to be the invention of Satan. I was last year at Blackheath, when the soldiers were discharging, only to exercise their skill, those mischief-doing instruments they call bombs, out of great mortars set up for that purpose. It is to be supposed that the prodigious noise and havoc which follows upon their bursting would suffice to unman the *mobile*, though its passions were never so enraged, and only a handful of soldiers stood to their pieces.

MR. BLEDLOE. I wonder what they will be at next. Our natural philosophers have so wonderfully increased the sum of human learning, as it seems Providence would in a short time from this have no more secrets to hide from us. I hear Mr. Boyle is in great hopes, he will find some way to bring about the transmutation of metals.

MR. MITFORD (*fatally returning to the subject Mr. Bledloe is always trying to avoid*). Mr. Boyle, besides that he is the most ingenious of our philosophers, is further notable in this, that he has a great disrelish of controversy in religion.

MR. BLEDLOE. I hope that is no very uncommon disposition of mind.

MR. MITFORD. Why, Sir, it is observable that most men will cry out against the differences of religion that have been since Luther's time. In part, because these have been fertile of wars and rebellions; in part, because the Roman Catholicks take to themselves much comfort from seeing what ill results follow (as they think) from leaving off obedience to their Pope. I hear the Bishop of Meaux, a very ingenious writer, has but now finished a book of prodigious length, which is nothing other than an exact history of these our disagreements. But when men talk after that fashion, each one of them commonly means no more than this, that he would have all Christians leave off their disputing, and agree in all points with himself. Sir, this is not to strive after the beatitude which is ascribed to peace-makers. He that would heal the divisions of the Christian commonwealth must rather consider with himself, that all sects do but aim at the truth by conjecture, and no man, not even himself, can be certain that his own conjecture lies nearer to the truth than his neighbour's. He must be ready to agree, if need arise, and not merely to be agreed with.

MR. LILLY. Sir, I think your friend Mr. Boyle will do well to bestow his pains on transmuting the metals. He is like to labour therein more fruitfully, than in seeking to bring about agreement between Christians.

MR. MITFORD. You will not persuade him to leave off his purpose so easily; and indeed, he has already made some shift to publish these his singular opinions. It is no secret, it was he set on Sir Peter Pett to write his *Discourse concerning Liberty of Conscience;* and I have heard him say, if he found himself a rich man when he came to make his testamentary dispositions, he would willingly endow a lecture in perpetuity for confounding the enemies of the Christian religion, with this further provision, that no man lecturing on his foundation should say one word in dispraise of any other Christian sect.

DR. GARSIDE. He will have the thanks of all honest men, if he so makes disposal of his worldly goods. It is very observable in these days, how many authors do not scruple to insinuate atheistical conclusions, making little less havock thereby than the papists themselves. Nay, the very papists do not stick at putting out works that are infected with the poison of Socinus; as witness one Father Simon, of the Oratory in Paris, whose *Critical History* was not long since translated into our tongue; a very damnable book. But, for what you say of the healing of divisions between Christians, it has fairly astonished me. Let us see now; suppose we had here one of the Quakers, who should tell us, it was in no case lawful for any man to bind himself by an oath, or an Anabaptist that would not have his children christened, would we tell him *his was very reasonable doctrine*, all the customs of this realm and of Christ's Church notwithstanding?

MYSELF. . . .

MR. LILLY (*chuckling hugely*). Ay, Sir, you were best; else the Quaker dog would be taking off all his clothes, here in the Common-room, and telling you, *That he went naked for a sign;* which is their beastly custom, as a friend notifies me, who hath been much in the plantations. (*To Mr. Mitford.*) No, Sir, you will not content these sneaking, fanatical Pharisees by linking arms with them and telling them, *We are all fellows at football.* We that are older have made trial of the sectaries, at what time the Parliament men overthrew all government, and most barbarously murdered his sacred Majesty King Charles. I have been put out of my fellowship, Sir, by these canting conventicle-men, and seen the old books burned in the College quadrangle. For my part, I think King James hath betaken himself to a very desperate shift, in procuring liberty of conscience for a whole pack of Ranters and Muggletonians, only because he hath a tenderness for his fellow papists, and seeks a colourable occasion to promote such to commissions in the army, or summon them as burgesses to Parliament. This is as if a man should make a gap in his hedge, because he would let his friends come at him more commodiously, and thereby should let a great roaring bull loose in his field; whereas he might very easily have fashioned a stile for his friends to climb, and no ill consequences to be apprehended. I am an old man, and shall not long outlive Mr. Provost; but you gentlemen that are younger will see whether King James have not stirred up a worse plague than ever Pandora did when she opened Epimetheus' box; only that then Hope was left remaining, whereas there is little hope for England, as I conceive, now that these ranting Tom o' Bedlams have been suffered to set up their tubs at every street corner.

DR. GARSIDE. There is but too great reason to fear what you prognosticate. The news from London is, many indeed of the non-conformists still hang back, and will not avail themselves of their new liberties, fearing, as Laocoon did in Virgil's Aeneis, the gifts that come from an enemy; but others are become very much emboldened. As for instance this Faldo, a Brownist as I suppose, who preaches every Lord's Day to as much as two thousand people together in Rope-maker's Alley; and the parish church at Deptford is almost empty of worshippers, so powerfully are men affected towards the Dissenters' meeting-house in that place. Yet would I not tremble so much over the issue, if I were sure that his Majesty's advisers are indeed peaceably minded, and do not rather comfort the sectaries out of practice.

MR. TRUMPINGTON. Sir, I think you do very ill to doubt the liberality of his Majesty's intentions. They say *Necessity makes strange bed-fellows;* nor is it great matter for astonishment if the Roman Catholics, that have these many years been ground down with heavy fines, and moreover seen their priests condemned to a horrible manner of extinction, should feel their bowels moved with compassion for such Protestant sectaries as have endured the like affliction.

DR. GARSIDE. It may be so; God forbid that I should speak ill of his anointed, and that without cause. It is nevertheless observable, how the papists are from day to day creeping into high preferment; and some of those giddier spirits, that will ever tack about to please the Court, are already forsaking the religion they were baptized in, to become professed papists. So that, honest men being quite neglected, a rabble of nobodies climbs into office and preferment, no more ashamed than the boys here, when they carry off the biscuits from the table after we are done with our supper.

MR. TRUMPINGTON. He is not of necessity a sycophant, who makes an exchange of his obedience when there is favour to be had at Court by so doing. There has not a year passed, I conceive, since the change of religion in England, that some few have not embraced the Catholic profession; only these were but few, like the first flowers of spring which do courageously appear, when they find no better welcome than cruel frost and the rage of boisterous tempests. But when spring advances, and the sun imparts more freely his generative influence, as he did this year all too late, see how they blossom in every field and hedge-row! So it is with this sun of royal favour, which now shines brightly on those, who have experienced but very ill weather heretofore. It is no marvel if generous resolves, long detained by the frosts of persecution, shew their heads at last. Men were formerly of opinion, that the sun bred life; the ingenious discoveries of this last age have persuaded us rather, that it can do no more than set free what life is already present. Which serves for a parable——

MR. LILLY. Yes, Sir, we have understood your parable well enough. You have invited us to the conclusion, that England breeds papists no otherwise than as meat breeds maggots.

MR. MITFORD (*coming to the rescue*). Nothing hinders, but that two men should be drawn into the same course, one honestly, the other somewhat out of sycophancy. Nor do I know that it is our part to judge, what must certainly be judged hereafter, whether of the two did right, or if both.

DR. GARSIDE. Sir, I cannot find any honest pretence upon which a man could desert the Church wherein he was baptized, and go after another.

MR. MITFORD. I think he might be drawn by little and little to such a conclusion, from overmuch absoluteness in determining matters of religion. As I think, Mr. John Dryden did, who in his discourse of the *Hind and the Panther* has defended the faith he now holds with uncommon dexterity.

MR. LILLY. John Dryden? Why, he hath tacked about most villainously; first crying up the Lord Protector, then setting his course by the new fashion of the Court, and now an avowed papist! Sir, if the Princess Mary were crowned to-morrow, John Dryden would be on his way to welcome her the day after, with a Protestant Ode in one pocket of his coat and an encomium of the

Dutch in the other. They bred him at Cambridge; thank God we did not father his hinds nor his maggots neither. I detest a Cambridge man, and it is Cambridge men everywhere in these times; John Dryden rhyming in dispraise of his betters, and Stillingfleet at Paul's, lying about the ancient British Church, and one Newton, that sets the Royal Society agape with theorems he hath stolen from Dr. Hooke; I would give more for this empty bottle than for a Cambridge man.

MR. BLEDLOE. What is your opinion, Sir, why Cambridge is more fertile of poetic gift than Oxford? There was Mr. Milton in the last age, and Mr. Cowley, and the ingenious Mr. Crashaw; and now you have Mr. Shadwell and Mr. Dryden, both very much thought of.

MR. LILLY. You have forgot Mr. Settle; who never proceeded here, but was formerly a member of Trinity. His drama of the *Empress of Morocco* was a very pretty piece, they tell me. You will find Elkanah Settle's name is still remembered when Dryden's is quite put out of men's minds.

DR. GARSIDE. It is not the office of a University, to make men into poets. A poet may learn his trade with very little grounding, except in the grammaticals.

MR. LILLY. That is true enough, as is seen in *Hudibras*, the most incomparable work of our time. So long as our tongue is read, I think there will be only one Samuel Butler.

MR. TRUMPINGTON. Why, Mr. Bledloe, I cannot understand what you will be at, to be always drawing away our talk from arguments of religion. Here is Mr. Mitford has moved a question that much imports us in these times, concerning freedom of conscience; and you do nothing but put him off with discoursing of philosophy, of poetry, and of much else. Come, Mr. Mitford, let us hear you satisfy Dr. Garside, who but now looked very ill-favouredly, as I thought, upon the notions of your friend Mr. Boyle. You are for saying, that we ought to tolerate other men's opinions, because we can have no certainty whether they be not in the right of it, and we in the wrong?

MR. MITFORD. Sir, you put forward a parable, but now, most suitable to these airs of spring-time; give me leave to offer you another in the same vein of invention. It is a fair prospect that you enjoy as you sit here, now it is warmer and the windows are set open; and what has most gratified my eyes when I looked out was the parterre, all set with beds of very curious shapes, and each of these planted out in a regular fashion with tulips. What a well-disciplined herb is your tulip! How stiffly it bears itself, like a soldier standing to the word of command! Upon which the late Mr. Marvell—alas, Mr. Lilly, there is yet another ornament of Cambridge—wrote in his description of a garden:

> Each regiment in order grows,
> That of the tulip, pink and rose;

you see it was the tulips he had in mind. Your gardener here must be a virtuoso, that he can force nature to such ready compliance with his will. But, Sirs, as I rode out yesterday to wait upon a friend that has a fair house beyond Eynsham, the humour took me (for the day was still young) to tie up my horse beyond the bridge, and ramble across the water-meadows, then for the most part firm under foot. And so it was that I came upon a field of those flowers they call fritillaries, purple and white both, most delicately veined; each of itself a proper study for the curious mind, and yet no less notable for the multitude of them with which the whole meadow was diversified. By this appearance I was very strangely affected; and I believe that I did the more admire them, for wanting that art with which your parterre of tulips is so ingeniously disposed.—Gentlemen, I have made a great matter of my poor parable. But you will see whither it tends. He that will make an anatomy of the Church of Christ will commonly so present it, as if it were expedient and indeed necessary for every man's conscience to be trained and disciplined, until it is exactly conformable to his neighbour's, like a garden in which every flower is exactly matched with every other. To that end, rulers will not spare to force their subjects into conformity; by persuasion if that will serve, and if not by the imposing of pains and penalties. I conceive that this is the opinion commonly held among the fellows of houses in Oxford. But I met with some when I was lately at Cambridge that were of another mind, and would have it that the Church is rather an assembly of Christian souls freely living together, without prejudice to the liberties of each, and not caring greatly whether their several opinions in matters of divinity exactly jump together, so that in their diversity they may do God honourable service.

DR. GARSIDE (*he has been fidgeting a good deal all through this monologue, which has had the effect of putting Mr. Lilly to sleep*). Sir, if the Christian religion were of man's invention, and more than that, if its tenents were such as each man severally must needs discover for himself by experiment, you should have much profit of your wild garden. But since it is so, that Almighty God has made known to us most weighty counsels of his wisdom; which things it was not possible for us to know, his revelation wanting to us; who can doubt but it is man's duty to bend and frame his opinions conformably thereto? Whereupon we are warned, that if a man will not hear the Church, he is to be to us as a heathen man and a publican. It is for the King, then, unless he would bear the sword in vain, to enforce the right rule of Christian living. Not, by my way of it at least, that he should punish and restrain all such as are non-conformitant; only I think they should not be suffered to assemble together. But he is strictly obliged, not to admit to any kind of preferment, whether in Church or in State, those whom we are bidden to reckon as heathen men and publicans. Or would you not call him a vile worthless gardener, Mr. Mitford, who should neglect the flowers and set about watering the weeds?

MR. TRUMPINGTON (*to Mr. Mitford*). No, Sir, you will not find many in Oxford that make so light of antiquity and of Church order. In Cambridge, they have ever bred strange doctrines; being more obnoxious, as I suppose, to the winds of learning that blew from overseas; in Oxford, as I conceive, we live more by the memories of our past. (*To Dr. Garside.*) Sir, let me ask you with respect whether you would only blame his Majesty for bestowing preferment upon the sectaries, as when he suffered Peake, that was an Anabaptist, to be made Lord Mayor of London last year? Or whether you grudge him equally the right to prefer learned and discreet persons that are of the Catholic persuasion to public office; as when upon the death of Bishop Parker he destined Dr. Giffard to be his successor at Magdalen?

DR. GARSIDE. God forbid that I should blame his Majesty; are we not warned that we should not speak evil of principalities? Nevertheless I am much concerned that he has proud and bigoted advisers about his person to whom he lends himself overmuch. And as to that, it makes no matter to me whether they be sectaries or papists that are intruded into places of emolument; it is an uprooting of the religion which this kingdom has received, whereas his own father died most gloriously for the preserving of it.

MR. TRUMPINGTON. Why then, Sir, let me have your opinion of this. Here is the French King, who is sworn to uphold the Christian religion no less than any King of England was; and the Christian religion as he has received it is the unreformed Catholic religion. Is not he, then, obliged by all means to uphold and perpetuate, nay, if need be to enforce it? Must not he withhold preferment from all such as will not conform to it; ay, and forbid them to build churches and assemble themselves together, lest he suffer the weeds to grow in the garden he has care of?

DR. GARSIDE. This is not all the French King has done. It is notorious that within these last years he has proved very bitter against the Protestants, both harrying and imprisoning them, and at last driving out a great multitude of them from his dominions.

MR. TRUMPINGTON. This is not to our purpose; it may be King Lewis has erred by overmuch severity, but my question was, whether you would have made shift to excuse him if he had exercised no severity at all? Since there is but one way God would have us worship him, and it is the office of a ruler to see to it that his subjects shall not rather give place to their own fanatical megrims, what should the French King do but endeavour himself, as best he may, to set forward the Catholic religion in France?

DR. GARSIDE (*feebly*). That is not easily answered. If it so be that he has framed his conscience so sottishly——

MR. TRUMPINGTON. Ay, but there is no question here of a man's private conscience; for King Lewis, mark you, was crowned with all due forms of Catholic piety; he has received the homage of a Christian kingdom that is but little removed from being altogether of one mind in religion. Neither he nor his subjects ever yet received the Common Prayer, that is very evident. What must he do, if he would make good use of the sword God has entrusted to him?

MR. BLEDLOE. I cannot assure myself, Mr. Trumpington, that I see what is your drift now. Would you have us believe, that because King James is a Roman Catholic, like the French King, he ought therefore to be persecuting all such his subjects as are not Roman Catholics like himself?

MR. TRUMPINGTON. I meant no such thing. Let him order his private conscience as he will, his Majesty has been called by Almighty God to rule over such a kingdom, as has forgotten the old ways these hundred years and more past; during which time it is become notably overgrown with variegations of opinion. So that it remains for him, not to favour one sect against another, but rather to procure, if he can, that all shall live peaceably in accord. Have you forgotten what he said when he took leave of us after his visiting Oxford last year, when he took coach at the great door behind the Theatre in Canditch? *I must tell you*, said he, *that in the King my father's time the Church of England's men and the Catholics loved each other and were, as 'twere, all one, but now there is gotten a spirit which is quite contrary. There are some among you that are the occasion of those things, but I know them and shall take notice of them for the future.* This was royally spoken, although it may be somewhat in choler. I would not, then, have his Majesty, whom God preserve, alter his course by a hair's breadth. All I proposed to Dr. Garside was to know why, if an established Church may persecute, they of France may not do it equally well as his friends in England? And if he has bowels of compassion for the reformed religion in France, why he has none for those many who have long been persecuted in England, be they Catholics or Muggletonians or what they will?

DR. GARSIDE. I do not know after what fashion to

answer you. It is easy, I conceive, for you that are younger to tack about, as if it were all one whether a man sticks fast in the opinions he has ever held, or will turn papist one day and conventicle-man the next, as the wind of fashion goes about. You have not lived to see the Church as it is by law established made nothing of by the sectaries, and grey old men put out of their fellowships and preferments, as came about in the Protector's time. For myself, I would willingly see once again a king in England that would uphold the Common Prayer, and restrain whatever is contrary to it; if the French King will do the like by his Mass-book, then I will be no judge of him; to his own Master he standeth or falleth.

MR. MITFORD (*smiling sadly*). No, Sir, if you would have had this people of England use no other service-book than one, you should have spared to root out the Mass. What has been changed, men will be for changing again; and what is framed to suit with the fashion of an age, with time will fall into discredit. You had best leave men to worship as they will, and see if Rome fall not by her own weight, as the poet said of her.

MR. BLEDLOE. Mr. Trumpington, you have been very forward to put Dr. Garside in the wrong; but you have kept pretty close about your own mind in this business. Will you tell us at last whether you are at one with Mr. Mitford here, and would have no man's conscience troubled, nor no tests prescribed for any manner of office or employment? Or will you tell us that the Roman Catholics do well to force men's consciences, as things are now ordered in France; and if King James shew favour to Anabaptists and Quakers, this is only done for expediency's sake, because the Roman Catholics are not so numerous that they can have their way with us all at present?

MR. TRUMPINGTON. *Imprimis*, you must not write me down as of one feather with Mr. Mitford. If I have not taken him up wrong, he is persuaded that there is no certitude at all in matters of religion, but each man must make shift for himself, to interpret both the Scriptures and the Fathers according to his own giddy mind; in the meantime agreeing, his neighbour that thinks otherwise may as well be in the right of it as himself. That is a very odd, fantastical notion. But, Sir, that I know myself to hold the true opinion and my neighbour a false, is no ground for putting him to the sword, or binding, or gagging him, but rather for persuading him by more excellent reasons that he errs. If I had my way of it, there should be no force put upon any Christian man, except only the force of argument. And I hold, as did the lately mourned Dr. Parker, it is most excellently thought upon that there should be one house at least in this University where the Catholic religion is taught; so that there is none can say, *The Pope's cause was not suffered to be heard in Oxford, for all he has so many of his religion in England.*

DR. GARSIDE (*shaking his head*). Ay, but when this same bishop of Rome, by many cunning shifts and sophisms, has stolen the hearts of this nation, do you not see how soon he will put off the sheep's clothing wherein he sneaks to and fro among us, and appear as a very wolf? As even now the news is from France, that he is setting on King Lewis to make havoc of his Protestant subjects, forcing them by means of dragoonades to comply with the unreformed religion?

MYSELF. . . .

MR. TRUMPINGTON (*rather pertly*). Sir, we will shew him a better example of mildness. But you, Mr. Bledloe, why is it you move this question so eagerly? I had thought you to be something well affected towards King James, and the restoring of the Catholic obedience.

MR. BLEDLOE (*smiling uncomfortably*). I think you will be Provost yet, Mr. Trumpington; you are so curious of other men's opinions. Why then, if you will have it, the reason why I exercise myself over the French King and his dragoonades is, I am much affected towards the Roman Catholic religion, and this news from France sticks in my throat. There were lately put forth, by royal command, two papers written by his late Majesty and found afterwards in his strong box, which contain very weighty matter for consideration; as, *That the Church of England would fain have it thought that they are the judges in matters spiritual, and yet dare not say positively that there is no appeal from them;* or this other, *If Christ did leave a Church here upon earth, and we were all once of that Church, how and by what authority did we separate from that Church?* So that being entangled with these and other the like perplexities, yet very ill disposed towards the French King and all his doings, I am in a great strait these many months past. I would I had lived in less uneasy times, that these dubitations might have concerned no one but only myself.

MR. MITFORD (*in a fatherly way*). Take courage, Sir; you shall find what light you need; from without or from within, it makes no matter.

MR. LILLY (*waking suddenly*). Why, what is this? I did not think I had been dozing. But so it was, for I have had a monstrous ill dream. It was of you, Mr. Trumpington; and my dream was you had turned Whig, and were become Provost of Simon Magus.

MR. TRUMPINGTON. Sir, the one thing is as far from my purpose, as the other from my deserts. Your dream came out of the ivory gate, that is certain, Mr. Lilly.

DR. GARSIDE (*suddenly*). O heaven, if it be not the bell tolling. Mr. Provost . . . he has slipped away from us while we sat over the wine.

MR. TRUMPINGTON. God have mercy on him.

DR. GARSIDE. God have mercy on this house. We are like to go heavily enough, wanting him.

NOTES ON CHAPTER IV

I have had the good fortune to discover, among the many parts of Thomas Hearne's Diary which have not hitherto been edited, some notices which refer to the subsequent history of the persons just mentioned. It hardly needs to be said that some allowance must be made, in reading these entries, for Hearne's notorious Jacobite sympathies, and also for the resentment he always felt over the loss of his appointment at the Bodleian. The following occurs under a date in the year 1711.

"This day died, to the great reluctance of all who knew him, my very good friend Mr. Richard Garside; at his lodgings in St. Aldate's; his distemper, a dropsy. I was with him about three days since, when he told me *he did not think he should go out this time,* notwithstanding he was far gone in his disease. Yesterday I waited upon him again, but found him much changed for the worse, so that when I asked if he knew me, he said 'No, no, you are not Tom Hearne; you are such a one', naming one that has done me great hurt, as I have set down elsewhere in these Collectanea, besides being a man of very damnable principles. Whereupon I concluded him to be raving, and so came no more to him, though I had been his great acquaintance these twenty years past. He was in the sixty-third or climacteric year of his age.

This gentleman was formerly of Sim. Magus College, where he matriculated about the age of sixteen, and went out A.M. in the year 1670, being a fellow of the same foundation. It was ever observed of him, that he conformed with the gospel principle, *Reddere ea quae sunt Caesaris Caesari* etc., being unwilling to strike in with those that would either set aside the establisht religion, or perjure themselves by acknowledging usurpation. It was upon his instance, as I have heard him say, that the old figure of Simon Magus (with his money-bags) in the first quadrangle was not done away with; tho' later it hath been removed to the garden on the North side of the College, what was only to be expected in these days when antiquity is so much despised, and learning languishes. At the time of the late revolution (or as it is more truly called, rebellion) he was put out of his fellowship very suddenly, without being even required (what he could never have been prevailed upon to do) to take the oath to K. William; and indeed it is much to be doubted whether he was not *de jure* fellow up to the time of his death, he having never resigned that office, tho' cut off altogether from its emoluments.

He was at that time in great straits, having no estate of his own, and the booksellers pressing him unmercifully. But an honest gent, Sir J. Conyers, who hath shewn much kindness besides to those who have suffered for their principles, made him tutor to his two sons, at Wormingham in the county of Salop; to their great satisfaction, for he was a very hearty facetious companion, as well as being much grounded in the study of the oriental tongues. (One of these was lately a gentleman commoner of Sim. Magus, and there ended his life suddenly, as 'tis feared, of drinking brandy in the morning.) But, his circumstances being eased shortly after (through the death of his kinsman, Mr. Amyas Garside, a gentleman that had an estate in Worcestershire), he returned to Oxford, and there resided in his lodgings in St. Aldate's, as before mentioned. He never married, and gave up to liberal studies what time he spared from his religious observances, of which he was an exact and cheerful performer. He hath wrote *A History of Sicily*, which is now difficult to be procured, as Mr. Clements tells me; besides putting out an edition of Tibullus, in which he was assisted, as 'tis said, by Dr. Huish. He also put out a Chronology, in which he hath interpreted the prophecy of Daniel amazing ingeniously; but he is not thought to compare with Sir Isaac Newton, being a very mean mathematician. Besides this, I do not know that he hath wrote anything else, unless it were an answer to Dr. Kennett; but this he never published, the bookseller desiring him to abridge it by two hundred pages, which he could never put force upon himself to do.

He remained in communion with the non-juring Church of England 'till the death of bishop Lloyd, which occurring about a year before his own death, he could not be perswaded that he would do an injury to his conscience by conforming to the establisht religion; in which I cannot reprehend him, having known several honest men that were similarly minded, though for my part I could not bring myself to it. I have not heard that any minister attended him on his death-bed. To be buried, as I hear, in the churchyard of St. Peter's in the East. He composed, shortly before his death, his own epitaph, in which he makes this claim (about the end):

REGI ORTHODOXO FIDEM DEDIT
ERRANTI PRAESTITIT:
OXONIAE DOMUM EXILIO MUTAVIT
CAELESTIS PATRIAE UTCUMQUE APPETENTIOR.

He was a gentleman of a very modest, cheerful disposition, liberal at all times to the poor, who greatly loved him. He was of a lively, ingenious disposition, and had learning above what is common in these times; I have heard Dr. Charlett say (who was no friend, it is well known, to the honest party) that the University had lost more by his deprivation than by that of any man who had suffered in these late troubles; by which comparison it is likely that he thought to put me down, who was present, but 'twas well spoken nevertheless. I wonder what is to become of Mr. Garside's books? 'Tis certain he hath left a pretty many of them, for all he had little room in his lodgings."

An entry, some years later, throws light on another of the old fellows, and his subsequent history:

"Last night lay in Oxford, at the Cross, a very honest man and my great acquaintance, sir Francis Marryatt. He hath been lately overseas, and reports that the R. Family are in good health; the Prince a fine child, excellently proportioned, and so like his ancestors that the silly canting stories put abroad by the fanatical crew, not long before the late rebellion, are now manifestly proved to be but idle forgeries. I was with sir Francis above two hours in his lodging, at which time he told me much of his late doings in the city of Paris, where he was excellently received, being well versed in the French tongue, tho' (as he told me) it is pronounced in those parts quite differently, and not at all as he was taught it. Among other things he told me of a visit he paid to the house of the Carmelite monks (he should rather have said, friars) in the city of Paris, which is justly famed for its observance and truly religious spirit, divers superstitions notwithstanding. In which place he had talk with one who is gone from Oxford these many years, tho' I have often heard him spoken of, viz. Mr. Eustace Bledloe, now styled father Bartholomew in religion.

This gentleman, being born at Northam in the county of Notts, matriculated at Hart Hall, but was afterwards a fellow of Sim. Magus, where he proceeded Master of Arts but a little while before k. James was (by the vile sneaking treachery of the d. of Marlborough and others) driven out from his kingdom. At that time he professed the establisht religion, tho' always somewhat inclined to extravagances of belief; this I had from Mr. Robt. Wood, nephew to the great Antony, that knew Mr. Bledloe formerly. He was nevertheless a man of great promise, and of a singular earnestness; there are some even who would have it that he is the author of *The Whole Duty of Man* (though this I take to be false, being more inclined to believe that Mr. Woodhead hath wrote the said book, or my Lady Packington). 'Tis certain that he favoured the Declaration, and seemed like to have become a papist when many others did, in k. James' time; but it appears he always boggled over it, being a man of very tender conscience, and a lover of old ways. But no sooner was the p. of Orange brought over to England than Mr. Bledloe threw over his fellowship, and went overseas. It was said by some that he had a hand in some political contrivance, but this I will not bring myself to believe, the multitude of pretended plots against the government being in these days so greatly increased, as that few honest men have escaped suspicion altogether, from the malice of their enemies and the great credulity of the vulgar. But, whatever the cause, 'tis certain that Mr. Bledloe went into France, and there falling in with a priest who worked upon his scruples of conscience, became a professed papist and afterwards, as hath been said, took his vows in a convent of Carmelite friars, what was thought a very singular thing, in one of his learning and attainments.

Sir Francis told me, he waited upon this father Bartholomew in the early afternoon, and was entertained in a great parlour, very richly hung, the place having been a gentleman's house before the friars had it. Father Bartholomew is a little wizened man, very sober in his talk, yet always wearing a little smile, as if he had his mind on something other than the matter in hand. This priest was very earnest with sir Francis, that he should leave off altogether from his present ways and become a papist too, bringing forward very weak injudicious arguments to perswade him in the matter. Stesichorus, he said, feigned that the Greeks did fight about the walls of Troy ten years for the sake of a phantom and no true Helen; so they of the true ch. of England were, by his way of it, sticking out for a point of honour that was altogether vain and unsubstantial. For the divine right (in which he had always sincerely believed) came not by any direct delivery from God; but Christian princes enjoyed it only as part of the general body of Christendom; which body having been altogether rent in sunder with the changes of religion in q. Elizabeth's time, such princes as had embraced the reformed principles could claim no more than the allegiance that was due to them from their election by the general consent of their subjects. It amazed me to hear of one who had formerly been so honest a gentleman crying up these canting whiggish principles; but 'tis very observable what cunning shifts a man will be put to, when he hath been trained by the jesuits, as father Bartholomew doubtless was. He did not scruple to conclude, that protestants who by their own profession denied the unity of Christendom had no business to boggle over the divine right, but the d. of Brunswick might serve their turn as well as another, provided he were kept in place by the general consent of his subjects.

Upon which sir Francis objecting, that men who had taken oaths of allegiance to a sovereign could not rightly withdraw their allegiance, unless himself consented thereto, this priest smiled, and said, It would have gone hard with the ch. of England, if her bishops had from the first been so nice about changing their allegiance without resigning their preferments; by which I conceive him to have meant, that archbishop Cranmer and others struck in well enough with the bishop of Rome for a while, but after deserted his cause, when k. Henry would have it so. But he added, that he had very great respect for those honest men who refused the oaths; only he wished he could see them embrace true principles in religion, instead of founding a schism of their own which must die out very shortly. (This is false; for we hear that the non-juring church in London gains ground every day.) Sir Francis said, he supposed it would be well if all men were of the same opinion in religion; but while that is not possible, we must make shift as best we can. Moreover, said he (for they spoke very privately, and there was no fear of any eaves-dropping), were it not best to wait till the k. should enjoy his own again, and then set ourselves to consider what rights the bp. of Rome should have accorded to him? At this, it seems, father Bartholomew smiled again, and said we must all do what God shews us to be right, be the consequences what they may; but as for its being his will that k. James should come back, of that we could have no certainty, providence often ruling our affairs otherwise than we expected, and rather bringing good out of evil than always letting the good prevail openly.

All this is very doating stuff, and I doubt whether the man's wits be not crazed with too much fasting and other like penances. It seems he hath the reputation of holiness, and there are some so far gone in credulity as to think he can do miracles. But for my part I think holiness is little consonant with the holding of these and other the like silly pragmatical opinions."

Finally, at a date very close to the end of Hearne's life, I find an interesting notice of Dr. Trumpington:

"This day I hear that the bp. of Barchester (that is a sneaker and a vile whig) hath confirmed the election of Dr. Trumpington to the provostship of Sim. Magus, he being the Visitor of that foundation. There were a pretty many among the fellows that had made interest for Mr. Holyoake, who, tho' a complyer, is nevertheless a man of very good principles, and hath some learning; and indeed he was at first declared elected; but, these proceedings being challenged (I could not as yet hear upon what ground, but doubtless 'twas some pettifogging scruple, as is in these days all too common), the matter was referred to the Visitor, and he, as was to be expected, hath declared for Dr. Trumpington, to the great reluctance of all honest men in the University.

This gentleman (a most vile, stinking whig) hath been a fellow of the College since k. James' time, when he was a great forwarder of all that was done to restore the popish religion, being much in company with Mr. Obadiah Walker and others of his kidney. Insomuch that, about the same time the Prince of Wales was born, he went to one Petre in London, a priest, and took upon himself the Roman obedience; nor would he, as some others, exercise the said religion privately, but went openly to Mass for all the University to see. For which, when the times changed, men thought they would see him properly served; and indeed the other fellows of Sim. Magus would have forced him to go off, if he had not saved himself by abjuring, not only the tenets of the ch. of Rome, but his allegiance to his lawful sovereign besides; I have even heard it said (by Mr. Potier) that he was one of the foremost to greet k. William, when he came to Oxford in 1695. So he became the pitiful, proud fanatic he hath been ever after. He was for a time at Bodley's library, and there did much mischief, so misarranging the books as it was the work of a pretty many months for honest men to set them in order again.

His learning hath been much cried up, but 'twill prove on examination to be sorry stuff that he hath wrote, mostly opinions taken from his betters, and other men's notes piled up without any attempt made to digest them. I have heard it said (by Dr. Grabe, who was a quere, whimsical man, but yet a good judge in such matters) that his observations on Polycarp were taken from a learned Dutch writer, and very ignorantly. Of his Antiquities of Glocestershire (since it is my purpose to say more of this book elsewhere, and in such manner as, I hope, to expose it for ever to the just indignation of the learned world), I will here set down no more than the opinion of my friend John Purcell esq., of that county, that he was lately with a travelling tinker that hath more knowledge, says he, of Cirencester than Dr. Trumpington hath shewn in all his whole book. But in these days learning is sunk so low, as that any braggadoccio who will set his name to a riff-raff of false conclusions, and inscribe his work to a whig Lord that should by rights have stood, some years back, in the pillory, is pronounced by all the other blockheads in the University to be a ripe scholar, which is only to be expected where false principles abound, and honest men get no preferment.

'Twas he that preached, not many years back, before the University at St. Marie's, on the 28th of May, this being the day on which the d. of Brunswick was born, who is falsely styled k. of England; and spoke of the true R. family so extreme disrespectfully, as that many could with difficulty keep their seats; and he was like to have been burned in effigy next day in the quadrangle at Brasenose, but that the vice-chancellor got wind of it, and so forced the young gentlemen to go quietly to their beds. They say he is a man of very mean origin; and indeed I never heard of one of his name that was at all regarded in the University before this. He is already very far gone in age, being well above seventy, so that Mr. Holyoake will not have to wait long for his provostship; but they say creaking doors hang long, and 'tis like that Dr. Trumpington will do an infinity of mischief, in a College where hitherto all hath been in good order, and sound learning and honest principles have flourished."

CHAPTER V

LOST CAUSES: 1738

MR. SHILLETT. I wonder, who is to have the professorship of poetry?

DR. THEWES. They will put in some very mean man, depend upon it. It is not to be expected that the Heads of Colleges should do otherwise.

MR. SHILLETT (*maliciously*). There was Mr. Watson not long back, that held it for a second term, when Randolph would have had it.

DR. THEWES. Ay, Watson was an honest man; but he would not have had it a second time if another than Randolph had put up against him; Randolph, Sir, was a sorry dunce. Though I believe (*lowering his voice and looking for a moment at the Provost, who sits staring into the fire*) he would have had the Provost's voice, in spite of it.

MR. ACKROYD (*a young fellow with pleasant manners, privileged evidently, raises his voice and addresses the Provost in a bantering tone*). They are asking, Mr. Provost, whether you would accept of the Professorship of Poetry, if the electors would have you take it?

PROVOST TRUMPINGTON (*shaking his head sadly*). No, Sir, it will not do; it is a burden that would sit upon my shoulders too heavily. I am getting to be an old man now, and poetry is for the young; for the sparks that would make favour with their wenches, and the clever spirits that would set the world to rights by inditing satyrs against its manners. This Mr. Pope sets my head spinning; he is too clever for me—it is not like what was wrote in my youth.

> "That which her slender waist confined
> Doth now my joyful temples bind"—

that was poetry, Sir; or we thought it such; you could read it with your feet on the hearth. But the University will not want to listen to an old man talking about what was wrote in his youth; what does Homer say? Something about the song that is newest ever finding the best favour. What was I saying? I think there is very little learning left in the University now.

DR. THEWES (*eagerly*). Tell us, Mr. Provost, what do you make of that? How is it that we are all in this Boeotian fog of ignorance?

THE PROVOST. What is that Mr. Thewes is saying?

MR. ACKROYD (*very loud*). He says, Mr. Provost, he would have you tell us why we are all such dunces nowadays.

THE PROVOST. Why, Mr. Thewes—Dr. Thewes, you will find in your Bible (I doubt if I could find the passage for you) that Wisdom says, "They that seek me early shall find me." And if we have lost her, it is because the young men are too fond of their beds. It is not so long since that Dr. Aldrich, the Dean of Christ Church, was up every morning to prayers at five o'clock. But in these last few years I think nearly all the Colleges have their dinner at twelve, not at eleven as it ever used to be, because no one is hungry before noon. There is no learning, where men do not rise gladly to their books.

MR. SHILLETT (*speaking in a comparatively low voice, so that the Provost cannot hear him*). For my part, I never took early rising to be anything other than a monkish superstition. What is time, but in the mind? If one of the gentlemen should climb up the tower, what is not at all improbable, and put the hands of the clock back from six to five, would not the Provost sleep soundly till six in his bed? Or, if he should put the hands on from five till six, would not Mr. Ackroyd and I rise willingly enough?

DR. THEWES. You will always be after your paradoxes. I hope I do not live to see you Provost. Come now, Mr. Ackroyd, let us hear your account of it, why the University is as it is.

MR. ACKROYD. I say the University is as it is because we are two worlds, not one; that we in the Common-rooms live our own lives, and the young gentlemen live theirs, as far from each other as China is from Peru. This is not to make the best use of our advantages.

DR. THEWES. Why, you would be for having all the heads of Colleges go the same way as Dr. Conybeare at Christ Church, that will have the gate locked at nine, and the keys brought up to his rooms, and hath put out, they tell me, all the bed-makers that were not either old or monstrous ugly! No, Sir, you will get no good out of pampering the gentlemen, as if they were children in the nursery. They must learn to order their own affairs for themselves; and if they will not apply themselves to their studies without the rod, they will reap the fruit of their own neglect. See now, if this be not the distemper from which we are suffering—that there are too many of these professorships and curatorships and the like, so that we spend all our time begging for places, like the Parliament men, and scheming to serve such an one, that he may serve us in his turn; so that the more part of our time is frittered away in politics, when we ought to be at our books. And, what is worse, all this contention for preferment has bred continual law-suits, so that either the Visitor or the King's judges are for ever meddling in our affairs.

MR. SHILLETT. Why, Doctor, I did not expect to hear you talk so lightly about the Visitors of Colleges. Are they not bishops for the most part? I had thought you, at least, would have agreed to think the bishops uncommon holy men, whose voice should be treated as the oracles of God.

DR. THEWES. Bishops, Sir? What bishops? It was but a few years back that the fellows of Magdalen had to appeal to the Visitor in the dispute over Mr. Burslam and Mr. Zinzan. What would be their case, if another like dispute arose, and they must needs carry it to the new Bishop of Winchester, that is a Cambridge man, and, of all the vile spawn of Cambridge, Ben Hoadly? Good God, the fellows of Magdalen, that, within the life-time of Mr. Provost here, have borne so noble a witness to their Protestant principles, to be at the mercy of a canting time-server like Ben Hoadly!

THE PROVOST (*roused by the louder tones into which Dr. Thewes' voice has strayed*). Hoadly is an able man. It is not to be thought that Dr. Sherlock has altogether put him down.

DR. THEWES (*putting down an empty glass and taking no notice of the last remark*). And you, Mr. Shillett, what remedy is it you would propose for our disorders?

MR. SHILLETT. Why, Doctor, I find myself in what is my usual case, of coming to the same point with you, but for the opposite reasons. There is too much, to be sure, of place-hunting and of politics in the University for my taste; but that is because I doubt whether the fellows of Colleges be fit to order their own affairs as they do. And as for the Visitors, there is little more to recommend them; for they have had all their training in Universities, and have little skill in governing. For my part, I would have the King in Parliament rule the Universities as he does the Mint or the Royal Navy, appointing his own officers and settling by his authority all contentions. Then, Doctor, as you have been saying, we should be free to mind our proper business of study.

DR. THEWES. Sir, those are very damnable sentiments. If you had proposed that his Majesty, as he is supreme governor of the Church of England, should rule the University by summoning Convocation, it had been a different matter. But you would have us forget that this University was from the first a religious foundation, and is yet much concerned with providing fit ministers for the Church. It would go ill with the Church, if the College fellowships all went to you and your Whiggish friends, so that the ministry was tainted at the source as it were by a sewer. No, Sir, let us compose our quarrels among ourselves as best we may; let us have no interference here from the Parliament men, who to-day are Whigs and may some years hence, for all we can tell, be very atheists or tub-preachers, so villainously does the world change about us.

MR. ACKROYD (*intervening peaceably*). Come now, Doctor, if we cannot prevent the world changing about us, were it not well to trim our sails and change a little with the world? It was but a dozen years since, as I think I have been told, that fifteen candidates for ordination in this University were denied orders for insufficient knowledge of their theology. And upon the other side, see how many gentlemen there are that come into residence here who will afterwards be highly placed in the commonwealth.

THE PROVOST (*taking notice again*). What is that Mr. Ackroyd is saying? I do not think there are many men studying here now who will come to anything, from what we see of them. The young gentlemen are too much given to drink and hunting; and they seem to me to grow fewer in comparison of this riff-raff of ostlers' sons and buttery-boys that are taking all the prizes now.

MR. SHILLETT. Will there be no place for them, Sir, in these days, when privilege goes for less than formerly? See if a man like James Craggs owed anything to the opportunities of his birth; yet he rose high, and might have risen further.

THE PROVOST. Ay, Sir, but he was a man of commerce;

you will not see these buttery-boys coming to anything, depend upon it. Why, I remember there was a young man at Pembroke, not many years back, whom the fellows used to cry up as something wonderful, and told us how he had quoted Macrobius when they admitted him. The truth is he was an idle scamp, and at the bottom of all the mischief in the College. I think his name was Jackson; yes, I recollect now well enough; Samuel Jackson. I have seen him myself standing outside the great gate of Pembroke and talking to a crowd of men as ragged as himself, like any tub-preacher. But he came to nothing; it sticks in my mind that he never took his bachelor's degree. It is ten years since, and we have heard nothing of him.

MR. SHILLETT. Ten years is not such a very long time, Mr. Provost. He may be upon some learned work, and we shall see the fruits of it later.

THE PROVOST. Oh, like enough he is become a printer's drudge, and will put forth a dictionary. But that is all we shall hear of him; he will come to nothing, depend upon it.

MR. ACKROYD. Yet my point holds: if the University is serving another office than what was at first intended, is it not time that she became the handmaid of the nation, not of the Church? The more so, that on your own shewing the bishops (as witness my Lord of Winton) are coming to follow new fashions, and the Church itself is not like to remain long what you and your friends would have it be.

MR. SHILLETT (*rubbing it in*). Surely, Doctor, Mr.

Ackroyd is in the right of it. When I would have the King in Parliament control the affairs of Oxford, you are for interposing the authority of the Church. But to what purpose, if the Church itself is subject to the authority of the King in Parliament, as in these days is most evident? If his Majesty have power to rule the consciences of his subjects, and say what it is they shall or shall not believe, is it not within his province to order the affairs of the University, all its ancient privileges notwithstanding?

DR. THEWES. Why, Mr. Shillett, I ever took you for a Whig! What is this language you are holding now, as if the King had authority over the consciences of his subjects in matters of religion? Nay, Sir, do not interrupt me; let me say my speech out. If the King have authority over the consciences of his subjects, what is all this to-do you and your friends are making over the Nonconformists, as if they must be relieved of all their disabilities, because they cannot form their consciences so as to strike in with the opinions of the Church?

MR. SHILLETT. Sir, you have took me up wrong. My meaning was an argument *ad hominem*, nothing more. If was men like you, fifty years since, that told us we must lift no hand against the Lord's anointed, though he were a professed papist. And when we brought over Dutch William, all at once he became the Lord's anointed in his turn, and we must lift up no hand against him. What was this but to say the King could do no wrong, 'till we chased King James overseas; and then, when the Parliament men had brought in Dutch William, to say that the King in Parliament can do no wrong, in Church or State? Yet, when I proposed to you his Majesty should busy himself in the affairs of the University, you cried me down for a sneaking reformer. Come, Doctor, tell us what we are to make of all this? Is King George, God bless him, in your mind the supreme governor of the Church in this realm? Or will you fetch the Pretender back, that is a papist like his father before him, and will have nothing to say to you, nor yet to your Church?

MR. ACKROYD'S GUEST (*a* MR. HERRIES, *breaking in on the conversation nervously, with a slight cough*). Gentlemen, it is a great honour to drink wine with the fellows of Simon Magus, and I vow I would not willingly intervene in these discussions of learned men. But this much I cannot leave unsaid—I have been with a gentleman of very good family who has but lately returned from overseas, having—having some business there. And he told me it is common talk in the city of Paris that the—the Chevalier, as they call him there, is by no means so besotted a papist as rumour has made him out to be. Nay, they will have it that he secretly adheres to the established Church of England, although he is forced, out of courtesy as I suppose and it may be somewhat out of policy, to conform to the religion of those parts, until there be some change in his fortunes.

MR. ACKROYD (*rallying Dr. Thewes*). Come, Doctor, this is a piece of excellent good news for you. You have told us a score of times that you would have recognized King James for your lawful sovereign, if he had not apostatized most scandalously from the reformed religion.

And here is Mr. Herries tells us that the son is come back into the true fold again; will you not fall upon his neck, and kill the fatted calf for him?

DR. THEWES. Sir, let us have no more of calves. Do you take me for a lousy Puritan, that you would put me in mind of calf's head after my dinner? To your story, Sir (*he turns to Mr. Ackroyd's guest*), I take it to be no better than moonshine. The Frenchmen are never content, but they will be putting about silly gossip such as you have been listening to.

MR. ACKROYD (*who does not like Dr. Thewes, and is anxious to stand up for his guest*). Nay, Doctor, you shall not put Mr. Herries down so. You and he are of one kidney; and I doubt not, if the Pretender comes back, you will be drilling together of nights in the University Park. Only Mr. Herries is a man who travels much; and he may well have better news than you of your friends overseas. Come now, will you not humour him thus far; let us put the case that a certain gentleman overseas, who is no Duke of Brunswick, should make up his mind London is worth a Communion service, and conform to the Church of which he is supreme governor, would you not be for recognizing him as your lawful head in matters of Church and State? Mr. Herries, I warn you, will be extreme provoked if you say otherwise.

DR. THEWES. What, Sir, are you for baiting me with supposititious cases? I do not know that I am obliged to answer your If's. Why, I might as well ask you what the University would do, if one of the boys should climb to the top of Dr. Radcliffe's library, and hang a piece of bunting there? You will not persuade me that your If is not equally extravagant as this.

THE PROVOST (*re-entering the conversation unexpectedly, on a favourite tack*). Why, if it were one of our gentlemen, I would see to it that the University did not punish him; upon my word now, it would be an uncommon suitable thing, what you talk of. (*To Mr. Herries.*) You will have seen Dr. Radcliffe's Camera, that is in building, Sir? It is a very mean piece of work; and if anybody should venture to climb it, I am not sure but it would come tumbling about his ears. Have we not enough space already in Bodley's for all the books that are like to be written, in these days especially, when the fellows of Colleges put out nothing but a riff-raff of old sermons now and again, and men have nothing to read but Bishop Burnet? If Dr. Radcliffe's will was for piling up a great store of medical treatises, this should have been done in the fields outside the North Gate, instead of spoiling one of the fairest pieces of ground in Oxford, and fetching in a papist to cumber it with his volutes and pilasters. Sir, it is of a piece with all the University does nowadays.

MR. ACKROYD (*in a low voice*). See now, Doctor, what you have got by your queer fancies; you had nearly thrown Mr. Provost into an apoplexy. Come now, you were telling us but a few days since that you were a loyal subject of King George, because King James unchurched himself when he turned papist, and the Crown passed into the younger branch as by natural inheritance. Are you still of the same mind? And will you not say that King

James' son would come into his own again by right, if the impediment of religion were to be removed?

DR. THEWES. Ay, but we cannot be for ever chopping and changing. If Parliament has settled the Crown on the younger branch, there it must remain, whether or no they of the elder branch are obstinate in their errors.

MR. SHILLETT (*eagerly*). It is true, then, by your way of it, that it is from Parliament the authority of the Crown proceeds, since Parliament has the bestowal of it?

DR. THEWES. Hold, Sir, hold; I distinguish. That Parliament must provide for the succession when the throne is vacant, I admit; that the authority of the Crown proceeds from Parliament, I deny. Why, Sir, is it not the Crown that must appoint, when a bishoprick falls vacant? Yet it is not from the Crown their authority is derived, but from the apostolical succession which they have inherited; there is not a boy in the University but knows that.

MR. HERRIES (*who has been drinking steadily, and is now less overawed by his company*). Sir, they told me you were a complyer, but I had not guessed that Oxford kept so little loyalty to the old ways; it astonishes me to hear you speak so. The article says very plainly, that the unworthiness of the minister hindereth not the effect of a Sacrament; and if a priest does not unpriest himself by his evil living, shall a king unking himself by turning papist? Pardon me, Sir, but you have spoke like a rank Anabaptist. For my part, I never could bring myself to understand how the fellows of this University will take their bread from the Duke of Brunswick, when Scripture plainly forbids us to lift up a hand against the Lord's Anointed, and King David pronounced sentence of death against the Amalekite that had put King Saul out of his troubles, his express permission notwithstanding.

DR. THEWES (*glaring at him*). Sir, we live in better times; we are not Amalekites. The Amalekites, depend upon it, were a nasty, brutish sort of folk, and God had other dealings with them; so I answer you.

MR. ACKROYD. Nay, Doctor, you shall not put down Mr. Herries so easily. If the Israelites wandered forty years in the wilderness, and we can pass from Oxford to London in a couple of days by coach, will you tell us that the ten Commandments are no more in vigour?

MR. SHILLETT (*eagerly joining in*). But there is more than that, Doctor; look well what you are saying. You tell us that King James unchurched himself when he turned papist; who is to be the judge of that? You will not find the Pope of Rome holding such language, I doubt. Who is to judge, if it be not the Commons of the Realm? And if the Commons of the Realm may judge the King, does not the supreme authority lie with them? Who, as you were saying but now, are a set of Whigs to-day, and to-morrow may be tub-preachers.

DR. THEWES. Ay, you will all bait me like a badger; I am all of a sweat with your quibblings. (*He takes off his wig and fans himself.*) To you, Sir (*he turns to Mr. Shillett*)—are you telling me that an honest man may not decide for himself whether King James, that was a professed papist, had a right to name Dr. Hickes Bishop of Thetford? Must I wait for an Act of Parliament to be carried, before I can see the nose in front of my face? It was but a matter of five years back that Handel, the German, was allowed to play at the Commemoration Act with his crew of lousy musicians, to the great discredit of the University. Am I not allowed to judge for myself that what we heard in the theatre was but pitiful jamblings and discords, and not true musick? Do I need an Act of Parliament to tell me that? Damn me, Mr. Shillett, I had thought better of your reasonableness.

MR. ACKROYD (*intervening as usual*). Come, Doctor, your case does not run parallel. We were speaking of authority, and it is very well agreed that authority does not bind, if its claim be not evident to the consciences of all who are subject to it. We cannot have Tom, Dick and Harry each deciding for himself how he will be ruled in Church or in State, and then justifying himself for disobedience by protesting that Dr. Thewes told him otherwise. If King James had no right to name Dr. Hickes, as you have been telling us, let us hear what right King George had to name your good friend Ben Hoadly, when he presented him to Winchester.

DR. THEWES. Sir, you are a very good host. Everybody knows you and Mr. Shillett for a pair of stinking Whigs; yet when your guest here pipes to the tune of *The King shall enjoy his own again*, you both strike in with him to anger me. Look now, I will answer this gentleman—Mr. Herries, is it not?—and see if I do not put him down. Your sovereign, Sir, is irremovable, that is plain; what will you say of your bishops? As thus; when King William put Dr. Sancroft out from being

Archbishop of Canterbury, had he the right to do that? I mean, granted he was the true king; *dato non concesso*, if you will.

MR. HERRIES. I see no room for dubitation here; I do not think, though he were ten times rightful sovereign, King William or any other man had the power to put out Dr. Sancroft, unless it were some council of the Church, convoked upon grave cause to that end.

DR. THEWES. I had expected you to say as much. And now tell me this; had Queen Elizabeth the right to put out Dr. Heath from being Archbishop of York, above a hundred years earlier? Look well what reply you will make; for if you say Ay, you will be for denying the admission you made to me this minute; and if you say No, you will be a confessed papist, for we had had no Reformation, if Queen Bess had had regard to the queasy stomachs the bishops had in those times. I think I have held you to a dilemma.

MR. ACKROYD. This is what will give the College a very bad name, if I cannot invite an honest friend to dine with the fellows, but they will be making a papist of him before the afternoon is out. You should have more respect for your cloth, Doctor, than to serve my guests so.

MR. HERRIES (*more interested in politics than in theology*). Are these, then, the notions you breed here? Is that University, which little more than twenty years ago must be kept down by a troop of horse, or they would have come out in favour of the honest cause, sunk so low that it will cry up a Whig government, and——

DR. THEWES. Watch your words, Sir; I did not say that I had a mind to strike in with the present government of England, a very beastly government, a vile, stinking government, Sir, which I would see drowned and damned if the raising of this glass would do it. Only my meaning is that the time is past when honest men should be for fetching back the house of Stuart, as if that were the only hope of better times. I believe, Sir, we in Magus are before our time; if you had been dining in Balliol, now, you would have found them wishing the King back, as you call him, very besottedly. Mr. Shillett would never have had a fellowship at Balliol, depend upon it. (*He glowers at Mr. Shillett, as if there was something to be said for Balliol after all.*)

MR. HERRIES. And the young gentlemen, Sir? If Prince Charles should come across the sea, like his father before him, what part do you think they would take?

THE PROVOST (*shaking his head and wagging a finger at Mr. Herries*). You need have no fear about the boys, Mr. Herries; they are very foolish, very foolish indeed. They will sit in the taverns drinking to King James, as they call him, so boldly as would cost them their liberty, if they were grown men, and in London. But you are to consider that these boys will always be for putting down the party that is in power; they are young, and will have a change at all costs. Besides, they like to fancy themselves grown men, and to meddle with politics, yet knowing well enough that it will cost them nothing, except perhaps to have their degrees deferred for a year or two at the worst. But, for what you say about the Pretender venturing over sea again, that is not to be thought of. The government is very well informed about his movements, and it would not be possible for him to stir a finger but he would be prevented before any harm came of it. No, Sir, we shall see no more trouble of that sort.

MR. ACKROYD (*mischievously*). What, Mr. Provost, do you think the young gentlemen would turn Whig all of a sudden, if his Majesty should call in my Lord Bullingbroke to advise him, and the honest party had the upper hand again?

THE PROVOST (*chuckling*). That is a very improbable supposition, Sir; I do not know that I am called upon to answer such a fantastic question as yours. But yes, Sir, if it should fall out in two hundred years' time (I will humour you as best I may) that the Tories should have their own way, then I am very willing to believe that the boys would run clean contrary in their sentiments, and would be crying huzza and jambling the bells for any party-man that would make head against them. It is of their nature to be contradictory; but let it pass, they will grow wiser when they have older heads upon their shoulders. A man must be a fellow of his College before he begins to ask himself, whether it were not well to move with the times.

MR. SHILLETT (*who has been sitting with his head buried in his hands, with the air of one trying to recover a lost thread in the argument*). You were saying but now, Dr. Thewes, that the bishops derive their authority from the apostolical succession, not from the Crown; or did I take you up wrong?

DR. THEWES. This is a sorry thing, that I cannot sit here drinking my Madeira, but I must be plagued all the time with your riddles.

MR. ACKROYD. Nay, Doctor, it was you that were posing Mr. Herries but now with a dilemma; will you not answer in your turn?

DR. THEWES (*with an effort*). Yes, Mr. Shillett, I did say as much. I only marvel that one who has determined so lately should need to be taught by an older man in the rudiments of theology. A bishop gets his authority for preaching the word of God and for the laying on of hands from his consecration by his fellow-bishops; and if he does homage after to his Majesty, that is only for the temporalities of his see, all the world knows that.

MR. SHILLETT. Why, then, I am not sure but you are in a worse case than Mr. Herries. For there is no doubt, when King James appointed Dr. Hickes to be Bishop of Thetford, Dr. Hickes was consecrated with all due forms by true bishops of Dr. Sancroft's communion; who, since he inherited the apostolical succession, inherited also the authority you speak of. If you had held a benefice in those parts a few years back, would you have acknowledged the Bishop of Thetford, or the Bishop of Norwich? For, that one did homage to King James and the other to Queen Anne, makes no matter, by your way of it. And if the godly monitions you had got from Thetford had been other than those you got from Norwich, how would you have resolved your conscience between them?

DR. THEWES (*after pausing a little for reflection, with his hands on his open knees*). Sir, you talk like a blockhead.

You have not learned to distinguish between authority and the exercise of authority. That a bishop can possess authority without being in any sort obnoxious to the Crown for it, I admit. That he may in conscience exercise such authority, unless the King gives him licence, I deny. Have I answered you?

THE PROVOST. Sir, you have answered him extreme wisely. This was ever the right of secular princes, to empower the bishops to exercise that authority which lay in them; this was not to usurp it. Did not the emperor Constantine take it on himself to convoke the first council at Nice; and not, as the papists falsely say, the Pope of Rome that then was? But this is not to say it was Constantine who condemned Arius; you know well enough, Mr. Shillett, the case was otherwise.

MR. SHILLETT (*bows to the Provost, but continues to address Dr. Thewes*). Then, Sir, if I had lived under Queen Mary, I would have done right to burn Cranmer in the street yonder, because her bishops ordered it? But if I had lived under Queen Elizabeth, I had done right to hang the massing-priests, now the new bishops ordered different?

DR. THEWES. Why, yes, Sir. The bishops under Queen Mary behaved extreme bloody, that is certain, and they will answer for it at the seat of Judgement; but they were true bishops for all that, and it was the part of good Christians to obey them.

MR. SHILLETT. So the bishops must be obeyed, but only if the Crown is our warranty that they are true bishops; and the king must be obeyed, but only if

Parliament is our warranty that he is the true king? For myself, I had sooner make friends with the officer who has power to bid the men of the ordnance let off their piece, than with the men themselves, who cannot move till they are bidden. And I would sooner make friends with the Parliament-men, that have power to dismiss the king that has power to dismiss the bishops, than with the bishops themselves, who may be no bishops to-morrow.

DR. THEWES. That is very loose, atheistical talk. It is not to be wondered at, that men like Mr. Herries here should want to fetch King James back, if we cannot make shift otherwise to stop such canting Whiggish talk, and that in Oxford.

MR. HERRIES (*not pacified after his recent defeat, and still drinking*). Ay, but in my submission it is what you have brought on yourself, Doctor. No bishop, no king—that is well enough; but must not good Protestants say, No king, no bishop? And if Tom, Dick and Harry are to say who shall be king, are they not saying who shall be bishops, to the great confusion of all order in religion? Why, Sir, to-day you are for granting toleration to the sectaries; who can tell but to-morrow these sectaries may be turning Parliament-men; and your bishops will come hat in hand to a riff-raff of Brownists and Anabaptists, asking for their licence to ordain this and that, to forbid this and that, in God's Church? Nay, but hear me out, Sir——

DR. THEWES. You speak of what is not possible. God, I have had such a set of Ifs proposed to me this evening as, if they were nightmares, would make me sweat my night-cap off. Sir, you are all for putting me down with figments of your own fancy. As for this riff-raff Parliament which you vaticinate, it is no more pertinent to a debate such as this than—than——

MR. ACKROYD (*coming to his rescue*). Let us say, a *chimaera bombinans in vacuo;* someone has used that comparison, I think it was Locke.

DR. THEWES (*glaring at him*). You do very ill, Mr. Ackroyd, to make mention of such a name within the four walls of an Oxford Common-room. It is well known that Locke's philosophy is not received here, what is little to be wondered at. Locke, Sir, could not be content with oversetting all authority in government by his pernicious treatises; he must needs write his Essay, and take away from us all grounds of reasonable certainty whatever.

THE PROVOST. They tell me he is read at Cambridge. I remember Mr. Locke well, when he was a student of Christ Church; a very mild, harmless man, Sir, but I do not think he has said much that was new. I marvel why there has been so much talk of him.

DR. THEWES. Let me say this, Mr. Shillett; I think this Parliament of yours will govern England when Mr. Locke's Essay is studied by the young gentlemen in Oxford; then and not before, Sir, then and not before.

MR. SHILLETT (*mildly*). Why, I believe it was Mr. Herries, not I, that was to blame, Doctor, for this disturbance of your slumbers. For all that, I take it to be very pertinent, what Mr. Herries has said, that you were for founding the dominion of the bishops in the authority of Parliament, and that is nothing other than *Vox populi, vox Dei*. To that, I say Amen; I am not for the old times, like Mr. Herries.

MR. HERRIES (*to Mr. Shillett*). Come, Sir, I believe your principles are better than your professions. I was this day walking out with a friend by Seckworth, delighting very much in the shade of the trees and their reflection in the cool water. We climbed a little afterwards to the hill above Wytham, whence there is a fine prospect to be obtained of the Colleges; I have been there more than once in years gone by with Mr. Thomas Hearne, that was my great acquaintance; some of you gentlemen doubtless knew him. There was a little mist risen from the river, as I suppose, in the great heat; and the church spires and the towers of the Colleges rose out of it as if they had no more substantial foundation than air. You will think me a very foolish old man, Sirs, yet I could not help but think of the past, and how Oxford is its epitome. There were the walls, much overgrown with ivy, where the nunnery used to be at Godstow; and there was Binsey, with the well that men used to frequent for the cure of their eyes in the days of Popish superstition; there was the spire of St. Mary's and the tower of St. Martin's, there was Magdalen tower, and Merton, and the Cathedral Church; and with them some of these new-fangled edifices we have put up of late, which some admire more than I do, as Archbishop Sheldon's theatre and the Church of All Saints. And it was my humour to reflect, looking on them, whether we are indeed part of the past, and it of us; or whether that old Oxford of the monkish days is indeed something other, and we and our Church—I mean the established Church, although I am like to die myself outside its communion—a new foundation with but a century and a half of history, piled up on the ruins of the old. Come, Sir (*turning to Mr. Shillett again*), which is your way of it?

MR. SHILLETT (*clasping his knees with his hands and sitting awkwardly in his chair*). What, Sir, are you for embroiling me with Dr. Thewes? I cannot answer other than he would, when you ask me that. I would say that ours is the same Church we have ever had in England, only we have grown too old for our superstitions. Or —stay, let me give my meaning thus; if Mr. Provost, looking through the archives of the College, should come upon a document shewing that the founder provided for nothing here but the teaching of Hebrew, should we not all be bound by his trust, and needs become Hebraists as best we could? This would not be to disown our past; rather, we should be returning to our past by doing away with all the logic and the Latin wherewith we had abused the minds of the young gentlemen hitherto. It was nothing other, in my submission, the Church of England did when she put all her monkish follies behind her, and returned to the true gospel, as we had it in the first ages.

MR. HERRIES. Sir, I like your comparison excellent well. But come, if Mr. Provost should light on this document you talk of, would you all be at work on Aleph, Beth and Ghimel the same evening? Would not there be some here, Dr. Thewes perhaps, who would ask what proof there was the document was genuine; and supposing that it was, whether it was still binding, in these changed times and after so many years' usage to the contrary? I think my friend Mr. Ackroyd has told me, that the endowment which was intended for providing lectures in moral philosophy is by the present custom of the University divided between the two proctors; is not that as much as to say, that title-deeds in this University may be very strangely interpreted? And is it not certain that any statute such as the one you mention would have to be submitted to a court of law, or at the least to the judgement of the Visitor, before any regard was had to it? And by the same reasoning, I hold that the words of Scripture could not be used to condemn the abuses of the old religion, unless some juridical decision had first been pronounced upon the matter by a competent authority. What is the authority, then, which assures you that the old ways were unscriptural?

MR. SHILLETT. May not a man, then, interpret Scripture for himself?

MR. ACKROYD. If you allow that, you will have every Ranter and Muggletonian buzzing round you, saying that his interpretation is as good as yours. It was not a generation back, as I have heard, that Dr. Whiston was for expounding the plain sense of the Apocalypse, and would have it that the world would come to an end in nine years' time, upon the occasion of a solar eclipse. Which eclipse did indeed take place, shortly after the death of her late Majesty; yet we slept sound in our beds —I remember it very well—because Dr. Halley had wrote a letter very manifestly tracing it to astronomical motions upon which he had informed himself beforehand. Scripture is to be judged in these days by sober and cautious men, not according to superstitious fancies; we have learned so much from the observations of philosophy; what we owe in great part to such men as Dr. Halley, and Sir Isaac Newton.

THE PROVOST (*stirring again in his chair*). Newton, Sir, was a very mean chronologer. He had very little tincture of the classics, even for a Cambridge man. As for his mathematics, there was a great deal of stir made about him; but he had it all from Sir Christopher Wren and Dr. Hook; that everybody knows. He has his monument at the Abbey, but it is a poor thing. I am not persuaded that posterity will make much of Newton.

MR. HERRIES (*who has been following his own train of thought*). Come, Mr. Shillett, let me put you to the test over this matter of Scripture. In the old days, you will not dispute it, the Pope's word ran in England, and the bishops exercised authority under him. When times changed, the word was put about that the Pope's authority was usurped and unscriptural; but we had bishops yet. Now, Sir, who was it determined we should be governed by bishops, and not by a presbytery? For it is certain many learned men have interpreted the Scriptures as though there had been no bishops in the first age, but presbyters only.

MR. ACKROYD. I do not know that you are serving your own cause, Mr. Herries. You are for making Mr. Shillett say, it was the bishops determined that we should have bishops in the established Church, but no Pope.

I am not much of a lawyer, but I think it is good law that no man is a judge in his own quarrel; what is clean contrary to your notion, that the bishops had a right to establish episcopacy.

MR. SHILLETT. What is all this labour about bishops and presbyters? I think it is mostly to King James we owe it that we have bishops yet; for he had made trial of the presbytery in Scotland, and found such meat was very heavy on his stomach. If we have bishops, it is because they take better order for the welfare of the Church than a presbytery would, not for any other reason.

MR. HERRIES (*highly scandalized*). Why, this is worse than anything we have had yet. You talk as if you made nothing at all of the apostolical succession, and loved bishops only because they ordered things well in their dioceses; what is besides very questionable. Come, Sir, would a bishop be as good a bishop by your way of it, if no man invested with the apostolical authority had laid hands on him?

DR. THEWES (*joining in eagerly*). Yes, Mr. Shillett, that is what you must tell us. If Mr. Wesley, now, were to lay hands upon some of his followers and send them out to be bishops, would they have the same right in the sight of God as his Grace of Canterbury?

MR. ACKROYD. Mr. Wesley? I thought he had been in the plantations.

DR. THEWES. He is in London again; and I hear he has struck in with the Moravian missionaries there; what is much wondered at.

MR. SHILLETT. I find no matter for wonder in it. Depend upon it, Wesley would not remain in the plantations, but come back to plague us all. And as for the company he keeps, Methodists or Moravians, it is all one.

MR. HERRIES. Methodists? I thought they had been a kind of mathematicians?

MR. SHILLETT. No, Sir; I for one would have been confounded glad if they had been nothing worse. It is very evident you have been away from Oxford these ten years; or you would have heard of the Holy Club, and the nasty canting professions they made of living differently from their neighbours, fasting and examining their consciences and lending themselves to every kind of dangerous enthusiasm.

MR. ACKROYD. It is true, Mr. Shillett was always for running down the Oxford Methodists; but by my way of it they were a very harmless kind of persons, and more to be imitated than to be despised. I do not know that this University was ever meant to be the home of young sparks, that cannot spend their time better than in drinking coffee every morning at Lyne's, and exhibiting themselves in Merton Walks arm-in-arm with all the toasts of the town. This Wesley, Sir, would have used Oxford as a place for serious study——

THE PROVOST (*breaking in with some heat*). You will all see, Mr. Wesley will finish up a papist. I knew his father a little, that was a bad husband of his own affairs, and has wrote up very bitterly against the Nonconformists. And as for the son, it is true what Mr. Shillett has told you, that he is become a dangerous sort of enthusiast;

and there is no other way of it, but such enthusiasm will carry a man to Rome; which is what I anticipate for Mr. Wesley, and other the like coxcombs with him.

MR. ACKROYD (*changing the dangerous subject*). Why, here is a very extraordinary thing, that we have spent so much of the afternoon examining the principles of the Establishment, and can come to no point over it. Here is Mr. Herries cannot tell us, why Queen Elizabeth had a right to put out the bishops that were till then, yet King William had no right to put out Sancroft and the others that held to the old succession. Here is Dr. Thewes thinks the Crown has power to dispose of bishoprics, and Parliament has power to dispose of the Crown, yet would sooner die than see bishoprics disposed of by Parliament. And Mr. Shillett finds all that has been done these last two hundred years in Church and State very right and conformable to Scripture, yet he cannot resolve our doubts whether or no the Church of England, since such things came about, is the same Church still.

MYSELF. . . .

THE PROVOST. Sirs, you do ill to move such questions; there was never yet any end found to them. Depend upon it, this realm of England has found more benefit in meeting troubles as they came, and shaping its course according to what was needed upon each several occasion, than by questioning who had authority here or there, or by what right anything was done that was done. We are a plain people, and have no stomach for academical dissertations; that is the truth of it. I was like you in my young days, Mr. Shillett; I would reason with the other fellows of Magus till the sun set, and then go off to finish the argument in a tavern; but we never got much further forward, Sir; never much further forward. The air strikes chill in these afternoons; and I have ever dreaded them since the epidemical cold carried off so many, five years since. I will be for getting back to my lodgings, Sirs; there is no end to these controversies, depend upon it. (*He hobbles out, amidst general silence.*)

NOTE ON CHAPTER V

Fortunately, no arduous research is needed to bridge the gap between my dream of 1738 and my dream of 1788. I have only to print here the well-known dialogue between Dr. Johnson and his biographer, which beguiled the coach journey after their visit to Oxford in 1776:

"I could not forbear to express my astonishment, that whereas the University so abounded in the company of learned men, some only and not all should privately direct the studies of the juniors. For, if it be considered that *one man's meat is another man's poison*, and that our minds have affinities one with another, so that one will learn more from the society of this or that tutor than from twenty others besides, it is not probable that in a College where only a few are tutors, each of the undergraduates will find one that is capable of spurring him on to generous emulation. It has moreover been set on record by Mr. Gibbon, a man of acute mind although it was tainted by infidelity, that many fellows of colleges spend their time in the pursuit of indolent trifling. I said something of all this to Dr. Johnson as we sat on the coach together. JOHNSON. No, Sir, a College would not get much advantage from having more than one or two of these *pupil-mongers*. If a boy has a hunger for learning, he will do well enough; if he wants it, he will not profit greatly from the best tutor. I said, there was nevertheless the danger to be apprehended, the residue of the fellows would sink into idleness. JOHNSON. That is only the abuse of a system; they should be writing and lecturing. You will always have some *loungers;* but this is better, than that learning should be hampered by penury. BOSWELL. I hear at Cambridge they are for doing away with these *pupil-mongers,* because it is thought they shew undue favour when they examine their own men.' JOHNSON. Ay, at Cambridge (laughing).

He observed, that his visits to Oxford, or to any other town where he had considerable acquaintance, were an incentive to melancholy, because he always found some places there vacated since his last visit by the death of persons who had been his familiars. 'In London it is otherwise, where we creep to our graves unnoticed, but in Oxford I mark every vacant chair. There was Mr. Ackroyd, now, who was my good friend till lately; Simon Magus is not the same place for me, since he was taken from us. There was a great cordiality about Ackroyd; it made a man's heart warmer, to have been in his company.' I asked whether this Mr. Ackroyd, whom I never knew, had been a man remarkable for scholarship. JOHNSON. No, Sir, not above the common. But he spoke very judiciously; I do not think there are many men who are so often right as Ackroyd was. I asked whether they had been together at the University. JOHNSON. I do not think he entered till after I had left it. I never had much acquaintance at Simon Magus, but I received some kindness from Dr. Thewes, who is dead these many years. Thewes was a good man, but a heavy man; he could not endure that anybody should differ with his opinion, yet he wanted the capacity to jostle them down in an argument. There is nothing so frets a man's mind, as to be continually disagreeing with his neighbour, yet never able to get the better of him. I hear he was at one time engaged upon an answer to Hume, but it came to nothing. If he were alive now, he would be for answering Gibbon. BOSWELL. There are many of us, Sir, who are sorry you have written nothing against Hume. JOHNSON. Sir, that is to save yourself the trouble of *thinking* against Hume. There is no sooner a good answer put out to some book that shocks the conscience of humanity, than the world takes a holiday from reading either the one or the other. But I would have put out a better answer than Dr. Thewes, depend upon it. Thewes would have given him the point, debating with him in the manner of the schools; I would have knocked him down with common sense (pausing a little). Thewes would have liked to bring the Stuarts back. BOSWELL. That was great loyalty in him. JOHNSON. No, Sir, only a habituation of the mind.

I hesitated to ask my companion, whether he had any acquaintance with another fellow of the same house, Mr. Jonathan Shillett, who is much spoken of for his elegant treatise of Ornamental Gardens. But it seems his thought kept pace with mine, for he said after a little while, Simon Magus is not what Trinity is, *evergreen;* there is nobody left there now that is of any consequence. When you look to be made acquainted with some remarkable man there, they present you to *old Shillett*, who must be a man of seventy-two, as I guess. Sir, that is not a great age. And if he were a man of ninety-two, he would not be a remarkable man. BOSWELL. He would be a man remarkable for his age. JOHNSON. It might as well be said of one who had never had the tooth-ache, he was a man remarkable for his teeth. Such a man might well be felicitated, but only for a privation of unhappiness. A man who lives long is only a man who has not died; which is a mere accident of his state, and not an excellence to be admired in him. Although, to be sure, we might admire him for the temperance which kept him alive, when otherwise the gout would have got him; but that is not so with Shillett, they tell me he drinks very heavy.

No, Sir, there is nothing to make us talk of him, except that he is not dead; which is no matter for public rejoicing, in so pestilent a Whig as Shillett is. I said, smiling, perhaps it was a good thing he should live long, that he might have space for repentance. JOHNSON. No, Sir old men do not repent of their bad principles.

I said, Mr. Shillett had written very elegantly of gardens. He would not allow any merit in this; a garden is a thing (he said) elegant in itself, so that one who writes of it cannot choose but write elegantly. He would have more respect for a man who could write elegantly of something that was of its own nature horrid and barren, as, of a mountain in Scotland. He said things went ill with a College, when there was too much gardening and too little learning. Seeing that he was out of humour with Mr. Shillett, I could not forbear to enquire more curiously into his reasons, asking him (as well as I remember) whether it would be a reasonable action for a man to get rid of his gardener, though he were a good gardener, because he was a Whig. JOHNSON. No, Sir; he could not breed bad principles in the flowers. It is a much worse thing that he should be fellow of a College, and train up the minds of the young men in a detestable fashion. But that is not to say they have much respect for him; I am told he is little regarded; he is a very ignorant fellow. BOSWELL. He was a man that promised much in his youth; I was told in Oxford that *he might have done anything.* JOHNSON. Sir, he might have hanged himself.

I said, it was at least a credit to the College Mr. Shillett had never become Provost; from which it might be argued it was still a home of honest opinions. JOHNSON. Sir, you are to consider that Whigs have little love for one another. In a College like Simon Magus, each man is for himself, and would not move a finger to advance one that shared his principles. If they pass over a scoundrel, it is to elect a worse scoundrel, that is certain. Upon this I observed, that Simon Magus was still ruled by the same statutes as formerly, for all its fellows were so whiggishly inclined; there was nothing done to reform it. JOHNSON. You will never find Whigs reforming *themselves*. Sir, if Wilkes were made a fellow of any society in Oxford, you would not find its statutes more rigorously interpreted thenceforward, or its emoluments diminished. (Laughing very heartily.) We will propose it to the Government, they should intrude Wilkes into Simon Magus, and see if his wings are not clipped. There is a great deal of politics talked in Oxford, but things do not change there, for the better or for the worse; I do not know that Shillett is a worse Whig than old Trumpington used to be, who was Provost when I was here. He had been a papist, I think, before the Revolution, but afterwards proved a worse Whig than any of them. BOSWELL. Then he was doubly a renegado, both when he embraced the Roman Catholic religion, and when he abandoned it. JOHNSON. No, Sir, a man must follow his conscience. If he was sincere when he embraced that way of thinking, he did no wrong then; if insincere, he did no wrong when he abandoned it; you must not make him out to be doubly a scoundrel. But he was a scoundrel for all that.

I asked, whether any credit should be given to the stories we hear of the sea-serpent . . . etc. etc."

CHAPTER VI

THE UNCHANGING WORLD: 1788

DR. JENNINGS. This is very pernicious stuff that one Mr. Knox has been writing about the expenses of men at the Universities. No doubt it is done to inflame the passions of the populace, by representing to them the great disproportion there is between the wealth of the gentlemen and of the servitors here. But you will see, it will all fall out to the discredit of the University. The fellows who write in the Reviews will take up the matter, and we shall be told that the seniors spend all their time toadying the richer sort of undergraduates, the better to get preferment and to be received in polite society.

MR. HAMMOND. I do not think Knox is a very judicious author. It is remarked that in his *Amendments* he complains the stipends of tutors are at present too little; yet it was not long since he put out his *Treatise on Education*, in which he would have it that the tutor's office is lucrative beyond what is reasonable. You may use any stick to beat a dog, but not one that breaks in your hand.

MR. SHILLETT. Who is Knox?

DR. JENNINGS. He was formerly, I think, a member of St. John's. He is a very slight man, Mr. Shillett, who will save himself the pains of authorship by publishing elegant extracts from the works of better men; a preacher who will wheedle money out of silly women for charities; a man who has a smattering of everything; he gives out that he is a Doctor of Divinity, having come by that title from some University in Pennsylvania, and uses it still, although the men who gave it to him are now become rebels and foreigners.

MR. SHILLETT. There was a man bearing this name that wrote of Scottish fisheries. A man must be grievously at a loss for a subject to exercise his pen before he will write of Scottish fisheries.

MR. HAMMOND. No, Sir, that is not the same person. That was a Scotchman, John Knox; this Dr. Knox of whom we were speaking is called, I think, Vicesimus.

MR. SHILLETT. Good God, is he then the youngest of a family of twenty?

DR. JENNINGS. It is a pity his parents were not content with nineteen. I hope it will be a hundred years before we see any more Knoxes.

MYSELF. . . .

MR. WATSON (*evidently the youngest of the party; so much of a modern that, unlike the others, he wears his own hair*). Yet it is a question whether there is not too much extravagance among the commoners. This University was founded, I conceive, in the times of superstition, to make learned clerks out of the sons of poor men; and so in part it is still. With what horror, then, does your industrious scholar contemplate the drunken revels and the fastidious manners of those who are called gentlemen, yet should, in a University, be his equals.

MR. SHILLETT. There is much cant about the luxury of these boys. You will find there is nowhere a man can have his hair dressed more cheaply, than in Oxford.

MR. WATSON. Sir, the expenses they undertake may be less here than in London; that does not alter the circumstance, that there is great disproportion between richer men and poorer in the fashion of their living. If the extravagances we were speaking of are not restrained by statute, I see two evils following; sycophancy on the part of the poorer men, and foppish idleness on the part of those who call themselves their betters.

MR. SHILLETT. They are not altogether idle, Sir. I think there is less idleness among the boys than there was formerly, when I was first a fellow.

MR. HAMMOND. If they are not idle, it must be their native ambition that spurs them to it. It needs very little incumbence upon their studies, if they are to answer the questions for their degree.

DR. JENNINGS. Good God, man, you are not for holding annual examinations, like Mr. Jebb, who has been raising such a hornet's nest at Cambridge? If you younger men had your way, I believe you would have all the men, with no respect to their station and capacity, reading themselves crack-brained for three years; and then set down to answer questions with paper and ink, whether Berkeley had the better of Locke, and whether David Hume has not shewn us a better way than either to them, and a multitude of trash besides. Sir, this is not to polish the minds of the young gentlemen; you will not make them apt for affairs by filling their heads with book learning, and giving prizes to the one that has the longest memory and the quickest wits for holding his own in a disputation. I could tell you of many men, since I became a fellow here, who shewed mighty little promise over their books, and yet proved themselves men of uncommon excellence in public life.

HIS GUEST (*a* MR. WILBRAHAM, *who seems more fashionably dressed than the rest of the party*). I have ever been proud to boast, I was a member of this College; but things will go very different, if it comes to be thought a University man is of necessity a *bore*. To have too much knowledge of philosophy and the arts is no longer *bon ton*. I have some friends who will not let their sons go to Oxford or to Cambridge either; they will have them go abroad instead, where they will learn polite manners. If this talk of annual examinations goes forward, we shall be much decried.

DR. JENNINGS. Sir, there is no substance in the phantom you speak of; this talk of examinations belongs altogether to Cambridge, and even there not many, as I conceive, shew any forwardness to propagate such notions. It is only this Mr. Jebb; and his wife supports him by putting out essays in the *London Chronicle* under the name *Priscilla*; I do not doubt but you have read them.

MR. SHILLETT. She should have called herself Sapphira, being privy to these abominable designs of her husband. Would she not do better, Mr. Wilbraham, to call herself Sapphira? This Mr. Jebb is a very poor-spirited man, that got himself made a doctor of medicine by the

University of St. Andrew's, because he would not hold a living any longer after he was turned Socinian. It was at Bungay, I think; whether he believed in the Trinity or no, cannot be supposed to have signified a great deal to the people of Bungay.

MR. WILBRAHAM (*yawning*). The doctrine of the Trinity is not much canvassed in the polite world nowadays.

DR. JENNINGS. It would have been pardonable enough, if Mr. Jebb had scrupled to get up into his pulpit, being unsettled in his mind over this or that point of the Christian philosophy. It is true there are many persons in holy orders, who are less nice in determining their consciences; but I think it was at least an honourable weakness in him to throw off his gown, and take to physicking men's bodies instead of their souls. What is damnable, is that he and others with him are now making a cry for abolishing subscription altogether, both in the Universities and in other positions of preferment; which is great prejudice to the cause of religion.

MR. SHILLETT. It is great folly besides; I could never abide higgling over the exact interpretation of an oath.

MR. HAMMOND. For all that, it might be contended that if men will subscribe to the Articles without believing them, subscription does not answer the purpose for which it was first designed, and is ready to be abolished. If I put up an advertisement at the edge of my grounds, bidding my neighbours beware of trespassing on them, and these same neighbours continue to come and go without regarding it, then it is time that I pulled the advertisement down, or else took measures to secure that my men turned the neighbours back from trespassing. An obligation which goes unregarded is an offence to public honesty. This is what the Russians protested a few years back, when they denied to the Spaniards the right of detaining their trading vessels, unless they should make their blockade stringent and effective for all alike.

MR. SHILLETT (*uneasily*). Sir, these are but words. It is good counsel, *Quieta non movere*; if subscription does not prevent, but that worthy men should get the preferment to which their talents entitle them, then there is no ground for abolishing it.

DR. JENNINGS. You must consider besides, that there are some who are shut off from preferment by the necessity of subscribing; and those are such factious and besotted persons, whether papists or non-conformists, as are too stubborn in their opinions to comply with the reasonable conditions which the law imposes. It is not altogether an inconvenience, that there should be a barrier set up against these hot-headed enthusiasts; who, if they came into any credit or esteem, might infect others with their abominable principles.

MR. HAMMOND (*drily*). Ay, Sir, I can see what you would be at. You would leave preferment open to all trimmers and time-servers that have good pliant consciences, shutting it only to those who are honest enough to shrink from perjuring themselves.

MR. WATSON. I take it to be the genius of our constitution, that what is of no service in the commonwealth is not abolished, but falls by degrees into abeyance. There will always be a spice of perjury needed, where this is to be achieved. As for instance, we are now agreed that it is a savage penalty to hang a man at Tyburn for theft within a dwelling-house. Yet there is a statute, come down to us from the times of monkish superstition——

MYSELF. . . .

MR. WATSON. ——which prescribes that penalty for one convicted of stealing more than forty shillings' value. Do we then abolish the statute? No, Sir, but the juries forget their oath, and declare boldly that what was stolen was not of so much worth. This is reasonable enough; it is but following the order of nature, to allow what is unserviceable to fall into disuse; the withered limb has no need of an amputation. Since, then, the Articles of Religion are proved unserviceable——

DR. JENNINGS. You would say, the practice of subscribing to them?

MR. WATSON. No, Sir, I mean the Articles themselves. These are days of enlightenment, in which the most part of us are content to recognize that the Divine Author of our being exists, without making bold to quibble over *homoousion* and *homoiousion*, over grace efficacious and grace sufficient; we have seen the horrid contentions and wars bred by this sort of controversy, and we are minded to let it alone.

MR. HAMMOND'S GUEST (*a* MR. PICKTHORN, *who has been sitting quite silent, as if he were thinking of something else*). Your pardon, Sir; would you be understood as meaning that the tenets of the Christian religion, of which

I take you to be a minister, are become *unserviceable?* And that we only do not amputate or abolish them from our minds, because our belief in them is already so much withered away, that we may look before long to see it fall altogether into desuetude?

MR. WATSON. Sir, you take me up very sharp. I will not be answerable, nor I suppose any other man, for the dubitations of posterity. Whatever is superstitious and unreasonable in the notions that have been handed down to us, that certainly will henceforward be without credit. As we see that on the continent of Europe, and notably in France, the Romish Church is already much decayed, and, some think, in danger of extinction. Have we not seen, in these last years, the suppression of the Jesuits? If the Pope be thus willing to make short work of his best allies, it is a sure sign that he is trembling for his own authority; these are desperate remedies, as when in a ship-wreck men will cut adrift the boats that are their best hope of safety. It did not profit King Charles much, when he sacrificed to the indignation of a people the two ministers that had been the chief instruments of his tyranny. I cannot tell, but I think if I live to be as old as Mr. Shillett is, I shall see Rome without a Pope.

DR. JENNINGS. Sir, you will not frighten us with your cry of *Proximus ardet Ucalegon.* That my neighbour has his mulberries nipped by the frost is no reason I should fear for my apple-trees. If so ill-conditioned a fellow as this Voltaire was can make merry over the fables that are credited in the Church of Rome, it is not therefore to be supposed that the Protestant Church in this country can be put down with a few mincing epigrams; we are too generously rooted in the soil of reason and of Scripture for that.

MR. WILBRAHAM. In London, you hear very little talk of religion. As for the Roman Catholics, they have quite hidden their heads since the late riots; and there is so little elegance about the established Church, that the company of the bishops is not much sought after.

MR. HAMMOND (*to Mr. Watson*). Sir, you will not find religion so much neglected among the common people as it was formerly. See how Mr. Wesley and Mr. Whitefield have changed men's hearts, both here and overseas, putting them in great fear of damnation.

MR. SHILLETT (*chuckling*). I remember, Dr. Trumpington used to tell us in the old days, Mr. Wesley would end up a papist. It is very laughable, when a man comes to my age, to remember all the prognostications that were made in his youth, and how little truth there was in them.

DR. JENNINGS. Mr. Wesley has *cooked his goose*, since he began to ordain ministers for himself. This sort of enthusiasm will die down as it has flared up, in a very short time.

MR. WATSON. Hitherto he has got much credit among the common people. That is because their lives are so brutish, they will welcome any comfortable doctrine, so long as it is within the compass of their minds.

MR. PICKTHORN. It is true, the common sort languish into great misery at this time. You will see more of that, now the canal has come to Oxford.

DR. JENNINGS. Sir, they are entertained in a fashion which would seem very miserable to us, because we are habituated to a more elegant way of living. But they do not *languish*, because the discomforts they have are only what use has made familiar to them. I think there is less destitution in England nowadays, than in France.

MR. WATSON. The French peasants, from what I hear, are so damnably oppressed that it is not probable they will endure it much longer without revolting from their rulers.

MR. SHILLETT. No, Sir, the Frenchmen will not revolt. They are very mean, poor-spirited fellows who will always scrape and bow to their betters. There is much foolishness talked about the state of affairs in France.

MR. WATSON. I do not know what is to happen in France in these next years coming, or in England either. What I hold to be certain is that we have now entered upon an era of enlightenment, from which we ought to expect nothing less, than an improved general condition of humanity. The minds of all reasonable men have now come to such a point of independence, that they will not long suffer any abridgement of their liberties, whether it be here or in France or, as we have seen, on the continent of America. And as they will not be content, in respect to their worldly affairs, with ancient privileges and prescriptive rights which are not demonstrably founded in reason, so they will not be content in matters of religion to be ruled by tradition and precedent. They will not acknowledge themselves daunted by any bugbears of punishment hereafter, such as have hitherto been used with great profit to themselves by priests and ministers of religion; we are not children any longer.

MR. PICKTHORN (*bending forward suddenly*). Sir, shall I tell you what I call this independence and this enlightenment of which you have been speaking to us? Weeds, Sir; weeds that have overgrown men's minds in this last generation, for want of proper care and attention had to the cultivation of them. Nay, Sir, bear with me a little while I tell you more of this thought of mine. I was upon a visit until yesterday to a good friend of mine that has a cure at Kingston Lisle, just under the hills they call the *Downs*, not above twenty miles from this. And one morning he would have me come out to see a ceremony which they perform yearly in those parts, which they call the scouring of the White Horse. Why (said I) what is that? And then he shewed me a very ancient old figure cut in the side of the hill, all white chalk, so that it shews (as I guess) for many miles round; and they call it the White Horse, though in truth it is more like some gryphon or fabulous animal, to my way of looking at it. Well then, Sir, it was a bright morning of spring; and it was a very gracious sight to see the common people of those parts all lending their endeavours to pluck the weeds off from the face of this figure, that it might shew bright and clean as it did in their fathers' time before them. And it is so, Sir, with the minds of men. They will appear all overgrown, from time to time, with the weeds of their own proud imaginings, so that the old landmarks are in danger to be quite obliterated. But the weeds will be plucked out, Sir; God will send his servants to pluck the weeds out. The old poet said, I think, you might put out nature with a pitchfork, but she would come back again. And if this be true of nature, which is nothing better after all than the corrupt fashion of this present world, what of grace, Sir, which is nature's better counterpart? I tell you, you and such as you will try to put out grace from among us, but in vain. It will come back, Sir, it will come back. You may controvert it with a thousand reasons, you may disparage it with a thousand buffooneries, but it will come back.

MR. WILBRAHAM (*in an undertone*). This is very ranting stuff. I did not expect to dine with the fellows of this College, and be preached to by a Methodist.

MR. PICKTHORN (*overhearing the end of the sentence*). No, Sir, I am not a Methodist; it was you in Oxford bred the Methodists, though I think it has advantaged you little. I am from Cambridge, and there are men of my University that are Church of England ministers, but are yet preaching Christ's gospel to the poor in that fashion which is decried by the elegant for enthusiasm. Such is Mr. Simeon, of King's; such was Mr. Venn, and such is Mr. Berridge at Everton, whose preaching makes the rough workmen of those parts fall down in convulsions of penitence over their sins. And they are not content to scour the weeds at home; they are doing what our Church has long to its shame neglected, sending men out to convert the heathen. Yes, Sir, your age of enlightenment has seen the foundation of the Missionary Society.

MR. WILBRAHAM (*bored*). Sir, I wish them well of their labours. I hope Mr. Hastings has joined this Society?

His name should have great credit among the heathen in these times.

DR. JENNINGS (*to Mr. Pickthorn, as if apologizing for Mr. Wilbraham's rudeness*). Sir, we are much in your debt for what you have told us. Although indeed we have heard something of what is going forward at Cambridge; we are not altogether shut off from the world in Oxford. No doubt the labours of these gentlemen in their several parishes have awakened the consciences of the indigent poor, and turned their minds to thoughts of a blessed future state. But there is this yet to be considered about enthusiasm, that it is of its nature a transitory thing, flaring up and dying down, as I said, in a very short compass of time. Is it, then, to be anticipated that the favour at present shewn to religion will long continue? I recollect hearing when I was an undergraduate of the death of one Chubb, an infidel fellow that had been assistant to a tallow-chandler, but afterwards spent his time putting out pamphlets against religion, as was then commonly done. In these days, thank God, we hear less of Chubb and Toland and " Christianity as old as the Creation " than we did formerly. But if, which God forbid, these assaults upon the very foundations of the Christian religion should come to be renewed, do you think—this is what I would ask—that Mr. Simeon and those others who are your friends would be able to make any head against them? Or would not they, together with Mr. Wesley and his followers, be confounded and put to silence, when the very foundation of their doctrine, which I take to be the Scripture, was a matter of dispute?

MR. SHILLETT. Mr. Wesley would undertake to defend Christianity for you, and do it uncommon ill. He is a very injudicious man, and was led away not long since into writing about electricity, or some other foolishness.

MR. WATSON. There is no reason why we should wait for the assaults Dr. Jennings speaks of to be *renewed*. They only do not continue, because there is no need to continue them. The enlightenment of the present age has removed the darkness of superstition which those rush-lights of a former time sought, by little and little, to disperse. What Mr. Hume has written of miracles has done more than Toland or Chubb ever did to bring fanatical doctrines into disrepute. That these doctrines are not more forgotten among the ignorant and vulgar, is because such persons have not learned to read, and must still believe whatever the parson tells them. Sir, if you taught the workmen of Yorkshire to read their book as well, even, as the commoners of this College do, there would be no more heard of these convulsions.

DR. JENNINGS. David Hume is dead these ten years and more, and has left no philosopher of his school to succeed him. Beattie will be remembered very much longer than Hume. Beattie has exploded more infidelities than Hume would have been accountable for if he had lived to be a hundred.

MR. WATSON. Why, Sir, in England, and in Scotland too, we are all gone to sleep; you must have your eyes on the continent of Europe, if you would see the torch of reason and of liberty yet alight. Dr. Kant, now, in Koenigsberg—there is a man that will shake Europe, when his works are better known. Let us have no more of Beattie.

MR. SHILLETT. The Germans have a prodigious name for profundity, only because their language is so ill constructed that a man cannot follow their thoughts. But the Germans will never be anything in philosophy; Sir, they eat too much. A full belly goes with an empty brain.

MR. WATSON. I think this next age that is coming will be remembered as that which put an end to the dull superstitions of antiquity; in which reason triumphed over prejudice, and freedom over privilege, and there were no longer any wars——

MR. PICKTHORN (*losing patience*). And I tell you, Sir, it will be remembered as the age in which the minds of men turned back to the thought of their Creator, and their consciences trembled before his terrible judgements; the age which set a crown to the glorious work of the Reformation by bringing men's souls naked to the feet of God.

MR. WILBRAHAM. I protest I do not know why this age should be remembered at all. I find it vastly tedious.

MR. SHILLETT. It is ever the way with these younger men; they will have it the times they live in are times of great stir and importance. It was so fifty years ago, when I was but a young fellow; we all thought great things were happening and to happen, but it came to very little, Sir, very little. And I do not doubt but if Mr. Watson himself or Mr. Hammond here should reach to my age, he will find the state of England then, and the state of

Europe, much what it is now. You, Sir (*addressing Mr. Watson*), would have us believe that these are days of enlightenment, which have the power to raise our minds altogether beyond the compass of those who seemed to be wise men before us. But to my thinking the fortunes of mankind, and the fashion of their minds, travel rather in a cycle, coming back ever to the term from which they commenced. It was a great matter of concern to such as were my seniors, that government should have passed into the hands of the whigs, and they would foretell all kinds of lamentable consequences; yet if such a man as Dr. Thewes, for instance, were alive to-day, he would be well content with Mr. Pitt and his party. And, as for what concerns matters of divinity, I think it is true what Dr. Jennings was saying, that we let ourselves fall into too great disquiet over the infidelities of the deistic writers, who have much fallen out of credit. I think what is believed now is pretty much what was believed in my young days.

MR. WATSON (*quietly, with the air of a man scoring a sure point*). Yet it is to be observed, that within these last few years Mr. Herschel has been prying with his telescope, and has taught us there are millions of stars in the heavens, whereas formerly it was thought there were not above two thousand.

MR. SHILLETT (*irritably*). There is Mr. Watson making much of his Germans again. Sir, this Mr. Herschel was bred in Hanover, and played the hautboy for the Guards indifferently well. It is but lately that he began discovering stars, and dedicating them to important persons, in the hope he would get patronage from it. I do not doubt but he has much over-counted them.

MR. JENNINGS. For my part, I could never see that it made any matter whether there were two thousand stars or two million. They are all God's handiwork; and we should do well, by my way of it, to accept of them humbly without inquiring too curiously how they came to be where they are.

MR. PICKTHORN. Humbly, Sir? Will you not rather look up at them in all their multitude groaning and sweating with terror, to think how infinitely magnificent is the Hand that made them?

MR. WILBRAHAM. No doubt but astronomy is vastly entertaining. Yet I would give less, to be able to fashion stars by the million, than to have hit upon the notion of bringing into existence that droll creature we call Man. I am well assured nothing could be more remarkable than the mind of Man; (*dropping his voice*), Mr. Pickthorn's, for instance.

MR. HAMMOND. For all that, sheer multitudinosity has power to oppress the mind. Mr. Herschel says, we live in a retired corner of the universe.

MR. SHILLETT. How the devil can that have corners, which is infinite? You will not find anybody but a German speaking so.

MR. WATSON (*breaking out excitedly, with the air of one who has made a discovery*). I see what it is; those who went before us did wrongly to build Oxford upon a river. We are like men who lean over a bridge; from long custom of seeing the water slip away beneath us, making the same eddies and ripples, presenting still the same surface, although it never ceases flowing, we have dulled our minds into the fancy that nothing happens, nothing changes, all is as it was when we first took our stand there. And as for what goes on in the world generally, we see that reflected in this looking-glass of our quiet contemplation; so men leaning over a bridge see the moon and the stars only as a reflection, and have no taste to enquire what their nature is, or what courses they run. Oh that they had set down the University on a hill-side, far from all these sluggish mists and vapours which confuse our minds, and damp the ardour of our spirits! I am half minded to imitate the example of this Mr. Jebb, and set myself to learn physic, so that I should have an honest trade to support me, if Oxford, that has been an unkind step-mother to so many before, should prove unkind to me, and to such as me.

MR. PICKTHORN (*rather smugly*). Cambridge also is built upon the banks of a river.

DR. JENNINGS. Sir, your Cam is a brackish and inconsiderable stream. What thoughts it breeds in you, is not greatly to the purpose; they must needs fall short of ours in intensity, who are nurtured beside the greatest river of England, and the fairest, as I think, of any in the world. As for Mr. Watson's similitude, I conceive that it is wholly excellent; only I find its signification somewhat less lugubrious. Do not the generations of mankind indeed follow one upon the last, very much as each mile or so of Thames follows upon the last, troubled into the same eddies and ripples by the same currents and promontories? You will see slight changes in the course of human affairs; but the general configuration of our doings is the same. I have seen—I do not know what is the cause of it—a bulrush standing in mid-stream that is continually tugged by a current, dipping and bobbing without intermission; that I take to be a parable of those busy fellows you see now and again who cannot ever control their energies, but must still be feverishly working for they know not what, as if by their endeavours they could alter the course of events. And as a river washes away its own pollutions, so that you may drink sweet water some miles above Abingdon, although it was but lately contaminated with our sewers and conduits, so mankind expunges its own follies; and Chubb who was yesterday, to-day is not. Let the waters flow as they will, they cannot cease to reflect that canopy of heaven which over-arches them; let men doubt and question, they must still return to the affirmation of a celestial government which orders their affairs. It is the rustic, as in Horace, who waits doltishly for this inexhaustible stream to flow itself out; we that are philosophers will be content to acknowledge its permanence, and to admire its profundity.

MR. WILBRAHAM. Good God, Doctor Jennings, what a sermon you have given us! You should have put on your gown, man, and turned up the hour-glass, before you embarked on such a tide of eloquence. I thought, like the river, you were never coming to an end.

MR. HAMMOND. What is worse, Doctor, you have altogether turned Mr. Watson's fable inside out. You made out the river to be the world in general, and Oxford only the bridge from which a philosophic mind observes it. But Mr. Hammond's river was itself Oxford; or so I thought. And it came into my mind to ask him, if he thinks Oxford was always nothing better than a looking-glass, which reflected the world and did nothing to alter its destinies, or whether this is a disease of our present age; whether Oxford did not once influence the affairs of this nation, and may not do so again?

MR. SHILLETT. Why, Sir, as to that you have no need to consult the histories; it is a matter of living memory. I that sit here have spoken with an old man, I think he was called Mr. Bromicham, who could call to mind what was the state of Oxford when King Charles defended it against the Parliament. He said the river then by no means kept its banks in so orderly a fashion as Dr. Jennings would have desired, being let out in flood every way, so that a man could not approach the city at all by dry land unless he came from the North. Which is a parable of what the University did at that time, being very hot for King Charles and making levies for the furtherance of his cause. For that matter, it is but a hundred years since Oxford stoutly resisted the danger of Popery that threatened us under King James; in which Simon Magus was not at all backward, so Dr. Trumpington used to say, that was Provost in my time.

MR. WATSON. They tell me there is news come from Rome, the Pretender is dead.

DR. JENNINGS. I had not heard tell of it.

MR. HAMMOND. It is probable the fellows of this

College a hundred years ago were all in great concern over the birth of his father; so the world goes on. And now, Mr. Watson, let us hear whether there is any hope that Oxford will cut a figure upon the stage of history, fifty years hence.

MR. WATSON. I think it is a supposition hardly to be entertained. You might as well expect movement in a dead body, as in what Oxford will be then.

DR. JENNINGS. Well, Sir, you may live to see it. Only I think it is likely enough, by the time you have reached Mr. Shillett's age, your zeal for the advancement of human liberty will somewhat have cooled down, and you will be more ready to let things rest as they are. Sir, it is ill work prophesying; for all we know, they may be for bringing the Pope back again, before you are put by in your coffin.

MR. WILBRAHAM. I conceive they will have need of Mr. Watt's steam engine, to draw him in here.

MR. PICKTHORN. This is not a proper subject for jesting upon. It would be intolerable, if this nation should ever go back to the barbarities of Smithfield, or to that havoc that is wrought in men's consciences by confession of sins to a priest; as if one man could come between another man's soul and the forgiveness which it can hope to win by faith only.

MR. WATSON. Sir, it is worse than intolerable, it is impossible. I see we shall never be agreed, in this present company, how much the world changes and how much it clings to its old habit. But one thing is certain, we do not travel backwards. The prepossessions which formerly occupied our minds, once they have fallen into disuse, cannot return to plague us any more; they are like the bugbears our nurses used to frighten us with when we were children, which never regain the power to alarm us, once they are detected. Consider how the science of architecture improves, from one age to the next, our apprehension of beauty, so that the barbarous things which were formerly held in estimation no longer have power to delight the mind ! In Oxford, we are slow to relinquish what is outworn; as witness how Hawksworth, not so very long since, disfigured All Souls' by retaining there the Gothic style of building; but who will be found to admire such a prospect now ? So it is with these prepossessions I was speaking of; you will not persuade an Englishman to entertain in these days the notion of purgatory, or the silly fable of the Mass. And as for what will happen fifty years hence, it will be no matter for astonishment if certain things that are still believed among Protestants should no longer find credit. Here is Dr. Jennings greatly concerned, because Mr. Wesley has laid hands upon some of his followers, to make ministers of them. Yet it would be rash to prognosticate that in fifty years' time such a doctrine as that of the apostolic succession will commend itself to polite minds any longer.

MR. SHILLETT. You will not find much variety, from this generation to that, in what the generality of Englishmen believe. Divines, to be sure, will be ready to follow a fashion; as those of Archbishop Laud's time were very positive in what they affirmed, whereas of late the wind has set in the opposite quarter. But your common man goes more by the tradition of his countryside than by the latest doctrines which he hears from a pulpit; nor does he care much, whether the preacher wear a pudding-sleeve gown or the gown of his university. There is much tenacity of tradition in a rustic society. When I was first a fellow, we used to dine at twelve, and now some of you will not be content unless it is deferred till three; you would not find so speedy a change of fashion among the common people.

DR. JENNINGS. Sir, there is much weight in that; and yet, should we not do ill to make our *rule of faith* out of the prejudices of the vulgar?

MR. WATSON (*maliciously*). It is certain the country folk of England are for the most part good Protestants; it is equally certain that this tenacity you speak of makes the country folk of Ireland excellent papists. We shall hear more of that before long.

MR. SHILLETT. The Irish are very mean, poor-spirited fellows. I do not think we shall have much trouble with the Irish. Good God, is it so late? I must take the air before supper-time. If you gentlemen would keep your blood sweet with a little more walking in the afternoons, you would not be so dismally exercised with what is to happen when we are all under ground. Things do not alter much from what they are, depend upon it.

NOTE ON CHAPTER VI

Simon Magus of the late eighteenth century was so little distinguished in an undistinguished Oxford, that I had not much hope of obtaining any side-lights on the fellows of the period; *omnes illacrimabiles*, I murmured to myself, finding them only names preserved among lists of names, until at last, in an old *Edinburgh Review*, I came across the thing I was looking for—an article devoted to Mr. Watson, evidently by no less a *vates sacer* than the Revd. Sydney Smith. Poor Mr. Watson, or rather Dr. Watson, as he had then become! It was an unfortunate emergence from obscurity. Like many other Englishmen who had been caught by the notion of enlightenment, he ceased to admire it when he saw it at work, in the hands of the French revolutionary leaders. He was shocked into a rather dreary kind of Toryism; preached against the infidelity of Tom Paine, anathematized Cobbett, and worked industriously (if the Edinburgh Reviewer may be trusted) against Catholic Emancipation. His mediocrity might have shielded him, if he had not in an unfortunate hour published a sermon preached in St. Mary's on the occasion of a minor famine in Ireland; which event he seems to have interpreted as a "judgement" on the attempts then being made to secure the passage of the Catholic Relief Bill. The article is of considerable length; I quote here those parts of it which serve to illustrate Dr. Watson's career, leaving the curious reader to look up for himself, if he will, the more general and more telling passages.

"If the gentleman had remained content with delivering these sentiments from the secure ramparts of his pulpit, we should have felt bound to refrain from criticism. The abuse of the pulpit, by showering down from it sentiments which the layman disagrees with, but has no opportunity to disown, has for a long time been as fashionable as it is indefensible. If we had replied, in print, to the pitiful ramblings in which Dr. Watson has indulged from the pulpit, we should have been guilty of a kind of constructive brawling, and perhaps laid ourselves open to the censure of delicate minds. But since the complacency of authorship has driven him to give his views further publicity in the form of a pamphlet, he has come out into the open, and exposed himself to the animadversion of posterity. He has called attention to them of his own choice, and he cannot complain of ill-treatment if they get it.

What sentiments, then, are aroused in the generous bosom of this learned divine by the failure of the harvest in certain districts of Ireland? Does he commiserate with the wretched peasants over the privations which they are forced to endure? Does he counsel patience, and console them with the prospect of greater prosperity in the future? No, in a more adventurous spirit he sets out to 'justify the ways of God to men'. And what principle of justification has he selected? He informs the tenants of those miserable hovels, which you may see disfiguring the landscape of Ireland, that their rebellious tendencies have brought on them a divine chastisement. Had he been present, we need hardly say at a safe distance, when the tower of Siloam fell, we can picture the reverend gentleman going to and fro among the mangled victims of the catastrophe, pointing out to each, with a wealth of exact information, how his sins were more heinous than those of Tom, Dick and Harry, who had the good luck at the time to be some hundreds of yards off. It is fortunate indeed that Divine Providence, which so often conceals from us the purpose of its mysterious dispensations, should at last have found in Dr. Watson a confidant, who can be privileged with minute information as to why punishment fell here and not there, why Patrick suffered and Michael went off scot free.

But, if we may be acquitted of impiety when we enquire further into the character of this visitation, let us ask the reverend gentleman why it should have fallen on the poverty-stricken inhabitants of a land which has suffered for centuries through our neglect, rather than upon those champions of theirs, at Westminster and elsewhere, who are in truth far more responsible for the political currents that disturb him? It is an old principle that *quidquid delirant reges, plectuntur Achivi;* but this is a maxim of experience, not of abstract justice, of observation, not of formal theology. We have perused the learned treatise in vain to discover why it is that the divine indignation should have made itself felt only among the Irish, who are the beneficiaries of certain proposed legislative acts; not in England, where those acts are under discussion, lest perhaps Dr. Watson (impious thought!) should have gone on short *commons* as he sits over his comfortable breakfast.

If we were dealing with the author of an anonymous pamphlet, it would be vain as well as impertinent to inquire, what qualifications he has for pronouncing so confidently upon the designs of a creative Omnipotence. But since he has published, not only his name and degree but the circumstances under which his remarkable confidences were first made to the world, we may be pardoned for drawing attention to his own record, and seeking illumination from it upon the origin of his extraordinary sentiments. Let us hear *quo numine laeso, quidve petens* this modern Jeremiah has taken upon himself the mantle of prophecy. In the closing years of the last century, if memory serves us aright, Mr. Watson was distinguished among the fellows of Simon Magus College for his active sympathy with the cause of revolution on the further side of the English Channel. No post brought word of fresh commotion and outrage, which did not deepen his conviction that the forces of enlightenment were at last triumphing over those of superstition and tyranny. It was not uncommon for festive students to scrawl unfriendly comments over the door of his chamber, and to burn his effigy in the quadrangle. But in the year 1793 he discovered, with the legendary Plowden, that the case was altered. In that year, two highly-placed situations became unoccupied almost at the same moment; the throne of France, and the provostship of Simon Magus. It is not for us to speculate, which of these two events contributed more powerfully towards effecting a change of heart in Dr. Watson. The fact is undisputed, that he forthwith turned upon his former revolutionary allies, taxing them with abominable cruelty and with short-sighted methods of finance; that from that moment onwards he has more and more drifted into the Tory camp, becoming known as an irreconcileable enemy to all change, whether in the system of the University or in the affairs of the country. Perhaps it is not surprising that a man so remarkably sensitive to the way the wind is blowing should be the first to expostulate with our unfortunate neighbours in Ireland, counselling them to abandon, at the risk of further celestial admonition, what is so evidently a losing cause.

If it should so happen, in the inscrutable designs of Providence, that there should be a failure of our English harvest, and that the humble rustics whose tithe supports the fellows of Simon Magus in plenty and indolence should no longer be able to contribute to their support as formerly, will some parish priest in Ireland attribute so melancholy an occurrence to the anger of heaven over Dr. Watson's busy scheming against the agitation for Catholic relief? It must be confessed that the picture is an unlikely one; there are better manners, we believe, to be found among the simple curates who are educated at Maynooth. But, if the capricious wheel of fortune should take such a turn, Dr. Watson may be assured that he will receive no message of sympathy from us, when we see him paid out in his own kind. It will be our single endeavour to recommend to him, it is to be hoped not too late, the simple virtues of Christian charity and forbearance; which would be a more honourable crown for his grey hairs than the petty rewards he at present covets, to the dishonour of the position which he does so little to adorn."

Poor Dr. Watson! He achieved, in his last years, the provostship of Simon Magus, but at what a cost! To be remembered among posterity only for a trouncing in the *Edinburgh*, hardly less bitter than that which his obscure namesake received from the immortal Cobbett!

CHAPTER VII

FALSE DAWN: 1838

DR. HAYNES. I see by the paper, the Prince of Talleyrand has died.

MR. TELFORD. Yes; they say he made a Christian end of it after all.

THE PROVOST (DR. WATSON). That was to be expected. You must consider that he has changed sides a great deal all his life; and to die a Christian was the only way left to him, if he was to be consistent in his inconsistency.

DR. HAYNES. It is extraordinary, how much he did without sleep. You and he would never have got on well together, Dr. Greene.

DR. GREENE (*a stout man of full habit, strongly contrasted with the spare figure of Dr. Haynes*). If the Prince had come to live in Oxford, he would have wanted more sleep; I think it is a habit that grows upon us here. Though I suppose we shall all be as sleepless as Macbeth was, if we have the steam-engines here, drawing their trains of carriages into Oxford at all times of the night. What do you think, Mr. Provost; will the petition of Convocation have any weight, or will they carry the railway here from Didcot in spite of it?

THE PROVOST. I believe we shall be defeated; for that matter, we were already defeated when it came beyond

Wallingford. With such a government as we have now, a vote of Convocation goes for very little.

DR. GREENE. I cannot understand how they think there is any need for it. It was only the other day the coach went from London to Cheltenham in little over nine hours; the steam-engines surely cannot travel much faster than that without grave danger to life. If they did, we should have no peace; the men would be asking for leave to go up to London in the middle of term, and back again the same evening.

MR. TELFORD. I am always expecting to hear that one of them has done so already, out of bravado, on one of the new velocipedes.

DR. HAYNES. The truth is, Convocation is too fond of sending petitions to Westminster. We are within our rights to make a protest, when we are threatened with the noise and smoke of a railway; as we were when they founded this mushroom University of London in spite of us. But you see how it was; when the Prime Minister received our petition against the London University, he probably did not read it, thinking it was only another protest against Catholic Relief.

DR. GREENE (*rising to the bait*). I never heard such nonsense. Does it not touch Oxford more nearly than any question of railways or of new Universities, when Parliament is full of Barneys and Paddys that take their orders from Rome? When the city is represented by a Stonor, whose ancestors have been traitors for generations back?

DR. HAYNES. You are talking like the two-bottle men,

Dr. Greene. If you will be honest with yourself, you will confess you do not fear any disloyalty from the Roman Catholics, now that they have been given the common rights of citizens. What galls you is that the Church of England, with Oxford for its stronghold, no longer occupies the position of privilege which it used to occupy. Your mind still lives in an old world of privilege, which has passed away, believe me, in these last decades. A new spirit is abroad; new men are beginning to count; I dare say it will not be long before Mr. Hudson, the railway king, is wanting to send his son to Oxford as a gentleman-commoner. I believe I am no less a friend to the Established Church than you are; but I think it must now fight its own battles, not sulk ignobly behind the walls of prejudice.

MR. SAVILE. Yes, do consider seriously what Dr. Haynes says; *fas est et ab hoste doceri*, you know. Though to be sure we do not count Dr. Haynes or any other of the fellows our enemy; only we know what sort of men they are whom he supports and admires; men who would cut down the number of bishoprics and reduce the tithe-charge; so that we cannot help but be in opposition to them. In these times, when men are thinking of nothing but commerce, we shall not do much good by bombarding Parliament with petitions over this and that. Why, the bad example has spread so far that some of the under-graduates themselves signed a paper which was sent to Westminster at the time of the Emancipation; and there was another to be sent in in the opposite sense, only the proctors got wind of it and interfered. We shall only make ourselves laughable if we persist in using these weapons.

DR. GREENE. I do not know what other weapons you would have us use, Mr. Savile.

MR. SAVILE. Why, I would have the Church of England remember what she is; not a political party, or the satellite of a political party, but a living branch of the Church of Christ, with her own indefectible system of belief, her own divinely appointed superiors. We have to accustom men's minds to the notion that it does not matter what the politicians do, does not matter even if our bishops seem to betray us; we belong to a spiritual kingdom complete in itself, owing nothing to worldly alliances. It was so that the ancient prophets were always warning the Church of the Jews not to depend upon the Assyrians or the Egyptians, but to wait confidently for the divine help.

THE PROVOST. It is very certain we are beyond the reach of all human assistance.

MR. TELFORD. Why, Mr. Provost, you remind me of the worldly gentleman in a storm at sea, who asked the captain whether they were in danger, and when advised to take to his prayers, cried: " Is it as bad as all that ? " I don't think we are in such a bad way that we need to despair of the ship of state. But for all that, what Mr. Savile says is true; the Church is a spiritual body, and it is a thousand pities she has been confused, these years past, with one particular school of politics. I am not sure but if she were dis-established to-morrow, she would come out the stronger for the process.

DR. GREENE. This is what comes of letting Mr. Newman carry all before him. Don't, pray, vex me by talking of the Church of England as "she"; it is a Romish trick, which interferes, I assure you, with digesting my dinner. Now, what was it you were saying? You cannot really mean that you would like to see the Church of England dis-established; no, I don't think you can possibly mean that. Have you considered that, in that case, you might have Divinity professors here who were Unitarians, or even Roman Catholics?

DR. HAYNES. I don't find that so very terrible. Indeed, I think it would be rather an ornament to the University if we had such professors, just one or two of them.

DR. GREENE. I am sure you only say that to vex me, Dr. Haynes. But my point was against Mr. Telford, who I am sure does not wish to see heretics intruded into the professorships any more than I do. Let us try if he can answer this difficulty. Don't you see, Mr. Telford, that establishment is as it were the bond which holds us all together? Here are you and Mr. Savile talking like Newmanites, whereas I am of the old-fashioned school, and Dr. Haynes is a friend to the Dissenters, and you will find people in Oxford of Evangelical leanings who differ from all of us. Well, at present there is no great harm in this, for we all belong to the Established Church, and it has room for all our different opinions. But if we no longer had an establishment, on what principle should we remain *one church*? Can two walk together, except they be agreed?

DR. HAYNES (*sardonically*). That depends, whether at

the same time the Church is dis-endowed. So long as there are any emoluments remaining, I believe you will find churchmen sticking closer together than you think.

DR. GREENE. Pray, Dr. Haynes, let Mr. Telford have space to answer my question.

MR. TELFORD. Well, for myself I don't think the Church would be any the worse for a little blood-letting. I dare say, in the event we are discussing, the Evangelicals would prefer to throw in their lot with the Methodists—there is not a great deal of difference between them—instead of with us. Dr. Haynes and his friends—why, they would have to make up their minds once for all whether they did belong to the Church Catholic or not. And if they decided to *challenge honours*, then it would rest with them to prove that they held the doctrines of the primitive Church as we do; I hope they would not be *plucked*. But all this would not happen at once; it would take place, as you see, *by degrees*.

DR. GREENE. I don't think this is a proper subject for jesting, Mr. Telford. And there is one point you still have not made quite clear; you talk of "we" and "us", as if it were certain that you and your friends hold the true tradition of the Church of England, and nobody else does. How do you propose to convince the world that this is so? That your movement, which was born only yesterday, is in the right, and all the rest of us, older men who have grown up in the bosom of the Church of England, are quite beside the mark?

MR. TELFORD. I am glad you should admit the Church of England has a bosom, Dr. Greene. I don't think we should find much difficulty in proving our case to a set of lawyers, if it came to that. We could shew that we held the doctrine of the Laudian divines—though, to be sure, they expressed themselves rather cautiously in those days, for fear of offending the Puritans—and that has ever been reckoned the golden age of the English Church.

DR. HAYNES' GUEST (*a* MR. COTTINGHAM, *a youngish fellow from another College*). I hope I shall not intrude if I interfere in the discussion. Is there not another objection to be raised to Mr. Telford's *purge* that he proposes? I mean, that the Church of England, instead of representing a great preponderance of the English nation, as it does now, will have shrunk to a very small body of people by the time he has finished with it—in fact, will consist only of Mr. Newman and his admirers? I remember, not many years ago, riding out to Ot Moor at the time when it was being enclosed; and I saw a sight there which impressed itself very strongly on my imagination. I mean, a set of country fellows, armed with nothing better than scythes and pitchforks and what they could lay hands on, banded together to resist the enclosure, and having to be dispersed by the Yeomanry. I shall not easily forget it, the mellow September sun brooding quietly over that mysterious marsh land which has remained so little disturbed through the centuries, and this sudden intrusion into it of human life and human passions. But I was going to say, if the peasants will rise to defend their old dykes, would they not rise in revolt, perhaps, against Mr. Telford and his friends, complaining that they had come to remove spiritual landmarks, not less dear to them? You will have to reckon with the common people of England, Mr. Telford.

MR. TELFORD (*a trifle uneasily*). You will not persuade us of your reasons, Sir, by allying yourself with a rabble of country bumpkins like this. Was it not about the same time that the peasants, in many districts of England, set about breaking the threshing machines, because the use of them put men out of work? I do not suppose, to be sure, that we should carry the ignorant people with us at first. But although we ourselves might be few in number, we should have this excellent advantage—we should be able to seek re-union with the Catholic Church of the West, which has so long regarded us as schismatics. We might, indeed, have to submit to re-ordination; but we should not have much difficulty in persuading them that the doctrines of our Church, properly interpreted, had a Catholic meaning.

MR. SAVILE. Hold, Mr. Telford, I am not sure we could all follow you there. Ought we not to think that the English Church follows a *middle path* between the Romans on one side and the schismatics on the other? And would she not, by separating herself violently from the latter and allying herself with the former, be false to what is her proper office? I mean, in God's good time to re-unite *all* Christians in a single communion?

MR. COTTINGHAM. It makes my heart glad, Sir, to hear you say that. But, if that be the object you have before you, I think you and Mr. Newman's followers generally are going too fast. For myself, I believe Oxford is too full of *views*; it is *viewy* people who have stirred up all the trouble in these last few years, from the time of Dr. Hampden's professorship onwards.

DR. GREENE. But Dr. Hampden's lectures were full of heresy. He wrote as if the doctrine of the Trinity had never been defined, or ought to be undefined again; he has been convicted with chapter and verse.

MR. COTTINGHAM. I don't think that was his intention. What he laboured to shew, was that the Christian religion is too much tied down by the dead hand of an Aristotelian philosophy. He thought it should be liberated from that; and not much wonder, in these days when thinking men are so much occupied with the speculations of Kant, the Königsberg professor.

DR. HAYNES. Kant? I don't think he will exercise much influence; his matter is too difficult. But Mr. Mill, now—there is a man who will carry the world with him, when his writings are a little better known. Mill's little finger, you will find, is thicker than Kant's loins.

MR. TELFORD. And Kant, I dare say, is a *stout* fellow. I am sorry, Dr. Greene, I had forgotten there was to be no jesting this afternoon. But I was going to say, if it be necessary to define Christian doctrines, I think the Pope is better company to be in than either Professor Kant or Mr. Mill.

THE PROVOST. It is five years now, I think, since Mr. Maurice of New College published a book which he called *Popery in Oxford*. We all told him then it was very fantastic stuff; now I am not so sure. Only our error, it seems, was that of the Trojans; we were expecting an attack upon our walls from without. Now we find Mr. Newman and his friends are a kind of *wooden horse*, that has insinuated itself into our citadel while we slept. When Dr. Faussett preached on the Revival of Popery the other day, I came near to forgetting where I was and applauding him; he spoke very weightily, did Dr. Faussett.

MR. TELFORD. Are you one of those, Mr. Provost, who think that Mr. Newman will turn Romanist?

THE PROVOST. Who, Newman? No; he is a man that is always changing, and will never nail his colours. He might perhaps become a Unitarian, as Blanco White has; he is very apt to push things to extremes.

MR. SAVILE. You see what comes, Mr. Telford, of your unguarded habit of speech; you have thrown the Roman claims into the discussion, like the apple of Eris, and we are all at sixes and sevens. We were not talking of Rome, but of the Church of England as she is and ever has been, a part of the Catholic Church.

MYSELF. . . .

DR. GREENE. I must beg of you, Mr. Savile, that you will not refer to the English Church as if it were some female of your acquaintance. I tell you, I cannot digest my dinner if you will talk so. A man's first duty is to his digestion.

MR. SAVILE. I am sorry, Dr. Greene; I had forgotten my manners. I was so vexed with Mr. Telford for leading off the conversation into controversy. But, my dear Sir, do pray tell us what your notion is of the English Church; whether you think of it as a political cause, which the Duke and Mr. Peele have abandoned, so that it must look for leadership somewhere else; a political cause, which must defend itself by seeing that so many members are returned to Parliament who will vote favourably to it? Or is not this to degrade our whole notion of it; and should we not rather see it as built upon the foundation of the apostles and prophets, a spiritual kingdom, as we were saying, which has derived from them an incorruptible tradition of doctrine, and a continued life which depends upon the laying-on of hands in the ordination service?

DR. GREENE. Why, of course it has come down to us from the apostles; that is a matter of common observation. But it has come down to us in our history as a part of English life, as the religion of a nation, adapted to its temper and modelled by its history; it is from that that it derives its substance; it is the religion of Englishmen or it is nothing. You and your friends are pursuing, as it seems to me, the phantom or ideal of a Church, which has no substance in reality; it is neither fish, flesh, nor good red herring. You will admire all the errors of Rome, and then call the Romans schismatics for no better reason than that they will have nothing to do with you. You will despise the Dissenters because they have no bishops, and then you will raise a cry against our bishops, that they have betrayed the Church. We all know of the dog in Aesop, who dropped his bone while he jumped after what was only a reflection in the water. So it is with you gentlemen; you neglect to preserve the Church of England as it is in fact, while you are running after an ideal church which is not there.

MR. SAVILE. It surprises me very much to hear you talk so about *substance* and *shadow*. You speak of the English Church as if it were one and the same thing with the religious life of the English nation. There was some reason for this in the old days, when Englishmen were not allowed by law to worship God in any other way than what the book of Common Prayer prescribed. The Nonconformists might meet in their conventicles, the recusants might celebrate their mass in obscure garrets and kitchens, but all this you affected not to observe; there was no public worship of God but what was conducted by ministers of the Church of England. Now, nearly all those old disabilities have been removed, and Dissenters and Romanists count equally with ourselves in the eye of the law. Is not your Church of England, then, disappearing and dissolving before our eyes? Unless, indeed, you count the Dissenters and the Romanists as somehow part of it, which would be sad nonsense. That is why men like Mr. Newman are trying to justify the existence of the English Church, no longer as a privileged body that is connected with the State, but as a receptacle of divine truth which, though it may not be perfect, has at least been preserved from those errors into which the others have fallen.

DR. HAYNES. There is a great deal of sense in that, Mr. Savile. But, my dear Sir, if that be your notion of the Church of England, why are you still so jealous for the privileges of the Establishment? Why do you raise so much outcry when it is proposed, for example, to diminish the number of bishoprics; and why does Mr. Keble get up at St. Mary's and tell us that all this amounts to a *national apostasy?*

MR. TELFORD. I don't think it is difficult to find the answer to that. We believe that the English Church would still remain the Church of God, even if it were shorn of all its privileges and emoluments; but that is no reason why we should stand by and applaud, while you and your friends do the shearing. A man may believe his wife to be so beautiful, that she needs no adornment to set off her charms; but we should think badly of him if he let thieves filch away her jewellery for that reason.

THE PROVOST (*with sudden animation*). Ay, but who are the thieves? Dr. Haynes' friends, who would rob the Church of its revenues, or Mr. Newman's friends, who would rob it of its Protestant faith? Stripped and wounded, Sir, like the man in the parable; stripped by the Whigs and wounded by the Newmanites.

MR. TELFORD. Oh dear, you are very difficult to please, Mr. Provost; you think every man's hand is against you. But indeed, we think we are doing the English Church a service by restoring much that has fallen out of use since the time of Archbishop Laud, or even earlier; the saying of matins, for example, and of evensong in the parish churches. We think people are less likely to turn Romanist, if we shew them that they can have all the pious practises the Church of Rome has, or most of them, without joining it.

THE PROVOST. It is not the first time people have talked so. Jeremy Collier, the non-juror, was wont to say, " We must come as near the papists as we can, that they may not hurt us "; so old Mr. Shillett used to tell me, whose memory went back to that time. The nonjurors did not come to much, after all, and I don't suppose we shall hear a great deal of this new movement, when it has ceased to be a *rage* among the young men.

MR. TELFORD. Then should you not, like Gamaliel, be content to leave it alone, since it is not likely to come to anything, unless it be of God?

THE PROVOST. Sir, in Oxford we are responsible for the faith of the young men here committed to our care, as much as for their health. When the cholera broke out here, five or six years back—at least, they called it the cholera—and carried many off by death, it was thought by some this was because the sewers emptying into the river had contaminated the water. And in particular, this was said of the Trill Mill stream, which flows as you know next to Christ Church meadows. What did the students of Christ Church do? Did they let the matter alone? No, Sir, they built the wall which you will see on the Western side of the meadows, to keep the bad air away. And if this infection of Popery continues to flow in among us, it will be for the heads of Colleges to determine how they can build a wall against it and fend it away; you will see if that does not happen.

DR. HAYNES. Perhaps it was the bones of the old monks that caused the infection. We are told that both the Franciscan and the Dominican monks had their houses in that quarter.

MR. TELFORD. Perhaps it is the bones of the old monks that are bringing in this other infection you complain of, crying from their graves.

THE PROVOST. Ay, you will be invoking the old monks next. It is a nasty dirty piece of Oxford; I wonder Christ Church does not pull it all down.

MYSELF. . . .

MR. SAVILE. Come now, Mr. Provost, nobody doubts it is your duty to protect the young men from the peril of Romanism; but are there no other dangers which young men encounter in these times? It is not as if they stuck to their books, and read nothing except what was recommended to them to get them a good class in the Schools. They are drinking in, from other fountains, the spirit of the age. Only the other day I came upon one of my pupils sitting out in the garden, reading some poetry written by the unfortunate Shelley; and there is quite a *côterie* of them that cultivates the works of Lord Byron.

THE PROVOST. He wrote well of Sennacherib. He said he came down like a wolf on the fold, I think; that was a very powerful simile.

MR. SAVILE (*smiling on one side of his mouth*). To be sure, there was no harm in that. But you know as well as I do, Mr. Provost, that he put his name to many other verses, which are recommended only by libertines. And it is not only what the young men *read;* there is a spirit got abroad, owing to the unsettlement of the times, which is quite unfriendly to patriotism, to public order, and even to morality. Don't, pray, misunderstand me if I say that I don't think we can protect youthful minds against these malign influences, by telling them that they ought to be content with what is good enough for their seniors; that the constitution of our country is the admiration of the world, and that a mature taste finds higher poetic genius in Mr. Southey than in Lord Byron. They won't take it from us; they will only tell us we are old *fogeys*. But an influence like that of Dr. Newman, which provides a less reprehensible outlet for their youthful enthusiasm—surely you can see it is some such antidote which is needed? Unless you think I am all at sea in my diagnosis.

MR. TELFORD. That is admirable, Mr. Savile, but you have not said enough. Don't you think that the restraining influence which we older men exercise must be one which can speak to them, somehow, with *authority*, if it is to counteract the cheap, garish spell which the modern world exercises over them? We shall not be successful, I very much fancy, in withdrawing their minds from false ideals and pitiable enthusiasms, unless we can say to them, "Look here! This is certainly true, this preaching of ours; nay, it possesses a certitude which is *infallible*, demands to be accepted beyond all cavil or questioning, once the principles upon which it is based have been grasped by a candid mind." Now, tell us, Dr. Haynes—for I see that Mr. Provost has taken umbrage at my putting the point so strongly, but indeed, I don't know how I could have done otherwise—tell us, Dr. Haynes, what is the infallible authority you would claim as your warrant, in preaching the gospel of Christ to a generation so distracted by perverse notions as this one is?

DR. HAYNES. I don't think I am as anxious as you are, Mr. Telford, to use words like *certitude* and *infallible*;

there is a smack of the seminary about them which I don't like. But, if I am in doubt over one of my pupils, and suspect that he is being too much carried away by these youthful extravagances you speak of, I send him back to his Bible. I don't tell him to sit and brood over it, verse by verse, as the Evangelical teachers would; I offer it to him as a guide of life which has been accepted by eighteen centuries of men; a rule which appeals to all that is highest in us and will bring out, if we let it, all that is highest in us; and I tell him, I think Lord Byron's admiration for Levantine females is very callow stuff by comparison.

MR. TELFORD. To be sure; and nobody will dispute that you have hit on a capital retort, *if it can be shewn that the Bible is everywhere trustworthy*. That it is so, we have no doubt; the Church assures us of it. But will your young friend agree to treat whatever the Bible says as axiomatic? Won't he be for picking holes in it, and putting you down with smart objections to its veracity?

DR. HAYNES. Sir, you put me in mind of a young barrister cross-examining some unhappy witness, reminding him he is upon his oath, and asking him whether he can swear it was Tuesday and not Wednesday the pig was stolen. There is such a thing, would you not say, as reasonable certitude? As to picking holes in the Bible, to be sure that can be done; but it doesn't amount to very much. I dare say you were at Commemoration a few years ago, when the Duke conferred the degrees; and I dare say you had a good laugh, as many of us did, over the false quantities he made in his speaking of the Latin. But you don't doubt, I suppose, that the degrees that day were validly conferred; or that the Duke is an uncommon fine soldier, for all his Latin may be a little rusty?

MR. SAVILE. Come, Dr. Haynes, it is surely you who are playing the advocate now. Or don't you know that in Germany some of the scholars who are most looked up to are no longer content to point out *little* inconsistencies, or what appear to be such, in the sacred narrative; that they cast doubt on everything, and would leave the Church, if they could, without a rag of theology? It was only lately I heard Mr. Rose, of Hadleigh, talking about this very subject; how Paulus will have no miracles at all, and Strauss quite denies the Divinity of our Saviour.

DR. HAYNES. Well, if anybody should translate these *theorizings* into English, I don't doubt we have scholars who will make mincemeat of them. I am content to abide for the present by what our English scholars have to say about it; such men, I mean as Mr. Scott.

DR. GREENE. Hold, I think you go too far there in neglecting the authority of the Church. Just because Mr. Newman and his friends hold too high a doctrine about the Church, that is no reason why sensible men should forget its teaching office altogether. I don't think we need scholars to tell us whether the gospel be true or not. (*To Mr. Telford.*) I don't mean the Church of Rome, Sir, nor your ideal English Church, but the Church of England as it is, and has been these centuries past, as I have known it and am content to live in it and to profess its doctrines, please God, till I die.

MR. TELFORD. When you say " the English Church ",

I suppose you to mean the bishops or angels of that Church, according to the Ignatian doctrine?

DR. GREENE. No, I don't mean the bishops; at least, I don't think so; I should not be surprised to hear that some of these Whig bishops they appoint nowadays had gone off into infidelity. I mean the English Church as a living fact; the ploughman at his team quite as much as the bishop in his palace.

DR. HAYNES. Sir, the ploughmen are dolts. Have you not read in the paper how some hundreds of them, in Kent, are following a silly lunatic who calls himself Sir William Courtenay, and blasphemously gives out he will rise from the dead if he is killed?

MR. TELFORD. And will you consult the ploughmen of Ireland, as well as the ploughmen of England? They will have much to tell you, I fancy, about the teaching of the Church.

THE PROVOST. No, Sir, that will not do. It is a very fond, foolish argument.

MR. COTTINGHAM. For all that, I don't quite understand, Dr. Greene, how you will support this appeal to the many-headed. Don't mistake me, I should be the first to agree that laymen ought to have as much say in managing the affairs of the Church as clergymen; nobody is less in love with this modern affectation of *priestliness* than I. But, my dear Sir, I am afraid you will find your good Christian ploughmen sadly in a minority. Or don't you perceive how the whole face of the English countryside has changed, as it were " while men slept "; great ugly towns springing up everywhere, populated not by the old-fashioned country folk we are accustomed to, but by grimy mechanics who have no thought except for the drudgery of the life they lead, and the pleasure they can enjoy in pot-houses? It is these people, now-a-days, who form the greatest part of England, or will come to do so shortly. Do you think that such people care at all for the doctrines of the English Church? Some of them have been powerfully influenced by the preaching of the Methodists; but most of them, I am afraid you will find, have no religious notions in their heads at all. Are these the allies you will call in to settle disputed points of doctrine, and pronounce whether the learned Germans we have been speaking of are Nestorians or no?

DR. HAYNES. Come, my good friend, I think you exaggerate the decline of religion in manufacturing parts. What has caused it has been the increase of vagrancy among the shiftless poor. People won't go to church when their Sunday trousers are in tatters. Since the new Act, the Poor Law is being very much better administered; a sense of *independence* is growing up, as men see that honest toil is the only thing that will keep them out of the work-house. And in proportion as persons of the working class acquire some measure of self-respect, you will find that they will go to Church and send their children to Sunday School without much reluctance.

MR. COTTINGHAM. Well, there may be better times coming. But I confess I don't think we can expect plain folk to take kindly to religious observances, while we are all at sixes and sevens like this, quarrelling with one another first about Dr. Hampden and then about the

Tracts. Can we not all agree to put our differences by, and devote our energies to working for men's souls? What a wonderful sight it was, to be sure, this winter, when the river froze quite over! How interesting a spectacle it was, when they roasted an ox on the ice at Kennington! And yet it was more comfortable for all of us when the thaw came, and the river flowed between its banks as formerly, carrying the barges that brought us coal to light our fires with. I think Oxford is rather like this just at present; it has somehow got overgrown with a hard crust of intellect; our younger men are dazzling the eye with a prodigious amount of *theologizing*, and I dare say we attract more of public attention than we did formerly. But I for one would like to see this hard crust thawed away, and ministers of religion returning to their proper task of looking after men's souls, instead of kindling these fires of theological debate, and piling on faggot after faggot to prove their *orthodoxy*.

THE PROVOST (*warming to a favourite topic*). It is what comes of the new system of examinations, as some of us were wise enough to prophesy thirty years back. You get a generation of bookish young men coming to the front, and carrying away all the fellowships; they must put the Church of England to rights before they have been half a dozen years in orders; with no other ambition than, as it is called, to *set the Thames on fire.* Sir, if I had a son—they have let the Warden of Wadham marry now, and I dare say the next Provost of Simon Magus will bring up a family—if I had a son, I would not send him to Oxford. A lodge in a garden of cucumbers, Sir; I never hear that verse read but it makes me think of Oxford, as it is in these days of its decline.

DR. GREENE (*in an obvious effort to change the subject*). Well, Mr. Savile, I am still all in a fog about your ideal Church, how it is you will preserve us against these heresies that are to be imported from Germany, by reading the Common Prayer on week-days in every parish.

MR. SAVILE. For shame, Dr. Greene; I believe you to be wilfully misunderstanding me. You are not to think of us as having any *nostrum* for curing the troubles of the age. Only, when you tell us that we can trust to the common sense of the ordinary Englishman to preserve our Church from contamination by heresy, we answer, as Mr. Cottingham answered just now, that we don't think, more's the pity, the ordinary Englishman is a very safe guide in matters of theology. And so, although we love the English Church, and admire her ways and her discipline, we don't believe that she can stand quite alone, and be a law to herself——

DR. GREENE. Oh God, here is that damned female again.

MR. SAVILE. I am sorry; indeed I did not mean to tease you, Dr. Greene. Well then, we do not believe the English Church can be a law to itself; it must remember and acknowledge, as it has too much forgotten these last hundred years and more, that it is only *part* of the Church Catholic; that we can only be certain of the truths which it teaches, when we see that those truths are also held by the rest of the Church Catholic; as for example infant baptism, or the apostolic succession of bishops. There are many good men professing to be Christians, who say they can find no warrant in Scripture for either of those two doctrines. And our reply to them is, *Securus judicat orbis terrarum*, as St. Augustine said.

DR. HAYNES. You mean, you don't care whether such doctrines are in Scripture or not, as long as the universal Church teaches them?

MR. TELFORD. To be sure. Even if it could be shewn that they were not primitive, we should be bound to accept them, because they are Catholic.

MR. SAVILE. Hold, I don't think that will do. The Church says they *are* primitive; if they were not, she would have no right to enjoin them.

DR. HAYNES. What, are you in two minds whether you hold these doctrines because they are primitive, or because they are Catholic?

MR. SAVILE. Why, don't you see, they are Catholic because they are primitive; but we know them to be primitive because we know them to be Catholic.

DR. HAYNES. My good Sir, that won't carry you very far. Don't you see that the Romanists have just as much to say for themselves? They will tell you that all Catholics, that is, they themselves, hold the doctrine of the papacy to be primitive, and primitive therefore it must be—with just as good logic as yourselves.

MYSELF. . . .

MR. SAVILE. But you must remember the Greeks, Dr. Haynes; the Greeks will have none of the papacy, but they hold bishops to be of divine institution.

DR. HAYNES. Exactly, Sir; and therefore the Greeks are prejudiced witnesses in the matter of the episcopate, just as the papists are in the matter of the Pope's claims. The Presbyterians do not care a rap for the episcopate.

MR. SAVILE. The Presbyterians? But they are schismatics; surely you will not allow *them* to enter the witness-box, Dr. Haynes?

DR. HAYNES. You call them schismatics, because they haven't an episcopate. That is, your whole argument moves in a circle, and is without value. You must be able to tell us whom your Church includes, before you point us to what it teaches. And you have to tell us what it teaches, before you can tell us whom it includes. I don't think much of Mr. Newman, if he hasn't faced so simple a dilemma as that.

MR. TELFORD. But you don't understand, Dr. Haynes; our appeal is to the *undivided* Church; say, in the time of St. Augustine. We may not be able to prove conclusively from history there were bishops in the time of the apostles, but we can prove from history there were bishops in the time of St. Augustine. And where were your Presbyterians then?

DR. HAYNES. And where was your English Church then? Had not the Donatists bishops just as good as Dr. Bagot or Dr. Howley? Yet St. Augustine rated them soundly for disagreeing with the main body of Christians, which is what we do.

MR. TELFORD. But we do not divide the Church; it is already divided between East and West. It was against the undivided Church that the Donatists were rebellious.

DR. HAYNES. That is nonsense, Sir; a great part of the world was at the time Arian.

MR. TELFORD. The Arians? To be sure; but the Arians were heretics.

DR. HAYNES. Good heavens, are you back at your old tricks again? Don't you see that the Arians claimed to hold the tradition of the primitive Church, quite as much as the Greeks do? No, Sir, it won't do; you can't use the infallible teaching of the Church to prove your doctrines unless you belong to a single undivided Church, like the Romans. I don't think it will be long before we see you a Romanist, Mr. Telford; and I hope it won't be long before we see Mr. Savile give over talking about the undivided Church, and put his trust in common sense and sound scholarship like the rest of us.

MR. SAVILE (*getting up and standing in front of the fire*). No, I don't think I shall fit in with Oxford ways much longer. Perhaps in a living I might find work that wants to be done, and feel I could do it; I don't know. I should wish to remember my friends here, who have never failed in kindness to me; but Oxford herself, with all her easy-going ways, will always be a cruel stepmother to some of her children; for the life of me, I cannot understand why it is. Of this I feel certain, that the movement which has sprung up among us, and is the cause of so much alarm to some of you, may perhaps be identified with Oxford, but Oxford will never be identified with it. I dare say it will bear many kinds of fruit, but in another soil; *non sua poma*, this strange fertility of hers is something that she will disown. Virgil—he has the gift, has he not, of summing up in a phrase used at random the aspiration and the tragedy of minds he could never have understood; that is the real poetic genius; and you talk of Byron! I don't know why, it is as if something in the very walls of this Common-room haunted me; all this evening the first eclogue has been coming back to my mind, and the shepherd who was dis-possessed of his ancestral land; *sitientes ibimus Afros*, he says,—we shall be off into the cruel desert, men such as I am; and we shall remember the greenery of Oxford only as better things, no, not better things, more companionable things, are remembered in dreams. This ferment that is now working among us does not belong to the spirit of the University; we are changelings, it seems to me, in the cradle. The genius which broods over this place is one which bids us reflect, and criticize, and do nothing. To have resolved your mind clearly upon a matter of speculative truth, is to disqualify yourself for its citizenship. If I am still fellow of Simon Magus, it is not because I hope to conquer the hesitations of my colleagues; it is because I cannot conquer my own. In the day when I see clearly, as you would have me see clearly, the scenes that I have loved will be my walks no longer. I am sorry, Mr. Provost; I have been thinking aloud, and the fellows must have found me a shocking *bore;* I do hope they will forgive me.

THE PROVOST. You are yet a very young man, Mr. Savile, and you have to learn the lesson of patience. Most of us see things with different eyes, as we grow older. When I was your age, I fancied myself born to put the world to rights; that is long ago now, and the world is much what it was, Sir, very much what it was.

MR. COTTINGHAM (*being tactful*). I never heard, Mr. Provost, whether the rules that were proposed in the late statute, to prevent the men running into debt with tradesmen, had your approval? I do not know what you find here; but with us there have been several complaints about the rash use of credit, which the shopkeepers are commonly ready to give.

THE PROVOST. It was the tradesmen who prevented the passing of the rules you mention; that is certain. I don't think the boys, the men I should say, spend so much as they did formerly. There will always be young sportsmen, as they like to call themselves, who will drive tandem and drink pretty heavily; but I don't see why we should play the nursemaid to them. They must learn their own lessons by experience.

MR. TELFORD. There is a great temptation for the shops to encourage them in extravagance; especially those which have to pay stiff rents for their premises; in the High, for example.

DR. GREENE. You mean in the High Street?

MR. TELFORD. I mean in the High Street. They have to make what they can, in what is after all but a portion of the year. And they suffer a good deal from petty thefts, when their door-knockers are carried off, for example. What, Mr. Savile, are you leaving us?

MR. SAVILE. I must ask you to excuse me, Mr. Provost. My head aches a little; I expect it is the spring weather. I hope the fellows will not miss my company.

NOTE ON CHAPTER VII

Material for the history of Simon Magus during the last century is, of course, abundant; and Provost Telford was a man of real importance in the University at the time of the Commission. So well known was he, that Dean Burgon is said to have chosen him as one of his models in a projected work which he never lived to complete, under the title, *Lives of Twelve Small and Bad Men*. But, by a lucky chance, we are enabled to get a glimpse of Simon Magus from the outside at the very moment with which the last chapter deals, from no less acid a pen than that of the Revd. Mark Pattison. It is well known that certain passages were omitted from his *Memoirs* when they came to be published, and this is one of them. It seems probable that friends intervened, pointing out how easily the identity of Provost Telford would be recognized under the initial " T."; he was of course still living, and head of his College, when the *Memoirs* appeared. Evidently there was no love lost between the Provost of Simon Magus and the Rector of Lincoln; a fact which may seem surprising in view of the similarity that can be traced between their careers. Perhaps Dr. Johnson's remarks, quoted above (p. 143), may be regarded as relevant to the situation. Anyhow, it will be well to print Pattison's comments in full, since they illustrate so many characters of my dream. Obviously they should stand just before the words " All the while I was rushing into the whirlpool of Tractarianism " in chapter VI.

"I say I turned my attention towards Orders, but it was not with any intention of accepting defeat after the series of rebuffs I had experienced in applying for College fellowships. In spite of my constitutional self-distrust, I think I knew that my abilities were bound to secure recognition if some opening could be found for them in an election which depended on merit rather than on petty-minded intrigue. It seemed a singularly fortunate coincidence—indeed, I find that in my diary I attributed it to the designs of Providence—that a fellowship at Simon Magus should have fallen vacant at that moment. The occasion of the vacancy was one that could not have been foreseen; Savile, a young tutor who had fallen, like myself, under Newman's influence, determined to throw up his fellowship owing to a scruple of conscience about the Thirty-Nine Articles. It was the end of what seemed at the time a promising career; his mind, already warped by the influence of the Tracts, and perhaps by those macerations of the body which superstition imposed, seemed atrophied thenceforward to all powers of reasoning, and shortly afterwards he joined the Roman Church. He was never much in the world's eye since; but it appears from the testimony of friends who came across him that he continued to derive a melancholy satisfaction from the practice of the effeminate creed he had embraced.

His loss, however, was severely felt at the time; and it became known that Simon Magus was looking out for 'a good man', as it is called, to replace him. In some ways, my own chances appeared to be slender. It was notorious that Simon Magus almost always elected its own men; a habit which often leads, as it did in that case, to a kind of intellectual in-breeding. And it so happened that there was a candidate 'in' who had on the face of it better qualifications than myself, having taken a first in his final schools, Marrowby, a Hart Hall man and a great dispenser of hospitality. On the other hand, the College was notoriously divided between factions, whose incessant quarrels Dr. Watson, an insignificant figure who then held the Provostship, was quite powerless to control. And since it was certain that whichever party supported the claims of Marrowby would automatically arouse the opposition of its rivals, it seemed possible that a man like myself, in spite of what was on paper a less distinguished career, would be looked upon with a kindly eye by a considerable body of electors.

Marrowby was the choice of the Tories and the old-fashioned high churchmen; the 'two-bottle men', as we used to call them. He was a safe man who did not hold 'views', and he was well connected; I do not know what other qualities recommended him to the notice of Dr. Greene and his friends, although no doubt his first class impressed them, as such distinctions always do impress dull minds. The old Provost was considered to be in the hands of this party; but he was so far gone in senility that it was difficult to say which way he would vote when the time came. The opposing camp was led by Dr. Haynes, a sensible man who shared the Liberal opinions that were fashionable outside Oxford in the days of the Reform Bill. In Oxford, it need hardly be said, these views had less currency; but the domineering and arrogant personality of Dr. Greene had made him enemies in the Common Room, and these, for want of a better leader, attached themselves to the policy of his rival. It was Dr. Haynes, then, who asked me to call upon him one evening, and raised the question whether I would allow my name to be put in as a candidate for the vacant fellowship.

I was at this time, as I have already explained, much under Newman's influence, although I had not as yet allowed my intellect to be thoroughly debauched, as it was later, by the fanaticism of the Movement. But it fortunately happened that I was no longer living with Dr. Pusey, and there was nothing, consequently, which publicly identified me with the rising agitation of the Tractarians. I had to admit to myself that, if he had known where my sympathies lay, I was the last man on whom Dr. Haynes' choice would have fallen; he was notoriously anxious to prevent the spread, in Simon Magus, of anything like sacerdotalism. But then, I reflected, *caveat emptor;* it was Dr. Haynes' business to find out whether the candidate he supported was in reality the man he wanted, not mine to expatiate on the views I held, or question whether, if elected, I should add any strength to the cause of enlightenment and reform. And at the same time, in spite of the self-distrust I have already alluded to, I knew that I was the best man in, and that the fellows would not repent of having elected me when my gifts for influencing the rising generation were given free play. Accordingly, I told Dr. Haynes that I was very grateful for his kindness in having made the suggestion, and quite willing that my name should be considered. In the examination, I felt certain that this time I was destined to do myself justice.

But there were further cross-currents in the business. At Simon Magus, as in many other Colleges, the younger fellows had been partly caught by the influence of the Movement, and were thus out of sympathy both with Dr. Greene and with Dr. Haynes; they were disposed, too, to resent the domination of senior men, the latter's quite as much as that of the former. It seemed likely, then, that they would take a line, and if possible produce a candidate, of their own. But here the stars in their courses seemed to be fighting for me. The leader of this party of discontent, now that Mr. Savile had left them, was a person whose name I shall only indicate by the use of an initial letter; he is still alive, and in Oxford, and I should not like to rake up old sores by mentioning his name when I come to describe the shabby part which he played on this occasion. It was the very next evening, then, that T. (for so I will call him) came round to my lodgings and opened up the subject of the vacant fellowship. He must in reality have been well aware that I was Dr. Haynes' candidate. But this knowledge, for reasons which were only too apparent later, he was at pains to conceal; he told me simply that Marrowby was being put forward by the two-bottle men, and that the younger fellows were determined not to have him foisted on them. I was a man of acknowledged qualifications; I was also (as he knew, for we had met often in the rooms of Newman and his friends) in sympathy with the Movement; would I allow my name to be considered?

I felt a certain delicacy about the situation. I had been approached in the same sense, as I have explained, only the evening before by Dr. Haynes; I imagined, for I had no reason to guess otherwise, that T. was unaware of this. It never occurred to me, in my innocence, that the coincidence of the two requests was more than a bare coincidence, either party having been actuated simply by the desire to find the strongest candidate they could. Was I to tell T. about my interview with Dr. Haynes or not? Once more I decided that it was his business to find out the relevant facts, not mine to disclose them. I agreed to allow my name to be considered, and to stand for the examination. What I did not realize till afterwards was that T., not knowing my consent had already been won, was simply out to make sure I would let myself be put forward as Dr. Haynes' man. He himself, although his manner clearly implied that he and his friends meant to vote for me, was in reality preparing to run a third candidate of his own, a *tertius gaudens* whose only chance of election was a splitting of the senior votes between Marrowby and myself. This was a Magus man, Delisle, who was thought lucky to have got a second class in the schools, and was not much known in the University, though T. knew that his sympathies lay with the writers of the Tracts.

I do not wish to dwell on the duplicity of the part played by T.; I feel bound, however, to mention, that he went so far as to ask me to dine with him, that I might have the opportunity of meeting some of the younger fellows. I have written elsewhere of the magnetic influence I possessed, which seemed to give me a moral ascendancy over my fellow-men. This was at the time latent in me, from a morbid tendency which I had of underestimating my own qualities. But I could not help feeling as I sat among them that these younger fellows of Simon Magus were ready to look to me for leadership, and I was elated by the thought that they should so wisely repose their confidence in me. I now know, of course, that the whole affair was a sham.

When the day came for the examination, I did not suffer from any particular nervousness. I had had enough experience of these examinations to know what would be expected of me, and to put it down on paper with fair rapidity. Delisle's presence at the examination puzzled me, for I had had no intimation that he was standing, and could not imagine what backing he had; I supposed, though, that he was merely standing on his own account, as men sometimes did, without any official encouragement. I went back to my lodgings feeling that at last I had found a rest for the soles of my feet; Simon Magus was henceforward to be my home. I cannot describe the feelings of bewilderment, disappointment, and injury with which I heard next day, in conversation with a friend who did not know I was interested in the affair, that Delisle had been elected. He is long dead now, and it is not my purpose in these Memoirs to stir up any mud unnecessarily. But those who are acquainted with the later history of the College will not need to be told that his subsequent career proved the choice of the fellows to have been a thoroughly mistaken one.

At the time, then, bitter feelings were uppermost in my mind, and I could think of little but the way in which my innocence had been practised upon. But I came to realize later that the rebuff which was so severe a blow to my feelings was a blessing in disguise. Simon Magus was destined to be a backwater in the educational world of Oxford; and although some of my friends have been good enough to tell me that my influence, had I been elected in 1839, might have arrested this process of decay, I have always felt that a nature like my own must have languished in such an atmosphere of intrigue and petty jobbery as that of its Common Room. The blight of Tractarianism, to be sure, did not hang over the College for long; but it was killed, I have ever believed, rather by the lethargic dullness which is the curse of that institution, than by the keen airs of intellectual activity which have blown through Oxford since."

CHAPTER VIII

A REAR-GUARD ACTION: 1888

MR. MCNAIRNE (*the philosophy tutor*). I hope Mrs. Telford is better?

THE PROVOST. Thank you; I think she is mending.

MR. MCNAIRNE. It has been a terrible winter, with all these blizzards and snow-storms. Can you remember such a bad year, Provost?

THE PROVOST. There was a very severe winter not long after I took my degree, '38 or '39 it would be. I remember a lot of us went out to watch them roasting an ox on the Isis, at Kennington. But I don't think we had so many spells of bad weather. It has tested the constitutions of people like Mrs. Telford and myself, who are getting on.

MR. WAYNE (*the chaplain, a youngish man in a modern clerical collar*). Arnold's death was very sudden. I remember being told he had a bad heart, but I don't think anybody foresaw a danger like that. He wasn't any great age, either.

THE PROVOST. Arnold? No, he was a young man comparatively. He had a fellowship at Oriel in the 'forties—yes, it must have been in '45. I remember it was the same year that Newman was perverted. Nothing seems to kill Newman; he must be all but ninety.

MR. MCNAIRNE (*speaking to his neighbour; but it is obviously the sort of question that is addressed to the company in general*). Would you call Arnold a typical Oxford man?

MR. BATTERSBY (*the Provost's guest. Unknown to himself, he is being inspected by the Fellows, who are looking out for an ancient history tutor; they are not going to elect him*). I don't think one ever finds typical Oxford men except at Cambridge. Henry Sidgwick, now, wouldn't you say he was a typical Oxford man?

MR. FANSHAWE (*the Mods. tutor, slightly past middle age*). Arnold made literary capital out of his connexion with Oxford, but he was never true to type. He was too unorthodox to belong to the old Oxford which used to be so pleasant, and too fastidious to belong to the modern Oxford which is so intolerable.

MR. BATTERSBY. I think that's so true. He looked on civilization with the eyes of a school-inspector, and criticized it in a style only possible to a Professor of Poetry.

MR. WAYNE. I don't think you do him justice, Fanshawe; your phrase "literary capital" suggests that he wasn't sincere. I should have said that he had an *anima naturaliter Christiana*, but it wouldn't function, if I may so express myself, because it was hamstrung by the Rationalism of the world he was born into. He had the will to believe, as they say, but when he contemplated Christianity as a working religion, it somehow seemed too—too——

MR. BATTERSBY. Middle-class.

MR. WAYNE. I don't think that's quite what I meant. I should have thought it was more materialism that seemed to him, well, vulgar. I suppose he had enough literary imagination to be impressed, more than he wanted to be, by work like Renan's, and not enough patience with exact scholarship to sit down to Westcott. And yet he had to believe in the " power not ourselves making for righteousness "; what a good phrase that is, up to a point!

MR. ROBERTS (*the science tutor, young and rather quarrelsome*). It might mean almost anything, mightn't it? I mean, it rather depends on whether it has a capital P. I suppose you can detect a kind of bent towards goodness in human nature *au fond*, which mounts up in the aggregate to an influence working for righteousness— one couldn't honestly say you find it in nature as a whole; red in tooth and claw, and all that——

THE PROVOST (*who does not much approve of science tutors*). Yes, but it is a power *not ourselves;* that was the sense of the definition.

MR. WAYNE. Well, you know, Provost, I think there is something in Roberts' criticism. The definition does look to me as if it were dodging the question whether that which makes for righteousness can be described as a Person or not.

THE PROVOST. Words like " person " can be very misleading. I don't think we ought to use them more than we can help.

MR. WAYNE. I agree. One doesn't want to *press* terms like that. Only I was going to say——

MR. FANSHAWE. Tell me, Wayne, what do you mean when you say on Sundays that the Lord your God is a jealous God?

MR. WAYNE. Well, I suppose one has to take a phrase like that back into its setting. I mean, at that stage of their religious development the Jews would still be thinking of Jahweh as one among a number of possible Gods; and the idea of monotheism, or rather perhaps monolatry, would best emerge if they thought of one among these under the figure of a jealous Rival. And naturally Moses, or rather the compiler, would think in those terms; but that isn't to say that the words have no modern reference; we still haven't found a better way of expressing the theological fact that absolute Goodness is incompatible with any intrusion of lower motives—isn't that the sort of thing we mean? After all, the whole situation belongs to an order that has passed away; we don't feel any temptation, now, to worship other gods.

MR. BATTERSBY. Oh, don't you think one does? I do, often; I suppose because it's forbidden; but really it's very hard to get up any enthusiasm about them. (*There is a slight shudder among the Fellows, and his stock goes down several points.*)

MR. FANSHAWE. Then you don't believe that God, or the Power working for righteousness if you prefer it, visits the sins of the fathers upon the children, to the third and fourth generation?

MR. WAYNE. Really, Fanshawe, you've become very theological this evening; I don't know what's coming over you. I suppose that's more a question of fact really;

I mean, of experience; more in Roberts' line than in mine. I'm not much good at acquired characteristics and all that sort of thing; but wouldn't you say, Roberts, that it was possible for people to have an inherited craving for drink, say, as the result of alcoholism in the parents?

MR. ROBERTS. I should go slow about preaching that to the undergraduates. It might do 'em good, of course, but it isn't a bit certain whether it's true. Anyhow, we should only describe it as cause and effect; we shouldn't presume to say whether the power, if any, which arranged these things was working for righteousness or not.

MR. MCNAIRNE (*who rather suspects scientists*). Naturally you wouldn't. It's difficult to see how a judgement of value like that could come into your province. All the same, Wayne, I don't think you can get out of it that way. What Fanshawe wants to know is not really whether children in fact suffer for the sins of their parents; he wants to know whether it is right that they should, if and in so far as they do; and if not, why the Bible says they do. The judgement of fact's immaterial.

MR. ROBERTS (*inaudibly*). Of course. It always is.

MR. WAYNE. Well, I suppose one would say something like this, wouldn't one? That the Jews in pre-Exilic times obviously didn't believe in personal immortality; and therefore the only way in which the permanent consequences of human guilt could be expressed in the language of their time was to say that the effects of sin lasted on into the next generation. And the same with righteousness, of course.

MR. FANSHAWE. It strikes me as an uncommonly rum way of putting it. As a matter of fact, what put it into my head was turning over in the library this morning a pamphlet of old Watson's, a sermon I think preached before he became Provost, making out that the Irish were having a bad harvest, that would be some time in the 'twenties, I suppose, as a punishment for O'Connell's agitation. He didn't say anything about the third and fourth generation, but I wondered whether the troubles there just now would have seemed to him a vengeance of some kind; and if so who imposed it.

MR. BATTERSBY. Great Britain, no doubt. It is well known that in Ireland we are the power that makes for righteousness.

THE PROVOST. I remember old Watson. He had been a great Liberal in his youth, but the Revolution made him into a Tory. We younger fellows used to call him the *kothornos*, like Theramenes you know, because he had changed sides so much. I never thought Gladstone would let himself be dragged at Parnell's chariot-wheels as he is doing now.

MR. FANSHAWE. We are lucky not to have him as our member nowadays. But we should have thrown him out over the Disestablishment, I suppose. Young Chamberlain has done well for himself.

THE PROVOST. I don't think Chamberlain will come to anything. He's a man of no principle. Thank God, principles do count, in English politics.

MR. McNAIRNE. I was wondering about that interpretation of yours, Wayne, which I think is uncommonly ingenious; I was wondering whether you would explain passages in the New Testament on the same principle quite? I mean, there's that difficult passage, isn't there, about the devils going into the herd of swine, and their all running violently down a steep place and being drowned; would you think it possible that that was just poetical imagery? And that the devils, you see, went back to the place they came from, only the disciples, not being great hands at describing things as they saw them, made a good story of it?

MR. WAYNE. You'd probably find scholars in Germany who'd tell you that sort of thing. In fact, I'm certain you would. But I don't think you can afford to use that kind of explanation where the New Testament is concerned; it cuts too deep.

MR. McNAIRNE. That's a tiny bit arbitrary, isn't it?

MR. PEARS-SMITH (*a young Modern History tutor*). I don't see that, McNairne. When you're dealing with the New Testament, you're dealing with what profess to be eye-witnesses' accounts, which come down to us from days when people were accustomed to the use of paper and ink, and all that. Whereas with the Old Testament the probability is that poor old D or whoever he was was writing centuries after the things happened or didn't happen, and he may have been depending for his sources on ballads which had been sung about the countryside, and got corrupt, and all that sort of thing. Surely there's a *prima facie* case for the Gospels being more trustworthy?

MR. McNAIRNE. I wouldn't have minded so much if

Wayne had said " you can't use that kind of explanation"; but he said, " you can't *afford* to use that kind of explanation ". And that's the language of *a priori* reasoning.

MR. FANSHAWE. The point is, don't you see, that Wayne has committed himself, with all possible solemnity, to the statement that he unfeignedly believes the Old and New Testaments. What we want to know is why he thinks it worth while to believe the New Testament unfeignedly, if he believes the Old—well, so feignedly, if that isn't an unkind way of putting it.

THE PROVOST. You can't draw hard and fast rules like that.

MR. WAYNE. I don't suppose I can make you understand the sense in which that declaration is commonly made nowadays; we've had all that out before. But, my dear chap, I do want you to see that if you leave mere formulas out of sight, and come down to bed-rock, there's all the difference in the world between the criticism which corrects our ideas about the remote history of an obscure Bedouin tribe, and the criticism which sets itself up in judgement to decide what Almighty God would have done or wouldn't have done in revealing himself to mankind.

MR. BATTERSBY. I always thought that incident about the pigs was charming. It is so stupid of modern civilization to have given up believing in the devil, when he is the only explanation of it.

MR. WAYNE. I don't agree with you. Taken in itself, I think the story is one which raises more difficulties than it settles. But what is at stake is the credibility of the witnesses. If you are going to give a metaphorical explanation of the Gadarene swine, why shouldn't you give a metaphorical account of the Ascension, or even the Resurrection? The Germans, of course, don't stop short of that; Cotter Morison, who died the other day, poor fellow, might have written some of the stuff they turn out. If you are going to expunge the facts on which the whole of our Christian certainty reposes, then the story will have no more interest for us than, say, the *Annals*.

MYSELF. . . .

MR. BATTERSBY. I find the *Annals* much less plausible than the gospel.

MR. McNAIRNE. Oh, but, my dear fellow, we all see the difficulties that beset any notion of a revealed religion. You draw a blank cheque, as it were, by assenting beforehand to its doctrines, not knowing whether there will be enough assets to meet it when you come to look into your account. The wonder is they got on so long without, apparently, criticizing the Bible at all; a hundred years ago, or even fifty years ago, your position would have been unassailable.

MYSELF. . . .

MR. FANSHAWE. The trouble with you parsons is, you kept the Thirty-nine Articles going for centuries as a king of TRESPASSERS WILL BE PROSECUTED notice to warn off the wretched Nonconformists; now that it's taken down you find it hung round your necks, like the albatross. You always held a position of privilege——

MR. WAYNE. You forget, before the Commission we were a clerical body, and the question of excluding Nonconformists didn't arise. (*Smiling sardonically.*) We were protected, in those days, from the company of irreverent Anglican laymen.

MR. FANSHAWE. Certainly you were; you were protected from the company of everybody you didn't agree with. But I'm not talking of Simon Magus, I'm talking of the country in general. The Articles were only meant to be a dodge for getting rid of the bigots; papist or puritan, Queen Elizabeth didn't want them; it was the crack of a whip to keep the dogs off. Now they're forty stripes save one laid on the back of you and a whole lot of other well-meaning gentlemen who don't really believe quite all that, but have to tell us that you do. And meanwhile the world has grown more sensible, and your ring-fence of privilege has gone. The Roman Catholics have been emancipated, there are no more tests to worry the Nonconformists, the Jews, even, have been allowed freedom of conscience; and now here is Bradlaugh getting a bill through to prevent the unfortunate atheist having to pretend he believes in God when he appears in a law-court.

MR. BATTERSBY. I think that's so sensible. Because it's quite inconceivable that a Bradlaughite should have enough imagination to be a successful perjurer.

MR. PEARS-SMITH. I don't quite see what you're complaining of, Fanshawe. Granted the justice of your historical estimate—and if you don't mind my saying so I think it's rather superficial—I should have thought the position of the Anglican clergy is better, not worse, since the abolition of tests, here in the University for example. As long as you had lots of good men, Jews and Nonconformists and so on, being kept out of positions here because they couldn't subscribe to the Articles, it would have been monstrous for our clergy to pretend they believed in them when they didn't. I suppose a certain amount of that went on in the eighteenth century. But now that everything has been thrown open, I should have thought that *ex animo* assent to the Articles or any other Anglican formulary was less important than it used to be. I mean, there aren't so many pickings to be got out of subscription as there used to be; surely that's obvious?

THE PROVOST. I can't understand why people make such a fuss of Bradlaugh. He is a fanatical creature. Nobody is more fanatical about religion than the man who has left it.

MR. MCNAIRNE. I'm not quite sure if I've taken your point, Smith; but aren't you preaching a rather immoral sort of doctrine? I mean, you seem to think it makes no difference whether a man believes what he says or not, as long as he isn't growing unduly rich on it. Isn't that the same as to contend that there's no harm in lying as long as you're not getting money by false pretences?

MR. WAYNE. I don't in the least want to spoil the fellows' fun, and of course I know it's not the slightest good trying to argue with Fanshawe. But just as a point of personal explanation, as they say at the Union, I should like to protest against the idea that I'm a kind of Bishop Blougram, only believing half of what I say.

When all's said and done, I do believe in a historical revelation, and I do accept it on the authority of the Church. I don't mean that the Bible doesn't come into it; "the Church to teach, and the Bible to prove", I suppose that's sound enough. But after all the Bible is a document, and documents have got to be interpreted, whereas the Church is a living society which has, we are told, "the Mind of Christ". The Bible isn't simply thrown at us, leaving us to make the best we can of it, like savages on a desert island—I suppose I should say, a partly desert island—who have come across a copy of Bradshaw. I wonder what Bradshaw would be like, if it were edited by Bradlaugh and Fanshawe? But that's a digression. The point is that, as Pears-Smith says, the modern parson is poor but relatively honest. He doesn't want to prevent Jews, heretics and infidels taking their degrees here. But he does still value the Articles as being a rough statement, drawn up in times when our modern problems hadn't arisen, of what the Church of England stands for. And although he claims a certain liberty of interpretation, he doesn't think it would be honest to take orders unless one is at least in general sympathy with the doctrines they express.

MR. ROBERTS. Don't you rather exaggerate the liberty of conscience that one gets in modern Oxford? After all, the men are still made to go to Chapel.

MR. WAYNE. Unless they have some conscientious excuse; the Roman Catholics don't, for example. In any case, it's the Provost's rule, not mine. But I confess I don't think there's much harm in undergraduates having to go to Chapel even if they are not strict Anglicans. The services there are very moderate, after all; there's nothing in the Prayer Book service, as we have it, that's likely to create offence.

MR. ROBERTS. But if they don't believe in God?

MR. WAYNE (*shrugging his shoulders*). My dear chap, is it such a great hardship for a mere boy, who comes up here at eighteen, and can't have formed any very valuable ideas for himself, to have to recognize, once a week, the existence of the Absolute? It isn't as if Oxford philosophy were still under the dreary domination of Mill. Hegel, though he has made us all frightened of dogmatizing, has surely taught us that much—that Existence couldn't exist unless there were a Mind to think it, and therefore materialism simply cuts its own throat. You'd agree there, wouldn't you, McNairne?

MR. MCNAIRNE. I don't think I want to quarrel with that statement as you put it. But I'm not quite sure that I want to impose Hegel as a dogma any more than Haeckel; and I think anybody who's going to put up a case for compulsory chapel would be very ill-advised to base it, don't you see, on the dominance of one particular philosophy here at one particular time. I'd prefer myself to say that I regard Hegel as provisionally true, but I don't think he has said the last word—who can ever say the last word in philosophy? And you might find yourself in a very awkward situation in fifty years' time, if our apprehension of truth has shifted its angle, perhaps that's the best way of putting it, in the mean time.

MR. BATTERSBY. I always think Oxford philosophy is

so like a running sore. Bad enough as it is, I mean; but if it were to close up, it would simply fester. (MR. MCNAIRNE *has a good glare, but says nothing.*)

THE PROVOST. I don't think the Germans have superseded Mill. His questions remain unanswered. Hegel is more of a favourite with clergymen, but we shall come back to Mill.

MR. FANSHAWE. You see, Roberts, there is really no reason why the men should not be made to go to Chapel. Two hundred years ago, or a hundred years ago for that matter, the Book of Common Prayer served the purposes of the Anglican clergy, because it kept the Dissenters away from Church. In these more enlightened days it serves their purpose equally well, because it is so non-committal that no Dissenter can possibly mind it.

MR. WAYNE (*stung into personalities*). How would it be, Fanshawe, if you told us exactly why it is you go to Chapel on Sundays?

MR. FANSHAWE. My dear Wayne, I find it a very embarrassing position, to have to discuss my private religious opinions in the middle of Common-room like this. But if you really want to know, I think it is because I have never been sufficiently interested in Christianity to make up my mind whether I believe in it or not. It was about the time I took my degree Darwin brought out the *Descent of Man;* and since then I have been profoundly bored by a vulgar controversy between prigs who told me that I was, or wasn't, descended from a monkey. It would have been impossible for me to give up going to Chapel, however much I felt the tedium of it, without incurring the suspicion of having been influenced by something the scientists said; which would have been frankly intolerable. Anyhow, it would be rather narrow-minded of you, Wayne, if you objected to my presence in the sacred edifice, when you have just told us that the services as you conduct them are not calculated to bring a blush to the cheek of any youthful atheist.

MR. WAYNE. Of course, one can always trust you to put a thing tactfully, Fanshawe. What I was going to suggest was this—need I really be accused of hypocrisy if I sometimes read out a phrase from the Old Testament with certain mental reservations about its meaning, when you are sitting there affecting to join in the service, although apparently your only motive for being present is to annoy Roberts?

MR. PEARS-SMITH. I was thinking over what you said just now, Fanshawe; and really I think you draw a rather unreal contrast between what the Prayer Book used to stand for and what it stands for now. I suppose it's true that when the Act of Uniformity was passed the Prayer Book was a sort of Popish abomination to large numbers of Englishmen, because after all it was liturgical in shape, and they'd quite forgotten what the Mass was like, so they had nothing to contrast it with except their own improvised prayer meetings. Then, it was a living document, bristling with controversial statements. Now, its language is so much a thing of the past, and has become so much consecrated by usage, that we really don't attach any special significance to the theology of it; it just gives us a nice, restful sort of feeling, like looking at a familiar landscape. It's all a matter of background; the English mind gets easily accustomed to changes, after they've been at work a few years, and comes to regard them as part of the natural order of things. Look at all the fuss there was about the Corn Laws! And now the principle of Free Trade is so firmly established that it's quite inconceivable, I suppose, we shall ever go back on it. You can't go back on the Prayer Book, either; it has become a kind of national monument, like Stonehenge. Fanshawe likes the Prayer Book, really, just as he prefers cobbled streets to Macadam; he would be up in arms if anybody suggested revising it.

MR. MCNAIRNE. Aren't you rather forgetting, Smith, that as Wayne says the Chapel services are tempered to the shorn lamb? We don't have the Athanasian Creed here, for example. I don't know just what Wayne would feel about it, but I wouldn't mind seeing the Prayer Book revised a little, if only so as to cut that out.

THE PROVOST. I don't think we have much to gain from a revision of the Prayer Book. Of course it contains things that are repellent to an enlightened taste; that is natural, because it comes down to us from times when people were always squabbling about the external details of religion. But those things will disappear automatically as time goes on; it shews the vitality of a religion, if we can discard the features in it that have become out of date; the organ which remains unused grows atrophied, one might say. But it would be a mistake to start meddling with the Prayer Book, or the Articles either.

MR. ROBERTS. Atrophied organs can be very dangerous sometimes. They can poison the system.

MR. WAYNE. I'm glad to hear you say that about " vitality ", Provost. Because surely that's where Fanshawe has got his whole idea of the thing wrong; he will talk of the Church as if it were a mechanism, demanding mechanical observance and mechanical acceptance of formulas. Whereas we know that the Church is an organism, containing her own inherent principle of life, and therefore capable of adapting herself to any environment, shrinking here, putting out feelers there, harmonizing her creeds with the background, as Pears-Smith would call it, of contemporary human thought.

MR. FANSHAWE. Really, Wayne, that's very interesting. I expect you're thinking of natural mimicry when you say that; butterflies that acquire markings that make them indistinguishable from the boughs they live on,— no, Roberts, it's all right; I dare say they don't acquire the markings at all, but they go hunting round till they find the right kind of bough, or they all die except the ones that have the right kind of markings; don't let us get into an argument about that. The point is, anyhow, according to Wayne, that the Church has got this chamelon's instinct of always taking its colour from its surroundings, so that in the nineteenth century it has markings quite different from those it had in the sixteenth century, a very convenient dispensation of Providence.

MR. WAYNE. I suppose Fanshawe can be trusted to misrepresent any argument. Markings on butterflies happen to be the things we're interested in about them, and therefore your analogy makes it sound as if I meant that the Church could alter her doctrines, or her dealings with men, in vital and essential ways; of course I don't. Her message remains the same in each generation; it must, because it is something entrusted to her, not something which she evolves from her inner consciousness. But that message has to be translated, surely, into terms of different philosophies, just as much as the Bible has to be translated from Hebrew or Greek into other languages, if it is to be understood. That's why it's such a mercy we're not tied down with exact definitions of doctrine, as the Romans are, like some property which is encumbered with a lot of irritating restrictions by will, so that the person who inherits can never really enjoy it as his own.

MYSELF. . . .

MR. McNAIRNE. Of course that's how we should all like to see the Church behaving, Wayne; and some of us, I fancy, would be glad to see it exercising more liberty of interpretation than you would quite approve of. But, you see, there's this difficulty; just in proportion as you refuse to be restricted by title-deeds and formularies, whether it's the Articles or the Westminster Catechism it doesn't make any difference, in that proportion you've got to be able to point to some central seat of authority which can decide how far it's legitimate for you to go.

MR. WAYNE. Oh, my dear McNairne, I'm not going to embroil myself in the disputes of your theologians North of the Tweed; I should be putting my head into a hornet's nest. But, fortunately for us, in the Southern kingdom we stuck to the episcopate; and any question about what's legitimate and what isn't can be left in the hands of the bishops; they're the umpires, you see.

THE PROVOST (*fidgeting in his chair*). It's a great mistake to go hunting about for authority in religion. Before you know where you are, you've committed yourself more deeply than you meant to. My advice to young men is always to take things as they come, and not to worry about ultimate justifications.

MR. FANSHAWE. I don't follow the ecclesiastical news very closely, though I do sometimes see a copy of the *Guardian*. But didn't I hear some story that the Church Association, whatever that body may be, is proposing to bring an action against the Bishop of Lincoln, for behaving illegally in conducting some service or other?

MR. WAYNE. I don't think it will ever come into Court. But in any case, that only concerns the behaviour of one individual bishop; I was speaking of the bishops acting and consulting jointly, as a college. Of course there have been heretical bishops before now; anybody knows that. But it's the general sense of the episcopate that's our safeguard.

MR. McNAIRNE. And that's reasonable. Only, you see, there's just this difficulty still to be considered; where do they get their authority from? We should say it was from below, from the consent of the governed. But I expect you'd be more likely to say it came from above; there's not much sense in prelacy otherwise. Your Church Association fellows would tell us it came from the Queen; but I suppose you'd be hardly likely to agree with them there? More especially as her Majesty is by way of being a sound Presbyterian when she's in Scotland.

MR. WAYNE. You've got that right first time, McNairne; we shouldn't say it came from her Majesty, though she does have the appointing of the bishops. We should say it came to the bishops directly from God.

MYSELF. . . .

MR. FANSHAWE. My dear Wayne, what a refreshing change of heart! Because when you first came here you were wanting us to subscribe, if I remember rightly, to pay the legal expenses of some clergymen who were fighting an action against their bishops. But of course they were wrong.

MR. WAYNE. Obviously if the bishops don't use their spiritual authority, and fall back on calling in the police, they cannot expect to be obeyed as bishops.

MR. FANSHAWE. But if they did all put their heads together, and came to the conclusion that incense was wrong, incense would be wrong? I mean, there's just the chance that they might, isn't there?

MR. WAYNE (*with a rather ghastly smile*). My dear chap, the bishops of one part of the Catholic Church can't simply abolish ceremonies that are customary in the whole Church. Where East and West are agreed, we fall back on an appeal to the Church generally.

MR. BATTERSBY. That's right, Sir, don't give up incense for anybody. It has such a deliciously decadent smell. And a Christianity which doesn't suggest decadence loses half its appeal at once.

MR. MCNAIRNE. Do you know, Wayne, I sometimes find your thought very difficult to follow. I imagined just now we were to take it from you that the bishops of this country, or perhaps on state occasions the bishops of the Anglican communion generally, were in a position to deal with any doctrinal problem that might arise. Now it appears that the Roman Catholics and those curious Eastern people are to hold a watching brief for orthodoxy all the time. I don't mean to be eristic about all this, but do you ever consult them about their views on the criticism of the Old Testament?

MR. WAYNE. Hang it all, McNairne, you really mustn't expect a cut-and-dried answer to everything. There's a lot in what the Provost says; a healthy, living organism rejects what is unsuitable to its development by a sort of automatic process; it's useless to ask exactly why or on what principle or by what authority it retains this, discards that. After all, the Church of England isn't a scheme that's been worked out on paper, like one of those undergraduate societies which draw up long lists of rules beginning " That this Society shall be called the Browning Society ", or whatever it may be. It's a thing that has grown up and taken its mould from history, like— like Oxford. Oxford isn't a thing you can reduce to a chemical formula. If somebody asks you why it's a good thing to have been up at Oxford, or what exactly Oxford stands for, or what determines the evolution of its thought and its history, you can't give him an answer in black and white; the whole subject is too elusive. Let me put it in this way. Do you know that place in

Wytham Woods, where you can look between the trees, and get a view of Oxford which hides the railway station and all the vulgarities of the modern city, isolating, by a kind of fortunate abstraction, the spires and the towers and all the Oxford that one wants to remember?

MR. BATTERSBY. I know. Very much like that key-hole near Santa Sabina, isn't it, where you look through and see the dome of St. Peter's hung in mid-air, like a really jolly soap-bubble?

MR. WAYNE. I dare say. Anyhow, I was there the other day, and this sense of abstraction was heightened by an accident of the weather; some effect of mist cut off from view all that they rested on, and left the spires and towers floating, so it seemed, in the air. Well, one doesn't want to sentimentalize over that sort of thing; but, you know, it did somehow make me think of the past—I wonder how many people have stood there in days gone by, and felt the same emotion? There was Godstow nunnery, with its grey stone basking in the sun-light; and Binsey with its miraculous well; the spire of St. Mary's and Carfax and Magdalen and Merton, and Tom Tower with the Cathedral shewing behind it, and the Sheldonian and the Camera and the City Church. I couldn't help reflecting, as I looked at all that, how inevitably we in Oxford are bound to our past; how the old Oxford of medieval days is still a part of ourselves, and we part of it,—the associations and the traditions of the place are so intertwined that you feel, like a living thing, the continuity of its history.

MR. FANSHAWE. I didn't know one could see Godstow from Wytham Woods.

MR. WAYNE. I dare say I didn't see it from that exact spot, but I suppose the memories of my walk had accompanied me. Anyhow, that was the feeling I got; trite enough, I'm afraid, but it does illustrate, I think, what I'm trying to say about the Church of England and its formularies. Suppose we received, in Oxford, a visit from some inhabitant of the planet Mars—a bargee, perhaps, Roberts, from one of those canals you were telling us about—and he asked me to tell him what precisely was the constitution of the Church of England, and what were its doctrines, how could I explain it to him? My dear fellow (I should say), you mustn't think of everything in terms of canals. I should take him by train to Banbury, and point out the difference there is between the canal—artificial, commercially useful, quite stagnant—and the river with its delicate bends and loops, the result of centuries spent in tunnelling through the soil, its unequal flow, swirling rapids alternating with silent pools, its tangled screen of willows. There (I should say), the Church of England is something like that; a natural growth, not a design thought out in men's minds and prepared to a formula. Don't you think I should be right?

MR. ROBERTS. Well, of course, if there are canals on Mars (and we don't know anything about it), the visitor might just possibly know that canals aren't stagnant, but have to have a flow of running water in them. If he happened to know a little about terrestrial history, he might feel inclined to ask whether the English Reformation wasn't in fact an attempt to canalize the Christian religion, and whether it wouldn't be more accurate to compare the Church of Rome to the original river. But most of all, I think he would be likely to draw your attention to the railway you were travelling on, and point out that, since it came into existence, both canal and river were to all intents and purposes useless.

MR. WAYNE. Well, perhaps my canal wasn't a very happy illustration; let's go back to Oxford. I suppose it's impossible to look at a view of Oxford like that Wytham one without being reminded of the passage in Arnold's essay. You remember how he speaks of Oxford as having " given herself so often to causes not mine, only never to the Philistines ", isn't it? Well, anybody can see that Oxford has changed with the centuries, is changing all the time. And yet, " never to the Philistines ", there is a continuity of instinct running all through her history, which makes her always react in a certain way, just as an organic thing, however many changes it passes through, maintains itself by reacting in a uniform way towards its environment. Something unanalysable, but it's there!

MR. ROBERTS. My dear Wayne, I can't say I call the record a very impressive one. Apparently Arnold had to admit that Oxford had boxed the compass in every conceivable direction, except that it had never given itself to the Philistines; by which he seems to have meant that it was always ready to throw a brick at anybody who suffered from the disadvantages of a scientific education. Surely that is rather a negative kind of continuity? And if it is only that kind of continuity which your Church of England possesses, I don't feel any very abject admiration for your Church of England.

MR. PEARS-SMITH. Roberts doesn't do justice to your parable, Wayne; but then, I don't think one could have expected him to. The doubt that occurred to me was quite of a different kind; I was wondering whether you weren't begging the question a bit by drawing attention to the external, visible monuments of Oxford as one sees them from outside. Of course, *they* are unchanged; that is simply a matter of bricks and mortar. In the same way, there is an obvious brick-and-mortar continuity about the Church of England, which nobody in his senses would deny; Canterbury Cathedral is Canterbury Cathedral still. But surely the ideal continuity, whether of Oxford or of the Anglican Church—and mind you, I believe in it—ought to be something that springs from the inner life of the institution; and to impress the imagination with a vision of spires and towers is hardly fair. Let me put the whole question in a different way. Roberts was telling us about a man called Tainter who's invented what he calls a graphophone, and another man called Edison who's invented what he calls a phonograph. I gather they're slightly different from one another, but each has the same effect—to record sounds on a sensitive instrument which can reproduce those sounds afterwards as often as you like; isn't that it? Well—supposing that some contemporary scientist, Dr. Dee, let us say, had invented such an instrument in the sixteenth century; and that Sir Piers Collett had secretly installed one behind the panelling of this Common-room, wound up in such an ingenious way that it would record the conversation of the fellows in this room, say once every fifty years. And suppose that a chap who was mending the electric light had come across those records, I think they're called, as it might be yesterday. It would be of the highest interest, naturally, to historians like myself. But what impression should we get as we sat and listened to them? What should we think of the old dons? Should we find them exercised over the same problems, *mutatis mutandis* of course, which exercise us, and giving the same answers that we give? Or should we have to admit that really we have nothing in common with them; that it is only the oak panelling which goes on and does not change, while the men who sit under it are changing, beyond hope of recovery, all the time?

THE PROVOST (*missing the point rather*). I do not expect much of Mr. Edison's invention. No doubt it will catch on for a time, as any new toy will; but I think a man of science should devote himself to more important work.

MR. WAYNE. Yes, but, Provost, you haven't answered Pears-Smith's question. You must have read the Poet Laureate's latest, "Locksley Hall Sixty Years After"; do you think that, if our memories went back in the way Pears-Smith has been suggesting, we should find ourselves in sympathy, or out of sympathy, with the talk of bygone times?

THE PROVOST. My memories of the College do go back fifty years; not sixty quite. Old Watson was Provost then, and he could remember the French Revolution breaking out. I don't think I should feel at home if I were back there now, Wayne; Oxford was full of ecclesiastical gossip in those days, and party feeling ran very high; it was a regrettable state of things. And I dare say if we went back further we should fare worse; they were a lazy set of people, the old dons, and I should think they talked about very little except politics and vintages. In any case, no institution ought to live by an appeal to its past; it must grapple with the needs of the day as it sees them.

MR. FANSHAWE. It may be only a fancy of mine, but I've always thought I ought to have lived a hundred years ago. What a good time the dons must have had, when they had nothing to do and nobody expected them to do it! If we had their talk preserved for us on the graphophone, I suspect we should have to cut it down a bit before it would be suitable for Wayne's ears. And all parsons, too, in those days.

MR. MCNAIRNE. Aren't we rather losing sight of Smith's point? He didn't ask which period would have been the best to live in, but whether we should recognize a kind of continuity between the College as it was and the College as it is. My own opinion, for what it's worth, is that you'd have to go back a hundred and fifty years to reach the period at which Oxford said good-bye to its past—and perhaps the Church of England too, for that matter. I would say Charles Stuart was the end of the old world, and David Hume the beginning of the new.

MR. PEARS-SMITH. I know, it's hard to think of them as contemporaries. But then, I don't believe in the break. If I did, I'd put it fifty years earlier still. Oddly, I think James the Second is the link between the old world and the new; his religion a hundred and fifty years behind the times, and his policy of toleration a hundred and fifty years ahead of them. But I don't say that I'd have liked to be a fellow in 1688; Oxford must have been an uncomfortable sort of place, whatever your politics were.

MR. WAYNE. Yes, if I wanted to find cronies I'd go back to the earlier half of the century, before the Civil War; 1638 would just do me. That was the golden age, before Locke ever gave rise to McNairne, or Boyle to Roberts, when there was real learning going about, and the Church was fiercely loved and loyally served. It was the Oxford men of those days who prevented the Church of England from being swamped by Puritan ideas, and becoming a sect among the sects.

MR. BATTERSBY. But what hideously grim company they must have been, the Laudian divines! Quite as grim, to judge by their writings, as the wretched Puritans they persecuted, but having to pretend they approved of the cakes and ale, just as the modern curate has to pretend he is interested in foot-ball, for the sake of his boys' club. No, give me John Donne; he must have been at Oxford when the Armada was about; what an age to live in, when you could be a successful churchman with such a dirty mind as his! I think Oxford ceased to be Oxford when the scholar gipsy left it; and Arnold, if he'd had any sense, would have realized that the place has been in the hands of the Philistines ever since.

MR. ROBERTS. Well, there's no room for me to go back another fifty years, because I understand Simon Magus didn't exist then. So I'll part company with the rest of you by projecting myself fifty years into the future, which perhaps after all is my right period. I've faith enough to believe that by that time Oxford will be——

NOTE ON CHAPTER VIII

The memory of the interlocutors in the conversation just reproduced is still green; one or two of them survive, though only Mr. Roberts appears, now on the list of resident fellows. It might seem, therefore, unnecessary to recall their fame to the reader's memory. But, in browsing through the pages of an old review, published a little after the War and preserved, heaven knows by what accident, among my papers, I came across an anonymous piece, headed " The Dons of Salisbury ", which is so plainly relevant to my theme that I must not omit to quote it. There can be no doubt, in the mind of a contemporary, as to the identities of those who are described under pseudonyms. I have no means of tracing the authorship; were the style more exquisitely polished, I would cherish the belief that it was an early essay of Mr. Harold Nicolson's.

" I remember with some shame my first introduction to Leadbetter "—obviously Fanshawe. " It was at a meeting, held in his rooms, of some minor literary society; the Milton, perhaps, or the Shaftesbury. I never found much exhilaration in listening to the result, mildly tentative or blandly self-confident, of the announcement that Mr. So-and-so would read a paper. Indeed, I have no idea who was, on that occasion, the reader of the paper, or what (if anything) he talked about. I can only remember the odd circumstances that every now and then, in the middle of a paragraph, he would suddenly say, ' Oh, no, I didn't mean to read that bit,' and would shuffle the loose pages in front of him with a nervous gesture till his eye lit on something he really did mean. Heaven only knows what a wealth of immature speculation this diffidence of his must have spared us; to judge by the Sibylline torso which actually got across, the unexpurgated edition would have been a martyrdom to his audience.

But, as I say, I hadn't gone there to listen to the paper. I had gone there because it was being read in Leadbetter's rooms, and I wanted to see Leadbetter. He didn't really approve of undergraduates; he treated them as if they were a pardonable mistake. 'I don't like to see you walking over the grass,' he would say to them, when they permitted themselves the one delinquency dons really mind about. 'To walk on good grass is an art, and you haven't got it.' But there was a tiny coterie of favoured specimens whom he seemed not to tolerate merely but in some odd way to like; I suppose the president of the society, a young man whose languor was such that his chair seemed inconsolable when he rose to his feet, must have been one of them. I sat in a very remote corner behind a pile of cigarette-stubs, banana-skins, and lumps of skim that had been removed from the coffee-cups, heaped together on the kind of table which apologizes for its existence by protesting that it is only occasional. I watched Leadbetter. His features were finely chiselled, except that the chin was a thought too gross; the lips slightly parted, as if in ridicule of the remark you were just going to make; a slight collection of stubble in the cleft of his chin shewed that he had reached the age when men begin to shave a trifle uncertainly. You would have put him down for a successful barrister; a cross (I have sometimes thought since) between M. Delbos and Kemal Ataturk. He was fast asleep. . . ." (Here I have taken the liberty of omitting two paragraphs, which are entirely devoted to furniture-chat.)

"When the paper was finished, or when the reader of it had been unable to lay his hand on any more paragraphs suitable for general consumption, a discussion followed in the immemorial manner of Oxford, conducted almost entirely by Rhodes scholars. I wonder who did the talking at societies before the Rhodes bequest? The prevailing attitude of the speakers was one of heavy disagreement with a number of things which the reader had not said. The heat and haze had become so intense that a public-spirited member rose and opened the window behind him, letting in that confused sound of hunting-noises, owls and distant bells which haunts over Oxford at night-time. At last it was all over, and to my intense embarrassment Leadbetter himself came upon me bending down in appreciation of a very fair Fragonard print. I suppose I can say that in those days my education had begun; but I had not yet seen through Fragonard. I was not, as I should be nowadays, looking at it in order that my host should catch me at it. He said something which I couldn't hear; I was too nervous to ask him to repeat it, and fell back on a formula which can be recommended, though it sometimes lets you down, 'That's what I've been wondering about all the evening'. To this day I do not know what it was he said, but he seemed hugely delighted with my answer, and asked me to dine with him in Hall the following Sunday. All the way back to College I seemed to tread on air; two very drunk Bullingdon men pushed me off the pavement into the gutter, but I didn't mind. I was going to dine with Leadbetter.

I called at his rooms the next Sunday, with nervous over-punctuality. He came out of his bed-room, and greeted me—dons always do on such occasions—in his shirt-sleeves. I have a very fair memory for braces, and could have told you, at the time, a good deal about the secrets which lurked behind the coat-lapels of eminent scholars. Leadbetter's, I remember, were mauve, and seemed to work by a curious system of interdependent pulleys which gave him the air of a Heath Robinson drawing. One didn't drink sherry, in those days; I stood gazing in some discomfort at the printed notices stuck into the looking-glass over his mantel-piece, while he finished his toilet off-stage, humming to himself as lonely people do. He took me into a dark ante-room, where dons were struggling with the sleeves of their gowns, and introduced me to several by names which, in my acute nervousness, I either misheard or forgot. Then we went into Hall.

I hate facing the audience when I sit at High Table. Undergraduates with whom you are acquainted catch your eye, and register surprised recognition. I could fancy them saying to one another 'What's he dining with Ledders for?' The supposed enquiry derived added point from the circumstance that Leadbetter was taking no notice of me at all. He sat staring at the menu, sighing gently over its contents like a man who had been hoping against hope that *this* Sunday, anyhow, it would be different. Beyond him (he sat at the end of the table, opposite the Warden) was a man gownless like myself; not a fellow, then; I had been introduced to him by some name so ordinary that it refused to stick in the memory, and put him down for purposes of classification as Query Higgins. He must, I conjectured, be the guest of Lamplough, who sat next to him; Lamplough was all right—I had met him in Sligger's rooms, and we smiled at one another with that insecure presumption of intimacy one reserved for people one had met in Sligger's rooms. Beyond him, I think, was a clergyman of a neutral tint, who for some unaccountable reason appeared to find his soup too hot." (Lamplough, by the way, is almost certainly Pears-Smith.)

"I don't know why I conceived such an immediate distaste for the philosopher who sat next me. He was a man of kindly intentions, and it was not his fault if he was a philosopher. But his eyes, which were large and glazed, had a trick of looking at you as if he disapproved of you, and was certain that your next remark was going to give you away. This in itself would have been distressing enough to a shy undergraduate, dining with an apparently dumb host at a High Table which was supposed to be the most brilliant in Oxford. But he made it worse by asking questions; not the ordinary exchanges of small-talk, but leading questions about life in general, questions which sounded as if they had a catch in them. He seemed to have no other conversational technique than that of the viva. Also he was a Scot, and the slight traces he preserved of his native speech added a touch of theological odium to his apparent disapproval; one felt one was going to be excommunicated at the next Kirk session, for not being a philosopher, and for not being at Salisbury." (This was clearly McNairne; he held his fellowship till the War.)

"He began, for instance, by asking me whether I approved of sleeping with one's windows shut. I found it impossible to believe that he was appealing to me as an expert; it was not for me to regulate the hygienic caprices of Bardwell Road. No, it was I who was being weighed in the balances; I was to stigmatize myself, in his estimation, as the sort of fool who takes risks with draughts, or as the sort of degenerate young man who likes fug. The latter, probably, or why did he use the word 'approve'? I have always found something unforgivable in the assumption that cold baths and things like that imply moral superiority. I said something rather flat about the difficulty of getting to sleep if your rooms faced the Garden Quad. There was a short silence, during which the Caledonian was obviously marking me by some internal process; beta minus, I feared. Then he said, 'Do you think one can be said to enjoy sleeping?' This was worse than ever; I was being betrayed into a philosophical discussion. For some reason, this new turn in the conversation arrested the attention of Query-Higgins, who bent eagerly over the table without saying anything. As he did so his shirt-front, which was not built to stand any sudden access of emotion, came loose from its mother-of-peal moorings with a gentle pop, such as one makes by squeezing a fuchsia bud. It was a fortunate circumstance for me, because it left Lamplough free to join in the conversation. Evidently he was accustomed to my neighbour's method of approach, and mercifully prepared to knock up his blade when it threatened a fatal assault. 'Cameron,' he said. 'They're offering you the sherry.' Then he made some friendly remark about Sligger. I was saved.

By this time, Leadbetter had finished his contemplation of the menu, and put it down with the gesture of a man who is resigning himself to the invariable. He began to talk, not fixing me with his eye like my other neighbour—indeed, his gaze was mostly reserved for one or two undergraduates at the other end of Hall, who were throwing bread at one another with a kind of forced bonhomie—but letting a remark drop now and again in a gentle tenuous voice that encouraged confidences. He asked about my family and my friends at home; he seemed to know everybody in a detached sort of way, and to be a living register of births, deaths and marriages. He talked a little about pictures, since a picture had been our introduction; looking back, I should suppose he had a sound if rather unadventurous taste; at the time, he left me gasping. In fact, he talked, and let me talk, about a quantity of things; and for myself I played up to him feverishly, not only because I liked the overtones of his conversation, but because I was in dread of Cameron getting in some more questions. Not more than two, I felt, of Cameron's questions should be attempted. At Oxford entertainments there is, fortunately, no hostess to reshuffle the conversation just when it is falling into an interesting series of duologues. Leadbetter and I talked. At intervals, Query-Higgins would turn round as if to 'chip in'; but the gentle explosion of his shirt-front, going off like a maroon in an air-raid, warned us not to look at him.

There was one subject that recurred in Leadbetter's conversation, yet was never mentioned without a kind of nausea; and that was Oxford. When he heard what school I was reading, he said, 'Well, I suppose it can't do you much harm', like a doctor reluctantly permitting the use of alcoholic stimulants. When I mentioned one of the women's colleges, 'Let us think', he suggested, 'of happier things'. When I referred to a Union debate I had attended (I think it was the one at which Winston Churchill and 'F.E.' were visitors), he winced slightly and told me he had not been to the place for years; 'some of the young men obviously don't mean what they say, others sound as if unaccountably they did, and I don't know which kind makes me shudder more despairingly'. When I asked (foolishly enough) what was his favourite building in Oxford, he reflected for a moment and said he supposed the summer-house in Merton garden was 'rather prootty'. I got the impression, somehow, that he had never really had any vocation to the academic life, but had slipped into a fellowship as a young man, following the line of least resistance; that the inertia which the place breeds had held him, since then, an unwilling captive, and that he hated the place as a man will hate some degrading *amour* which he lacks the energy to relinquish.

Cameron, of course, took these criticisms to heart much more than I did. Not that I supposed he had any great love for Oxford; indeed, I didn't put him down as a great lover, somehow; but the expression of any strong prejudice obviously gave him the fidgets. Whenever he wasn't occupied with the man on his right he was listening, on a half-turn, to Leadbetter; he would make little starts, now and again, like a kitten waiting to spring, when he thought Leadbetter was going to reach the end of a sentence and give him an opening. But it seldom came off; Leadbetter knew his man, and always wasn't looking at him at that psychological moment when you must catch the man's eye, or you can't say it. I suppose Cameron got through his guard about four times; once was when he had committed himself to the statement that Oxford was a kind of isolation hospital, in which the English nation was well advised to segregate all the people who were intelligent enough to prove a nuisance if they went into public life. 'Would you say, Leadbetter,' asked Cameron, 'that the theoretical life has no value at all?' Leadbetter's reply was, I suppose, rude, but really it seemed fair enough to use any weapon in dealing with Cameron. 'I don't think that's a proper form of question,' he said. 'What I say is all very carefully thought out; and I don't like to have it invented for me by other people. I shouldn't, as a matter of fact, say it in Common Room, because I know it's the sort of thing you, Cameron, would be wanting to argue about. I hate arguing.' 'I agree with you, Sir,' said Query-Higgins unexpectedly, as he coaxed out the mother-of-pearl with a determined expression. 'Waste of time, that's what I always say.' I suppose he must have made other remarks during the evening, but this was the only one audible to me.

I only once met Leadbetter again; it was in Paris, at the Gare du Nord, when I was over there for the Peace Conference." (Two fascinating paragraphs are here omitted, as not bearing strictly on my theme.) "He had been working somewhere in the outlying filaments of that extraordinary spider's web the Foreign Office became during the War, and was now engaged, as far as I remember, in repatriating Armenians. He seemed to have shrunk a little, but his carriage was still erect, and that distinguished presence of his still imposed itself; his porter, I could see, had got him mixed up with Lord Balfour, and was wreathed in confidential smiles. We exchanged our news; Leadbetter still full of births, deaths and marriages, but principally deaths. I asked whether he would go back to Oxford when the Armenians had been returned to store, or whether he was tired of it. 'I have been tired of it,' he explained 'for nearly fifty years, but I know I shall go back. Whenever I get inside Paddington Station I take a ticket there automatically; sometimes I have had to give it back to the booking-clerk. The port, at least, should be tolerable; they have been drinking very little of it. Excuse me if I get on board the train; these foreign trains do not start with the delightful pageantry of ours.' And then, as he climbed on board, 'There will be a lot of vacant fellowships now, you know; if they offer you one, don't take it.'

'I don't suppose,' I said, 'that I shall.' "

CHAPTER IX

IN WHICH I WAKE UP

"—A PLACE no reasonable person should be expected to live in." I woke up, with a guilty start, from the last of my dreams, to hear these words addressing themselves to my waking consciousness. For a moment, I thought I was still dreaming, because they seemed to complete the last sentence of what I had heard the dons saying in 1888. Then I reflected that it was a somewhat lame kind of completion; perhaps coincidence had been at work. I looked up at the speaker, and found that it was old Roberts, who has been a science tutor at Simon Magus ever since anyone can remember. He grumbles, I think, at everything, except during those long intervals of Common-room life in which he says nothing at all. I wasn't interested to know whether he was talking about the traffic nuisance, or the degeneracy of the modern undergraduate, or the inadequacy of the grants which the University makes for scientific research; they are all favourite themes with him. But I knew he was the only living link that bound Simon Magus of to-day with that other Simon Magus I had been dreaming of; and the link seemed frail and inconspicuous.

It was plain, now, what influence had awakened me. In the growing heat of the room, some public benefactor had opened a window; and through that window selections from the music of *Snow-white* were pouring in, reproduced in a very raucous manner by an undergraduate's gramophone. That discussion, then, of Edison's invention which was still echoing down the empty passages of my mind was only something to be expected; it marked the familiar point at which external reality begins to invade our dreams, but can do so at first only by clothing itself in their imagery. And if the dons of 1888, as I had last dreamt of them, had turned self-conscious and were beginning to talk about what it would have felt like to live in still earlier times, that was because reason and the memories of waking reality had begun to assert themselves against the free play of mere imagination. I had dreamt, and woken as men wake from their dreams.

Somebody said, "Bill, you're supposed to be dean of this place; why the hell can't you persuade the young men to put a green-baize cover on their lousy instruments when they live just over the Common-room?"

The dean of Simon Magus is sleek and lackadaisical; some say, affected. "My dear Eustace," he said, "one can't stop people doing things. That's Carruthers, of course; I'm always fining him, but he's so rich that he doesn't mind. I shall probably haul him to-morrow for playing his gramophone out of hours; he will say that he didn't know the time, or that a friend from another College came in and played it while he was out. But for the Lord's sake don't imagine that I shall speak to him severely about interfering with the amenities of the fellows' Common-room. We don't count, nowadays; we just exist on sufferance. That comes of trying to be kind to the young men and calling them by their Christian names and all that. They have forgotten to believe in the legend that dons do a great deal of work, and mustn't be disturbed on any account."

At this point my host returned, voluble in his apologies and in his anathemas over the cheap night-rate for telephoning. His return coincided with a movement which threatened to be a general exodus; there was a meeting, it seemed, at the Town Hall, which was to be addressed by some politician or other on the Menace of Spain. Remote spiritual descendant of Mr. Richards! And not less dreary, I suspect, than he. But the dons of Simon Magus are, for the most part, laboriously progressive, revolving monotonously on the Oxford-Moscow axis; and they like to register attendance when Freedom shrieks, though it be at the most unconscionable hours. Some, as is the way of dons, walked out of the room suddenly without saying good-night to anybody, some lingered over apologetic farewells; but within a quarter of an hour the company was reduced to small and sociable dimensions. Apart from myself and Mordaunt, only half-a-dozen remained; and these grouped themselves around the fire-place in the very attitudes, as I thought, of the personages in my dream. Is it possible that our dreaming self reaches forwards as well as backwards, and that my sub-consciousness had borrowed, from the yet unborn future, the stuff of its imaginings? Or should it rather be supposed that our waking thoughts, without meaning to, falsify retrospect; that we come to believe we have dreamt thus and thus, influenced more than we know by subsequent impressions? Anyhow, it seemed to me that old Roberts was sitting just where the Armada Provost had sat, and Dr. Taverner, and after him Mr. Lilly; then Provost Trumpington, then Jonathan Shillett, then the egregious Watson, then Dr. Telford. And the others seemed to occupy familiar stations; I, too, was at my old post of disadvantage; only now my words did not stick in my throat as when I sat dreaming, but I was able to contribute (as will be seen) to the discussion which raged among my contemporaries.

Some account is due to the reader of these interlocutors, " and which they weren, and of what degree ", before I beg his leave to reproduce our conversation, as before, in dramatic *format*. Roberts, whom I have already mentioned, is a museum piece, an elderly don with those eccentricities we are prepared to forgive in elderly dons, but without that air of distinction you find (for example) in a Fanshawe. His long, rather scanty grey hairs are the frame to a face which suggests a secret sorrow when it is in repose; when you talk to him, he looks up at you with a sudden fear in his eyes, like a school-boy who is afraid of being ragged if he opens his mouth. His own utterances are blurted out with something of defiance in their tone; and he has a nervous trick of prefacing them, regardless of appropriateness, with the formula " Of course ". He is unmarried, and very much a recluse; he never seems to take any interest in the individual undergraduate, but he can outline for you the career of anybody who has matriculated at Simon Magus since the 'eighties; he is always on the College barge when a race is being rowed, but is never heard to make any comment. That science is the Cinderella of Oxford studies is an old conviction with him; you can put acres of ground under laboratories and not disabuse him of it.

A scientist also, but altogether of a different calibre, is Professor Beith; to give him his full title, the Rolls-Royce Professor of Genology. From casual encounters, he and I have a nodding acquaintance which is, I suppose, exquisitely tedious to both of us; we are always meeting in the street and having to salute one another, without any common background or the most rudimentary interest in each other's affairs. When I get into my compartment in a journey to London, he is usually there; we smile and say nothing, though once I went so far as to supply him with a match. He has nothing whatever to do with Simon Magus, so far as his work or his interests are concerned; but his Chair, which is of recent foundation, is combined in the modern fashion with a fellowship at that College, and he has a voice in its councils. He was bred, I think, at a Scottish University, and has held posts in Newcastle and Liverpool; he approaches Oxford somewhat from the angle of the Woodstock Road, where his wife dispenses hospitality on Sunday afternoons. The nature of the researches he conducts is obscure; perhaps only understood by himself, and one or two battered Colonials who frequent his laboratory. I did not know that he held strong views about science and its place in the scheme of things until I heard him take part, that night, in a general conversation.

Drechsel I had not met before, though I had become accustomed to the sight of him in my daily walks without being able to put a name to him; he does the economics lecturing at Simon Magus, and I think some of the history for Modern Greats as well. He is pleasant-looking, sandy-haired and freckled, but not somehow impressive; if you met him dressed for tennis you would take him for a suburban clerk, brisk but unimaginative. As a matter of fact he is (my host informed me) nothing less than Dictator of Great Britain in his day-dreams; he has a remedy mapped out for every social evil, plans for redistributing everything and pulling almost everything down so as to rebuild it somewhere else. He comes from Canada, but has been so long in Oxford that his speech hardly betrays him; for some reason, he has a mysterious vendetta against Roberts, and frequently says in an undertone at College meetings, "That man ought to go". I should have expected him to make his way, with the rest, to the Town Hall; but it appeared that the politician who was addressing the gathering held slightly different views about social remedies, and is put down by Drechsel as a charlatan.

Langdale is not, properly speaking, a fellow of Simon Magus nowadays, for the chair he holds—I think it is called the Martha Smail Professorship of Logology—involved the transferring of his allegiance to another foundation. But he had been, and still is, useful to the College in teaching the undergraduates such philosophy as they are capable of imbibing; he was allowed to keep his rooms, and is generally to be found at High Table. He was, I suppose, the senior member of the company next to Roberts. And, in some way which I feel a delicacy in explaining, he seemed to me the most old-fashioned. He belongs to a world in which philosophers were expected to go in for plain living as well as high thinking; took over the mantle of the clergy and practised, if only by way of setting a good example, that Puritanism which is the Englishman's substitute for asceticism. Langdale has never, I think, been to a cinema; he doesn't drink, doesn't bet, dresses badly as if on purpose; he wouldn't tell you that it is wrong to dance or to shoot, but you can see he regards such amusements, and a multitude of others, as a culpable waste of time. What his religious beliefs are, nobody has ever found out; it is certain that he goes to chapel, but the irreverence of his junior colleagues attributes this either to sheer love of mortification, or to a preference for being on the right side on the off chance that God might exist.

He had brought a guest with him; not a friend exactly, but a man he had been arguing with at some meeting of an obscure philosophical society; he is desperately broad-minded, and would never have you think that he dislikes you because he disagrees with you. This was a psychologist, a Cambridge man by origin and not belonging by preference to the academic world; I gathered that he lived in London and wrote books. He was introduced to me as Mr. Hartman, but

I am not certain how many N's the name should carry. I didn't like him much; I thought him rather unctuously polite in pretending to an intellectual inferiority which he obviously didn't feel. But I dare say this was only prejudice; Langdale assured me afterwards that he was a very interesting fellow, and Langdale always gives me an irritating impression of being right.

And then there was Peter Verey-Massingham, a fellow of another foundation; I couldn't quite make out whose guest he was, but he knows so many people in Oxford and dines out so much that you take him for granted everywhere. I always find a certain artistic pleasure in his conversation because in him the process of Oxfordization, if I may so call it, has really been complete; he seems to have been left without any illusions whatsoever. As a rule, you expect a man who has abandoned one set of beliefs to have picked up, in doing so, another set of beliefs which are scarcely more demonstrable; your crude materialist will prove to have a touching belief in the League of Nations, your Behaviourist suddenly launches out into a diatribe against the ugliness which defaces our English countryside. Verey-Massingham holds no briefs of his own, has no theory of life, no discoverable scale of values. The result is that, having an incorrigible love of argument, he will always take the opposite side to the one that is being put forward at the moment, and overtrumps the sceptic, whatever be his colour, with a scepticism yet more naked and profound. In all the conversation which followed, he took Langdale for his companion-in-arms, merely because his cause was the unpopular one; a circumstance which gave me a good deal of pleasure, knowing as I did how deeply Langdale disapproved of him.

They occupied the positions, often unconsciously they fell into the attitudes, of the old dons who had been the personages of my dream. Sometimes—I suppose I was still a little sleepy—the very expressions on their faces, the rise and fall of their voices, cheated me into the belief that I was back again among the figures of the past. Or at least that I was still dreaming; for there is something dream-like about our Oxford discussions, so remote are they from the crude actualities of life. Were we real people, I was tempted to ask myself; or was all this debate and speculation merely a backwash from the stress and urge of daily living, much as the psychologist would have told us that the greater part of our thoughts were only rationalizations of our unconscious desires? Once back in my own bed, in the great house over against Grampool, where the mill-stream washes down its memories of the old friars against the imperturbable stone wall that fringes Christ Church property, I found myself wondering whether I had been awake that evening after all.

So we sat and talked, while dusk closed in and the lights shone here and there in the windows of Simon Magus.

CHAPTER X

CHAOS: 1938

MORDAUNT. That blasted gramophone again! I wish somebody would tell me what you ought to do with a man like Carruthers. (*To Verey-Massingham.*) You don't know him, do you, Peter? I should have thought you would. He's quite charming, adequately athletic, and has none of the squalid vices. But I'm supposed to teach him, you see; and he's got the sort of mind you just can't establish any contact with. He sits in front of a book; I've seen him; but he doesn't begin to understand about working. The memory retains facts, and I suppose one or two formulas; but they don't colour his outlook; I'm not really sure that he has an outlook to colour. Ought we to take on those people at all, when they're just nature's thirds?

BEITH. That's the examination system; thank God, my men are all doing research. In my department, the whole thing works itself out quite simply; if a man's a dud, you spot it in less than a term, and you just tell him to go and read something else. Why can't you all do that, on an extended scale? Simply refuse to teach people if they're unteachable, and see how they like that.

MORDAUNT. Like it? You evidently don't know Carruthers.

BEITH. No, but seriously, why shouldn't it be up to a given undergraduate to find a tutor who will take him on? And if he can't, of course, he goes down. You'd hardly need examinations then. Education's nonsense, I've always said, unless there's some kind of bond between tutor and pupil.

MASSINGHAM. What a touching idea! You mean they ought to be soul-mates? And if at the end of a few terms the pupil seems to be slacking off, the tutor sends back all his essays tied up in pink ribbon, with a nice little note saying he sees he's made a mistake, and it will be better if they don't correspond in future. As a matter of fact, I haven't any bond at all with my pupils. If they seem hopeless, I'm very, very rude to them, and tell them they will plough. Which makes them so angry that they quite often pass, simply to spite me. I think kindness is wasted on the young.

LANGDALE. I don't think it's so much a question of passing and ploughing, or even of people slacking—one isn't responsible for that. The difficulty is about the people who simply don't take polish; they work like blazes sometimes and you pull their essays to pieces and shew them exactly where they were wrong, but it's all like painting without a medium—nobody's fault, only the thing doesn't take. There's something that just isn't there.

HARTMAN. Or possibly, don't you think, something that *is* there? Something, I mean, that oughtn't to be? Don't you ever find yourself up against that positive hostility to knowledge which comes, we're beginning to think, from somewhere very deep in the sex-life?

MYSELF. But surely that's not what . . .

BEITH. Yes, but why bother about them? They oughtn't to be here, those people. They're keeping the real students out. It's like when you're in a hurry to get a ticket and some fool woman will keep chatting to the booking-clerk about which is the best train to Didcot next Wednesday.

ROBERTS. Of course, you've got to be sure the real students are *there*, waiting to be taught. Of course, the College rooms have got to be filled somehow.

MASSINGHAM. I know my outlook's all wrong; but I must say I find students rather a bore. I so much prefer undergraduates.

LANGDALE. You would say that.

MASSINGHAM. It dates you rather, Langdale, that habit of identifying the characteristic with the untenable. No, but seriously, Beith, if Carrutherses are prepared to pay for the privilege of being uneducated here, why shouldn't we let them? All these ornamental young men form a kind of puddle, in which you and your friends can make a culture of pure students. They don't do much harm, and when they've finished playing here they can go out like good little boys and govern the Empire.

MYSELF. *Sitientes ibimus Afros*—yes.

BEITH. Pardon?

MYSELF. Oh, it was just a quotation that came into my head.

LANGDALE. The point is surely, if there are people who won't take polish when you try to teach them the humanities, ought we to give them up and let somebody else give them technical education, turn them into chartered accountants and all that? Or ought we to go on and on at them, hoping that the little they pick up will do them a little good?

MORDAUNT. I think Roberts' point is the sound one. Here are all these damnably expensive sets of rooms, which have got to be filled somehow. Until the Government or Huntercombe have put down enough money to fill them with impecunious students, we've got to go on being the playground of the moderately rich. The humanities do 'em no harm, and it keeps them humble, don't you know, to see the clever people running away with the firsts. Examinations aren't infallible, but they do help to expose the bogus intellectual.

DRECHSEL. What it does is to keep alive the old social system. The handful of students we have here are the gold backing which gives currency to the paper value of the Oxford B.A. The public, which has just been taught to see through the nonsense about the Old School Tie, is taken in instead by the legend of the B.A. gown. Along those lines, we still produce a ruling caste; that's the defence of our present Oxford system—or its condemnation, according to the way you happen to look at it.

MASSINGHAM. Then you'd let the moderately rich go on here until the money dries up? Well, they *are* here; what are you going to do with them exactly? Let them what's called suck honey from every flower (except Beith, of course, who's only open to *bona fide* applicants)? Or do you put them all through a stiff course of P.P.E., to prepare them for the Dawn?

DRECHSEL. I must say I think it would be rather a good thing if everybody here had to take a fairly stiff prelim. in economics and political history before he started reading for any school. There's no harm in their having the glimmerings of citizenship.

MORDAUNT (*to Drechsel*). I hope I shan't live to see you dictator, J.D.

DRECHSEL. Oh, good Lord, if I were *dictator*, there wouldn't be any of that stuff going. Only the *samurai* would be allowed to hear about economics then. The ordinary citizen would just have to do what he was told, and the ordinary undergraduate would be picking up useful knowledge, not bothering about economics. My idea for a Civics Prelim. was only for the transition period, till we get a planned State.

LANGDALE. I see. You don't believe much in liberty, then?

DRECHSEL. Does anybody nowadays? One talks about democracy, of course, because it's a convenient antithesis to fascism; but obviously it won't be any use till it paves the way for the enlightened dictatorship we're all wanting; you can't go back to the Manchester School.

LANGDALE. Yes. I expect I'm old-fashioned. But what you don't seem to see is that if we did make all the men do your prelim. in—what was it? Oh yes, economics and political history,—you wouldn't be a bit further on. You wouldn't have turned them into good citizens, or anything like it. Lots of 'em take economics in Pass Mods now, and how much difference does it make to them? My point is, about seventy per cent of the men don't absorb anything from what they read; they just mug up things and forget them again. Your prelim. wouldn't turn them into good citizens, any more than Divvers used to turn people into good Christians, when people bothered about that sort of thing.

MASSINGHAM. My God, Langdale, d'you really think it's the idea of education to *turn* people into something? I mean, I should have thought that had always been a mistake, at the best of times. But in these days, my dear man, you simply can't do it. The ideal product of education used to be the apostolic man, who rowed for the Varsity and then went out to do foreign mission work. Now, it's the apostatic man, who gets bunked from his public school for revolutionary tendencies and finishes up in Chelsea. The apostatic man learns by reaction from everything he's taught, and despises his teachers. You can't *turn* him into something; he isn't plasticine, he's india-rubber. Good idea, that, to describe this as the Age of Rubber; I must work it out.

LANGDALE. I suppose it would be pedantic to ask what is exactly the difference between saying you turn a man into something, and describing him as a *product*?

MASSINGHAM. Oh, but there's all the difference in the world. Education produces people, in the mathematical sense; it just exaggerates the ideas they started with, that's all.

MORDAUNT. Or the ears they started with, perhaps?

BEITH. That's good, that's very good. Like donkeys, what? But, you see, that's where we scientists score; we don't set out to colour people's outlook; we don't mind whether they absorb things or not; we just want them to know, and train them a little, of course, to make use of the knowledge they've got, so as to make it lead to further knowledge. We don't expect our pupils to become missionaries, wanting to convert the inconvertible, or novelists, wanting to—to——

MASSINGHAM. Mention the unmentionable?

BEITH. That'll do; yes, excellent. Man's become what he is, if you come to think of it, by finding out things the other animals didn't find out; he's an inventive animal. And our idea of education is to make him more inventive still. It's rather like training dogs to hunt, you know; one simply encourages them to exercise their instinct for nosing things out, and at the same time warns them which are the cold scents, what's worth nosing out and what isn't.

MORDAUNT. But isn't it rather the question we've got to settle, what *is* worth nosing out? Do you think scientific research is the only worth-while form of research, or would you allow people to investigate historical documents, and classical antiquities, and one or two things like that?

MASSINGHAM. And, as Langdale would say, if so why?

BEITH (*with an apologetic smile, as of one smashing an idol without wishing to hurt its feelings*). Oh, well, you know, from the scientific viewpoint it's rather difficult to defend what you might call promiscuous research. Because I think we're coming to see more and more that intellect was given to Man as a weapon, if you see what I mean.

MYSELF. Yes, but who . . .

BEITH (*continuing*). I expect you'll disagree with this, Langdale; but if you look at the thing historically, surely the intellect, which is just a kind of super-cunning, has only survival-value in the first instance; it's meant to tell us when we ought to go to ground and when we ought to shin up a tree, and so on. And as long as Man goes on discovering fire, and the lever, and the wheel, and so on, he's all on the right track; and so on through Galileo and Boyle and Koch and Einstein. But once you start trying to acquire knowledge merely for the sake of knowledge, it's . . . well, strictly speaking, it's the abuse of a faculty.

MASSINGHAM. If Einstein isn't acquiring knowledge for the sake of knowledge, what the hell is he acquiring it for?

BEITH. Ah, well, you've got to think of Science, ultimately, as a single body of knowledge; it's all building up an accurate world-picture, and you never know what'll come in handy, so to speak. But when you set people down to research into the causes of the Peloponnesian War, or something of that sort, that isn't going to help the human race survive, is it? It's side-tracking the primary purpose of the intellect, that's my point. Of course, I don't say there's any harm in it; only it's rather playing about, from our point of view. Like a kitten chasing a ball of string, which hasn't the nutritive value of a mouse.

LANGDALE. And philosophy, I suppose, is just the cunning of a hunted animal run to seed, as it were?

BEITH. Well, really, Langdale, I would hardly have liked to put it in that way myself, but that does just express it.

MASSINGHAM. And I suppose one could extend that principle, and say that the human intellect remains true to its proper function when it devises all sorts of unpleasant ways of killing people in war? Like that thing of Dr. Watts, you know:

> "Your little hands were never made
> To tear each other's eyes—
> You'll do it better with the aid
> Which mustard gas supplies"—

something of that sort. I mean, I know some scientists explain that those jolly little inventions are only hit on by accident. But I suppose you'd rather take credit for them, wouldn't you?

BEITH. I'd never thought of mustard gas, I confess, as contributing to the survival of the human race.

MASSINGHAM. Oh, not the race as a whole; but surely it's all part of the same process? From the strictly scientific point of view, I shouldn't have thought there was much difference between spraying Flit on flies and spraying gas on Abyssinians. Just the survival of the Flittest. (*To Mordaunt.*) Sorry, Charles, were you going to say something?

MORDAUNT. I was only going to say, in Beith's defence, that he *has* put up a show—he has given us his idea of what education ought to be and do. None of the rest of us seems to *have* any idea. Have you, Peter?

MASSINGHAM. Good God, no! I go on telling the young what I'm paid to tell them, and trying not to bore them too much; I've no theories. Let's see; where are we? Beith says, Man is by nature a nosy animal, and it is the function of education to make him nosier and nosier. Only we ought to teach him, as we teach dogs—perhaps more ordinarily called hounds—which smells are worth-while and which are only red herrings. Who's next? J.D., I think you ought to tell us about this. You're a sort of Director of Programmes for the new age, aren't you?

DRECHSEL. You mean my theory of education for the *samurai*, the people who are really going to be in the inner ring? Or for the herd-people?

LANGDALE. Why not tell us about the herd-people? I mean, I suppose you'll have some citizens (as Plato had) who aren't in the inner ring precisely and yet are taught something that isn't just technical stuff?

DRECHSEL. Oh, yes, Oxford would still function. And I don't think I'd be inclined to follow the modern tendency, and turn it into a second technical University, on the model of Cambridge.

ROBERTS. I always said you people who get interested in politics are the most obscurantist devils of the lot. You'd starve the Labs, I believe, if you had the running of this place, worse than Langdale would.

DRECHSEL. Well, you see, that's only a question of rationalization. One would have to see how the thing worked out; but probably it would be more economical to concentrate all the scientific teaching at other universities, devoting (say) Birmingham to engineering, Leeds to medicine, and so on.

MYSELF. But doesn't " University " . . .

DRECHSEL (*continuing*). After all, I think we'd be less in danger of getting crowded out by foreign visitors and research students, if it were quite firmly understood that Oxford only undertook to teach the Humanities. Only of course one wouldn't mean by Humanities quite what's meant by the term now.

MORDAUNT. The classics, I suppose, would have disappeared?

DRECHSEL. Yes, I'm afraid they would. I don't see how one's to eliminate class-consciousness without eliminating classics-consciousness. God knows why it should be so, but as a matter of observation it seems to me quite certain that the whole legend of the " English gentleman " has been built up on Latin and Greek. A. meets B. on the steps of his club, and says, " Well, old man, *eheu fugaces*, what ? ", and B. says " *Dulce et decorum est pro patria mori* ", and the crossing-sweeper falls on his knees in adoration of two men who can talk as learnedly as that. Nobody can really explain the ridiculous prominence the classics still have in English education except by admitting that what saves them is their snob-value.

MORDAUNT. Do you include Ancient History as part of the classics?

DRECHSEL. Obviously. The trouble about Ancient History is that it's all ancient history. These researches into the origins of things (I'd include there the philological side of the language Schools) don't get you anywhere, and they're liable to make people absorbed in a moonstruck admiration of the past. History is only useful when it shews us how we've become what we are; and all the individualist period of history—that is, down to the French Revolution—would be learned by school-boys, I dare say, at an age when one has no head for anything except names and dates, but it wouldn't come into the Oxford course. We've got to get away, you see, from a wrong orientation of the mind.

LANGDALE. And philosophy? Would that be relegated to Hull, or would it disappear altogether?

DRECHSEL. I don't see what we'd want to keep philosophy for. It's quite out of place in Modern Greats as it is. Teach the mind to be doubtful about its own processes, and you hamstring its usefulness. To do any good, one must be sure of oneself.

MASSINGHAM. Yes, J.D., I can quite understand your saying that.

ROBERTS. Meanwhile, I take it that I should have been removed to a concentration camp somewhere in the Eastern counties, to teach science. May I ask whether science would be allowed to go on on its present lines? Because really——

DRECHSEL. Oh, on its present lines, yes. But your salary would be paid by a State grant; and a reasonably planned State would naturally keep a watch on the work you were doing and direct it, if necessary, into useful channels. I don't think, I confess, that you'd find much encouragement in building up what Beith calls a world-picture. There'd be too much practical stuff that wanted doing.

ROBERTS. Of course, I'd sooner be shot than teach on those terms.

LANGDALE. Do you know, J.D., I'd never quite realized why I believe in all the things that make Oxford Oxford till I heard your reasons for wanting to get rid of 'em. Honestly, I find it much easier to be patient with Beith, who thinks the human intellect is just a hoax, than with you, who admit that it has power to operate freely, and then propose to shut it up in a padded cell so that it shall never do anything of the kind.

BEITH. I don't think you're quite fair to my point of view. I shouldn't describe the human intellect as a "hoax" at all; I should only regard it as a tool which you can use properly or improperly. You can use a half-penny for opening a bottle of Perrier, but that isn't its proper use; it was meant to be a medium of exchange. Drechsel, it seems to me, is prepared to sacrifice both its improper and its proper use, on the altar of a political theory.

DRECHSEL. No, damn it, that's not a fair way of

putting it. All I'm doing with this urge for discovery is to utilize it, to harness it, so that it can be used in the interests of the hive, not of the individual insect. Surely that's scientific enough?

MASSINGHAM. But what I can't understand is why either of you should *mind* the intellect being used for other purposes than just helping us to survive? I mean, what's wrong with it?

BEITH (*rather uneasily, I thought*). Well, just what I've been saying; it's not what it's meant for.

MASSINGHAM. *Meant?* How d'you mean meant? Meant by whom? I never knew one of you scientists yet that didn't talk naked teleology if one took one's eye off him for two minutes in an argument. If you're going to believe in God, say so, and we'll talk about what he meant the intellect for. But if you're going to keep to plain matter of fact, what on earth's the sense of talking as if it were right to use our intellect in one way, and wrong in another? It's just words.

HARTMAN (*coming to Beith's rescue*). Well, you could say this, couldn't you—that the validity of our intellectual processes is guaranteed to us as long as we only make practical use of them? Because if you use them right, you survive; if you use them wrong, you disappear. The kind of people who thought climbing a tree was a good way of dodging a jaguar *may* have been right, of course, but they aren't alive to tell the tale. Whereas the question whether (say) Time has any absolute existence can't be decided by any such simple tests. You can answer Yes or No without any fatal results to yourself. Surely that makes a difference?

MASSINGHAM. Yes, but that doesn't justify Beith in talking about a proper and an improper way of using our intellects. The fact that our intellect happens to come in handy when it's a question of dodging a jaguar doesn't mean that that's the only use of it or the proper use of it; it's just a lucky accident. I may use my walking-stick to keep off a mad dog, but that's not what I carry it for. I carry it because I like it.

HARTMAN. Have you ever asked yourself why? Have you ever considered why it is that a man who can't find his walking-stick will be miserable the whole afternoon because he hasn't got it, or will even refuse to go out for a walk at all because he hasn't got it? To say that you "like" a thing when you can't even pretend to find a reason for your preference may mean getting into very deep waters. Suppose it were a race-memory, coming down from the days when dogs were madder, which makes you "like" carrying a stick?

LANGDALE. I should have thought there was a much more deep-rooted objection to Beith's line of argument. You do or you don't believe in the validity of inference. If you do, then you've already parted company with Beith and the Pragmatists. If you don't, then the fact that the intellect is useful in the struggle for survival, if it be a fact, is an isolated fact and nothing more. You cannot infer that that is the only use of the intellect, or the primary use of the intellect, or the proper use of the intellect, because it is no longer possible for you to infer anything.

HARTMAN. But if you find that reason, when it becomes abstract instead of merely practical, leads the mind irresistibly to two opposite conclusions which contradict one another?

LANGDALE. There's no reason to worry over that, unless you believe in the principle of contradiction. And if you believe in the principle of contradiction, you believe in abstract reasoning.

MORDAUNT. It seems to me you people won't ever agree about a syllabus of education for this neglected University until you can make up your mind about fundamentals. Surely what's bothering you is not that you don't agree about theories of education, but that you haven't got any common approach to life. Why not, if you must argue, argue about that? What is the proper approach to the mystery of existence? Which are the loose ends that lead nowhere, which is the authentic clue by which a man might hope, if he can follow it, to unravel the whole skein?

MASSINGHAM. You're quite right, Charles; that's what's worrying 'em.

MORDAUNT. But not you, I suppose, Peter?

MASSINGHAM. Oh Lord, no. I gave up the riddle long ago.

DRECHSEL. But what's all this about riddles and mysteries? You don't know anything of skeins, Mordaunt; you aren't married. The other day, my wife spent the whole evening trying to unravel her skein of wool, and then went to bed, telling me to get it out for her and not to sit up too late over it. Well, of course, as soon as she was gone I picked out one or two of the leading threads, and whenever I got near the tangle I cut the thread off with a pair of scissors. The actual core of the tangle had to be thrown into the fire, I admit that. Meanwhile I got five or six longish threads, and told my wife the shop must have made up the skein wrong. The whole thing only took about ten minutes. Well, I suppose my approach to life is the same. I don't try to solve mysteries; I ignore them. Human happiness is the only thing that matters, in the long run; and my idea is simply to hack at the mess on perfectly obvious lines till you've straightened it out, and made the world a possible place for the mass of men to live in.

LANGDALE. Chucking into the fire any elements in the complex that resist your methods of treatment? Well, I suppose your system would work if, as we were suggesting just now, you were a dictator; but as I was saying just now, I hope to God you never will be. Tell me one thing; I don't mean to be offensive; but do you believe in honesty? Do you believe in a duty of the mind to love truth, and do you despise a man who deceives his neighbour over something that's important?

DRECHSEL. No, on the whole, I don't think I do. What I mind is the selfishness which commonly leads people to deceive one another, and the cowardice or idleness which prevents nine men out of ten from looking facts in the face. Truth and honesty, I think, are cant terms as a rule.

BEITH. Hang it all, Drechsel, you can't mean that. Granted that there is a very small area of the truth that can be discovered—I'm all with you there—there is such a thing as truth, and it deserves to be told. Otherwise, if you'd been a medieval Pope, and thought it more important for people to be happy in the next world than in this, you'd have been justified in hushing up the Copernican system, for fear of disturbing simple people's minds.

MYSELF. But surely the Pope . . .

DRECHSEL. Oh, he was perfectly right from his own point of view. I'd hush it up to-morrow if I thought that would get us out of the silly mess our economics are in. Truth—what's truth?

MASSINGHAM. Does your wife dream much, J.D.?

BEITH. Well, I don't suppose I'm easily shocked, but really, Drechsel, I never expected to hear a fellow of the College talk like that. Of course I've never really examined the Communist theory——

MASSINGHAM. Communism isn't a theory; it's only the mood of the disinherited.

BEITH. Well, anyhow, I hope I'm not narrow-minded about politics; but really, if people are going to talk like Drechsel, all I can say is, we might as well be back in the Middle Ages. Whatever else knowledge is or involves, surely it means that truth does exist, and is something to which we must bow, not something we can bow to our own ends. That's my approach to life,

I suppose. Yours is too . . . too cold-blooded—no damn it, I don't mean that; too revoltingly smug. How can you keep alive, man, without feeling there's something outside you that's independent of you; that always must escape your control? I forget if you ever go round Addison's Walk in the afternoon? I generally meet you in the Meadows. Anyhow, I was going round Addison's Walk this afternoon, and I saw the fritillaries; they're early this year. You know the way they hit your eye suddenly, a kind of lake of purple and white where everything was green a week ago? Well, I'll tell you what it made me think of; it made me think of an Italian gardener I read of in some book or other, who said of a flower that was growing all over the place, "It flourishes like the thought of Man." That's a fine sentiment, Drechsel; and you'll find Man's thought will flourish in spite of you. It's not like the tulips in the garden there, that you can plant out in beds all at regular intervals, and they'll grow up as straight as ram-rods for you. It will take its own direction, not yours.

MASSINGHAM. I suppose the fritillaries do really grow wild in Addison's Walk? I'd always rather suspected the hand of the Magdalen bursar.

DRECHSEL. Of course my point is that you pay too heavily for enjoying the colour of the fritillaries if it means that you have to live in a marsh.

MYSELF. But that doesn't quite . . .

LANGDALE. I wish I could understand your point of view, Beith. You quarrel with Drechsel's approach to life because it concentrates too much on progress or whatever it is, and is indifferent to truth. And you insist, very reasonably, that truth is something which has absolute claims of its own, so that it's wrong to try and distort it or bottle it up; probably futile, too. Or do you mean that it's *merely* futile, because sooner or later somebody will be sure to blow the gaff, like the child in the story of the Emperor's New Clothes?

BEITH. No, I think it's *wrong*. Look here, supposing I came across a discovery that might mean a great deal of misery for the human race—say a poison that left no traces behind it whatever. And suppose I was engaged in such an obscure by-way of research, that the chances were a hundred to one against any man of science ever passing that way again, for a century or more. Am I to hush up that discovery? I wouldn't.

DRECHSEL. Now you see, Roberts, why when I'm dictator I'm going to keep an eye on your experiments at Cambridge.

ROBERTS. Of course, I don't think any experiments I did would be likely to result in my coming across new poisons. But if they did, Drechsel, I can quite understand your not being keen about it.

LANGDALE. I'm not sure that Beith's imaginary example hasn't fouled the wires of the argument a bit. I wasn't trying to involve him in any abstruse cases of conscience. I was merely going to ask him, when he says it would be wrong to suppress truth, what exactly he means by " wrong "?

MASSINGHAM (*in an audible aside*). Oh, *Lord!*

BEITH. I'm not quite sure that I see what you mean.

LANGDALE (*smiling*). Well, of course there has been a discussion before now on the Meaning of Meaning; but I don't suppose you'd want to go into that. Put it this way; when you say suppressing truth is wrong, do you mean it's wrong in the same sense in which it's wrong to match mauve with electric blue? Or wrong in the same sense in which it's wrong to throw a baby out of the train when it annoys you by screaming? Or wrong in some sense different from either?

BEITH. We-ell, it's not just aesthetic; you can rule that out. And if I said it was morally wrong, you'd ask whether it wasn't even more wrong to let loose a Holmes-proof poison on the world. You see, I'm not by way of being a philosopher, but I know you, Langdale. Upon my word, I think it must be a third kind of wrongness, that's different, as you say, from either.

LANGDALE. Well, there you are—surely when you say that you admit that truth is absolute. It has a claim on us that's got to be considered, without reference to your likes or dislikes, without reference to the reasons of State that Drechsel would lug in. If it's absolute, how can you try to pretend that human reason is just a twopenny-halfpenny faculty designed to help us in our struggle with environment? How can you pretend that its processes have no value, except where they happen to be practically useful? *Your* approach to life seems to me to be a mix-up of two quite different world-pictures. You must follow out the implications of your own logic.

BEITH (*attempting geniality*). Ah, well, you see, Langdale, I never had the advantages of an Oxford education.

MORDAUNT. It occurs to me, Langdale, that you haven't put much of your own in the pot all this time. Why shouldn't we have your approach to life, or world-picture, or whatever it is? 'Tisn't fair for you to sit there sniping at other people; you ought to come out into the open.

MASSINGHAM. Yes, Langdale, do tell us; are you pro-God?

LANGDALE (*pressing his hands to his temples and then looking up*). That question of yours, Massingham, is one I don't think I could answer without drawing a lot of distinctions which would bore the rest of the company. But anybody's welcome to cross-question me about my approach to life, if he'll tell me what the words mean.

HARTMAN. I don't want to look as if I were turning on the hand that fed me, after such an admirable dinner, too. But I really would like to hear more about this business of absolute truth. Isn't the idea behind absolute truth or absolute beauty or absolute anything simply an attenuated relic of the earlier belief in God? I mean, you start with the human mind—a certain type of mind, rather—projecting (as it were) its own shadow on the screen of existence and calling it " God ". Where the urge comes from that makes us want to do that, hasn't much importance for what we're discussing now; I suppose it's really a kind of back-formation from our sense of inferiority. Anyhow, people did that; they thought up a God who was originally just a Big Man, and then by degrees turned into an Unlimited Man. And then philosophers had enough penetration to suggest that an unlimited Man was a contradiction in terms, and it was nonsense to think of God as being a Person like ourselves——

MYSELF. What exactly . . .

HARTMAN (*continuing*). And so the edges of the shadow got more and more blurred, until all that was left was what you may call the late-Victorian Absolute, with a capital A. Surely what you and your friends are doing, Langdale, is simply to write "l.c." in the margin of the page, utilizing the absolute with a small "A" for the purposes of your philosophy, but not connecting it at all with going to chapel and that kind of thing. All this idea of something outside yourself that's got a claim on you, as you call it, whether you like it or not—isn't that in fact a superstitious relic of the belief you people once had in a divine Being, like the dead body of the Cid, you know, tied onto a horse so that it could lead the army into battle?

LANGDALE. Usedn't there to be a story of some Dean or other who was asked by a heckler, "Where was your Church, Sir, before the Reformation?" and floored him by asking, "Where was your face, Sir, before you washed it?" I should have thought that was really the answer to your question. If people in an earlier stage of civilization went wrong by deifying the absolute, that doesn't prove that the absolute has no value for philosophic thought. You might as well say that because people in the first century thought Augustus was a god, that is reason for thinking Augustus never existed.

MYSELF. But Augustus didn't. . . .

MASSINGHAM. You know, Langdale, I should think it's quite likely dons of Simon Magus in the old days used to argue about the Church of England; and one would say "Where was your face, Sir, before you washed it?" and another would come back with some wise-crack about emptying out the baby with the bath. Which was right? I suppose we don't very much care nowadays. But see how one thing leads to another; here are you comparing the absolute of philosophy to a face which has been washed, and your guest, if I may presume to interpret him, comparing it to a bath with no baby in it.

LANGDALE. I don't see that you help much towards solving the question by introducing flippant metaphors.

MASSINGHAM. Oh, but I haven't started solving the question yet. In fact, I don't know that I want to much. But, look here, Beith was telling us just now that the human reason was quite valueless when it wasn't inventing things or discovering things in nature. And you ticked him off for acknowledging the validity of reason, but only where human reason served the interests of science. Why shouldn't I tick you off just as well for acknowledging the existence of God, but only where he serves the purposes of philosophy? You told Beith to follow out the implications of his own logic; what about yours?

LANGDALE. You will observe that I haven't yet stated

what my theological views are. And meanwhile, I want to get at Hartman here and find out exactly what he's saying. (*To Hartman.*) I want to get you pinned down to something. Here you've got three different approaches to Life, materialist, pragmatist, intellectualist. To Drechsel, the human reason is just a drudge; to Beith, she's a kind of *haus-frau*—it's a *marriage de convenance;* to me, she's my romance. Now, make the judgement of Paris; which of those is your choice?

HARTMAN. Oh, but you see, I stand outside all those quarrels. To me, you're just three types; and, if I may say so, admirably true to type all of you. Drechsel wanting to dominate, and you wanting to be dominated, and Beith running away from his conclusions—it's all perfect. Your reactions to reason are much more interesting to me than reason itself.

MASSINGHAM (*chuckling*). It's no good, Langdale, here's a fourth approach. A whole foursome of you, and none of you has the least idea where the green is.

LANGDALE. Well, as usual I suppose I have to console myself with reflecting that the other people have to assume the validity of reason, in order to deny it.

MYSELF. And you have to . . .

DRECHSEL. Well, it doesn't seem to get us any further. Tell me, Roberts, did the fellows spend a good deal of their time having arguments like this, in the 'nineties?

ROBERTS. Sometimes—yes, I think sometimes. Of course, Fanshawe would argue about anything; he was a great man for arguing, was old Fanshawe. Of course, I think we had more in common in those days; got to grips more, instead of standing about sparring each in his own corner. I may be wrong, but that's my impression.

MORDAUNT. Don't you think perhaps the background of classical education had something to do with it? I know this'll annoy you, J. D., but I do sometimes wonder whether we haven't lost something by not having a common classical culture, as we used to. Oh, of course I know that if it comes to doing a cross-word, Beith can supply the name of any of the Nine Muses without stopping for breath. But that's not quite the same thing, somehow, as being saturated with the classics, using ancient Greece and ancient Rome as two windows from which we can look out on life, frame all our experience in them. I think in the old days it was the classical grind they'd been through that gave them, in part anyhow, a common meeting-place of the mind.

MYSELF. You don't think perhaps . . .

DRECHSEL. Well, don't be discouraged about it, Charles; in a generation or so, as I was suggesting, perhaps we shall have got rid of the classics altogether. And then we may find that our total ignorance of Latin and Greek gives us what you call a common meeting-place of the mind.

MASSINGHAM. With modern Germany for one window, and modern Russia for the other; oh God, yes. Meanwhile, here's the unfortunate Carruthers looking up and not being fed; or rather, we feed him nothing but husks, like that cardboard stuff women eat at breakfast when they think they're getting fat.

ROBERTS. Of course, it doesn't really signify much. Because after all the next world-war is scheduled to break out in July, isn't it? And after that Drechsel will have his revolution, and we shall all have to toe the line. No use quarrelling with the inevitable.

MORDAUNT. Is anything inevitable? If you come to think of it, the fellows of Simon Magus, just three hundred and fifty years ago, must have thought the Armada was going to win, and it never did. And two hundred and fifty years ago, they must have expected England to go Papist again, and it never did.

DRECHSEL. Yes, and a hundred and fifty years ago, they weren't expecting anything to happen; and by God, didn't it?

MASSINGHAM. Well, anyhow, it shews it's a mug's game, prophesying. I say, I'd no idea it was so late. That nasty little piece of work must have finished his lecture at the Town Hall, and I promised Eustace I'd go round to his rooms and meet somebody. Good-night, Charles; thanks awfully for looking after me.

MORDAUNT (*getting up and emptying out his pipe into the grate*). Good-night, Peter.

· · · · ·

And I awoke, and behold, it was not a dream.

Date Due

~~FEB 15 1972~~			
~~MAR 15 1974~~			
NOV 29 1990			
DEC 0 6 1990			

CAT. NO. 23 233   PRINTED IN U.S.A.

LF 509 .K6
Knox, Ronald Arbuthnott,
Let dons delight : being varia

0 1163 0205986 4
TRENT UNIVERSITY

LF509 .K6

Knox, Ronald Arbuthnott

Let dons delight

DATE   ISSUED TO

84839